# MARK WAID · MARCIO TAKARA

# INCORRUPTIBLE

## VOLUME 4

**BOOM! STUDIOS**

ROSS RICHIE Chief Executive Officer • MATT GAGNON Editor-in-Chief • FILIP SABLIK VP-Publishing & Marketing • LANCE KREITER VP-Licensing & Merchandising • PHIL BARBARO Director of Finance
BRYCE CARLSON Managing Editor • DAFNA PLEBAN Editor • SHANNON WATTERS Editor • ERIC HARBURN Assistant Editor • ADAM STAFFARONI Assistant Editor • CHRIS ROSA Assistant Editor
STEPHANIE GONZAGA Graphic Designer • CAROL THOMPSON Production Designer • JASMINE AMIRI Operations Coordinator • DEVIN FUNCHES Marketing & Sales Assistant

A catalog record of this book is available from OCLC and from the BOOM! Studios website, www.boom-studios.com, on the
Librarians Page.

BOOM! Studios, 5670 Wilshire Boulevard, Suite 450, Los Angeles, CA 90036-5679. Printed in China. Second Printing.
ISBN: 978-1-60886-056-2

01:23:20AM
CA -N47R
Doe, Jane EY-411
OVRBRK-PD 916 4212
12-12-2010
GARRY BROWN

CREATED AND WRITTEN BY:
# MARK WAID
ARTIST:
# MARCIO TAKARA

COLORIST: NOLAN WOODARD
LETTERER: ED DUKESHIRE

EDITOR: MATT GAGNON
ASST. EDITOR: SHANNON WATTERS

COVER: CHRISTIAN NAUCK

DESIGN: BRIAN LATIMER

INCORR

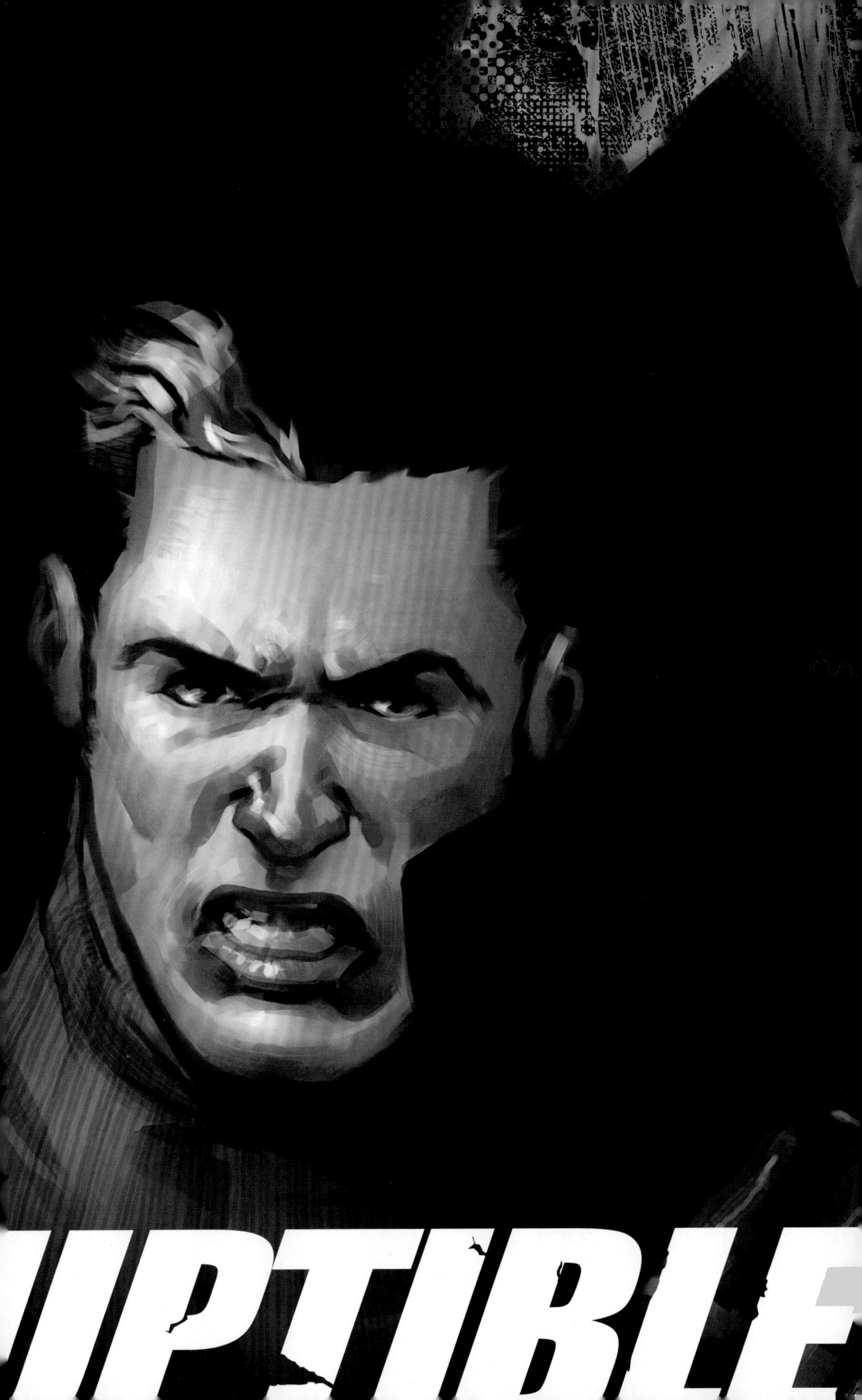

# CHAPTER 13

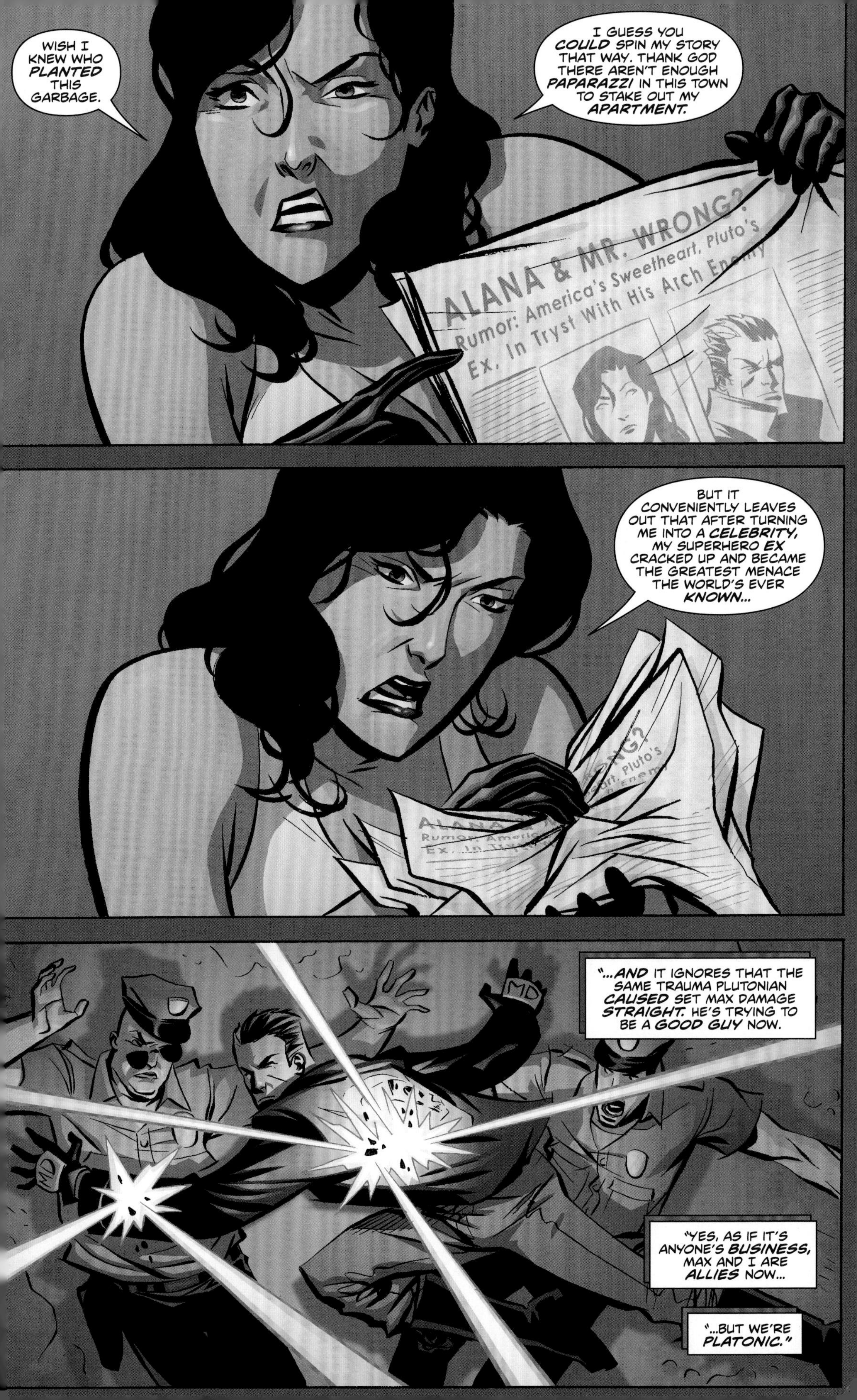
WISH I KNEW WHO PLANTED THIS GARBAGE.
I GUESS YOU COULD SPIN MY STORY THAT WAY. THANK GOD THERE AREN'T ENOUGH PAPARAZZI IN THIS TOWN TO STAKE OUT MY APARTMENT.
ALANA & MR. WRONG?
Rumor: America's Sweetheart, Pluto's Ex, In Tryst With His Arch Enemy
BUT IT CONVENIENTLY LEAVES OUT THAT AFTER TURNING ME INTO A CELEBRITY, MY SUPERHERO EX CRACKED UP AND BECAME THE GREATEST MENACE THE WORLD'S EVER KNOWN...
"...AND IT IGNORES THAT THE SAME TRAUMA PLUTONIAN CAUSED SET MAX DAMAGE STRAIGHT. HE'S TRYING TO BE A GOOD GUY NOW.
"YES, AS IF IT'S ANYONE'S BUSINESS, MAX AND I ARE ALLIES NOW...
"...BUT WE'RE PLATONIC."

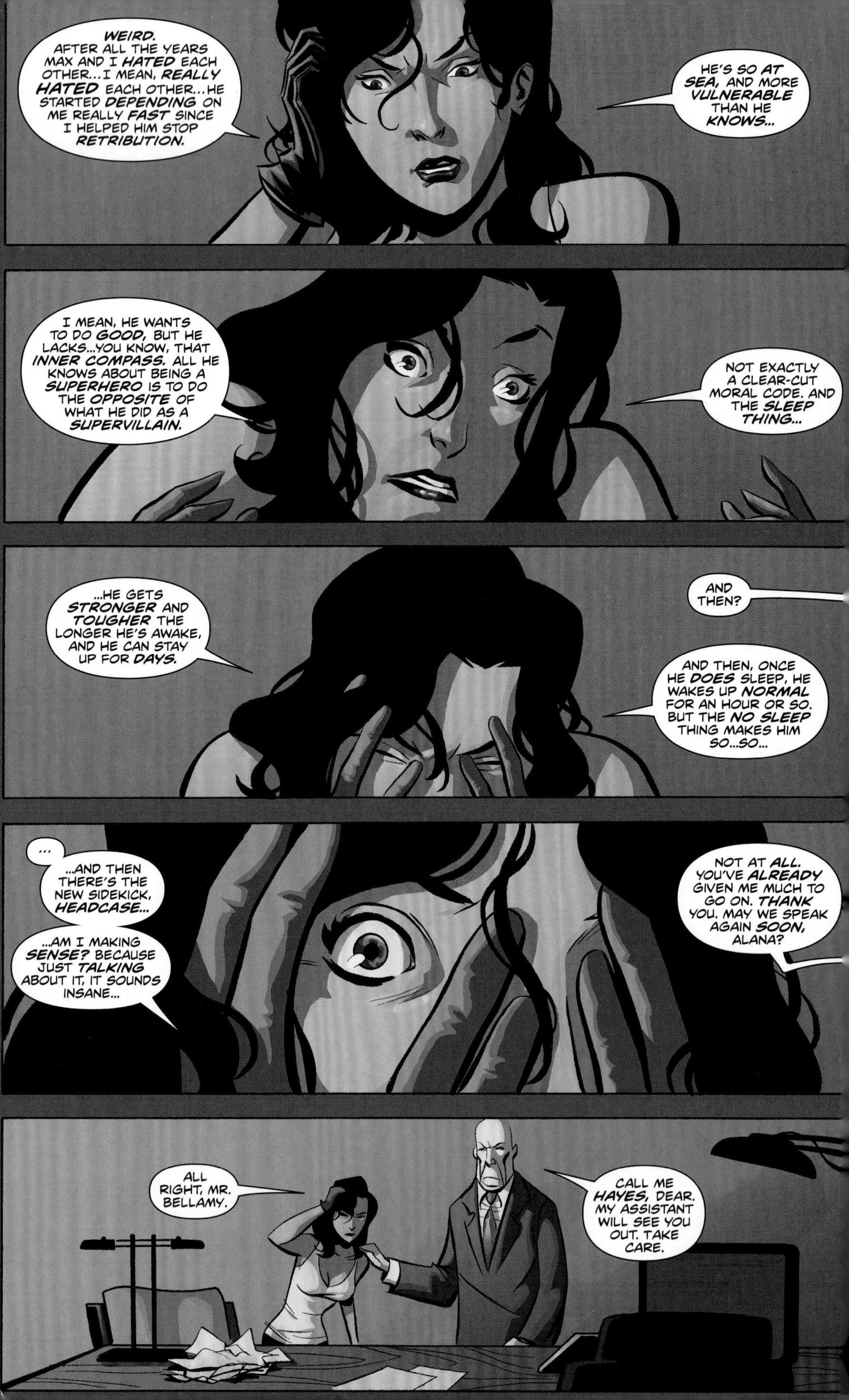
WEIRD. AFTER ALL THE YEARS MAX AND I HATED EACH OTHER... I MEAN, REALLY HATED EACH OTHER... HE STARTED DEPENDING ON ME REALLY FAST SINCE I HELPED HIM STOP RETRIBUTION.
HE'S SO AT SEA, AND MORE VULNERABLE THAN HE KNOWS...
I MEAN, HE WANTS TO DO GOOD, BUT HE LACKS...YOU KNOW, THAT INNER COMPASS. ALL HE KNOWS ABOUT BEING A SUPERHERO IS TO DO THE OPPOSITE OF WHAT HE DID AS A SUPERVILLAIN.
NOT EXACTLY A CLEAR-CUT MORAL CODE. AND THE SLEEP THING...
...HE GETS STRONGER AND TOUGHER THE LONGER HE'S AWAKE, AND HE CAN STAY UP FOR DAYS.
AND THEN?
AND THEN, ONCE HE DOES SLEEP, HE WAKES UP NORMAL FOR AN HOUR OR SO. BUT THE NO SLEEP THING MAKES HIM SO...SO...
...
...AND THEN THERE'S THE NEW SIDEKICK, HEADCASE...
...AM I MAKING SENSE? BECAUSE JUST TALKING ABOUT IT, IT SOUNDS INSANE...
NOT AT ALL. YOU'VE ALREADY GIVEN ME MUCH TO GO ON. THANK YOU. MAY WE SPEAK AGAIN SOON, ALANA?
ALL RIGHT, MR. BELLAMY.
CALL ME HAYES, DEAR. MY ASSISTANT WILL SEE YOU OUT. TAKE CARE.

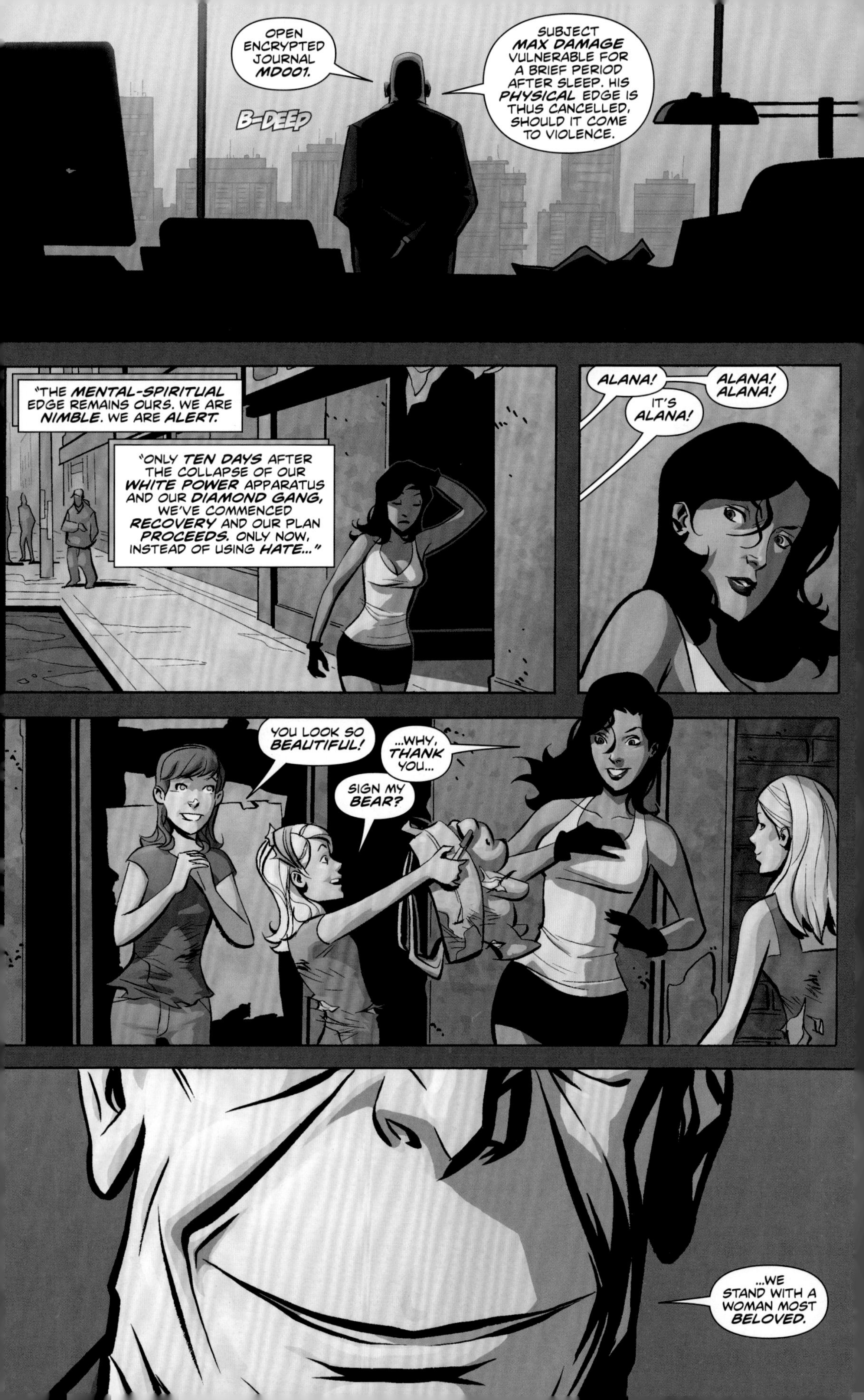
OPEN ENCRYPTED JOURNAL MD001.
B-DEEP
SUBJECT MAX DAMAGE VULNERABLE FOR A BRIEF PERIOD AFTER SLEEP. HIS PHYSICAL EDGE IS THUS CANCELLED, SHOULD IT COME TO VIOLENCE.
"THE MENTAL-SPIRITUAL EDGE REMAINS OURS. WE ARE NIMBLE. WE ARE ALERT.
"ONLY TEN DAYS AFTER THE COLLAPSE OF OUR WHITE POWER APPARATUS AND OUR DIAMOND GANG, WE'VE COMMENCED RECOVERY AND OUR PLAN PROCEEDS. ONLY NOW, INSTEAD OF USING HATE..."
ALANA!
IT'S ALANA!
ALANA! ALANA!
YOU LOOK SO BEAUTIFUL!
...WHY, THANK YOU...
SIGN MY BEAR?
...WE STAND WITH A WOMAN MOST BELOVED.

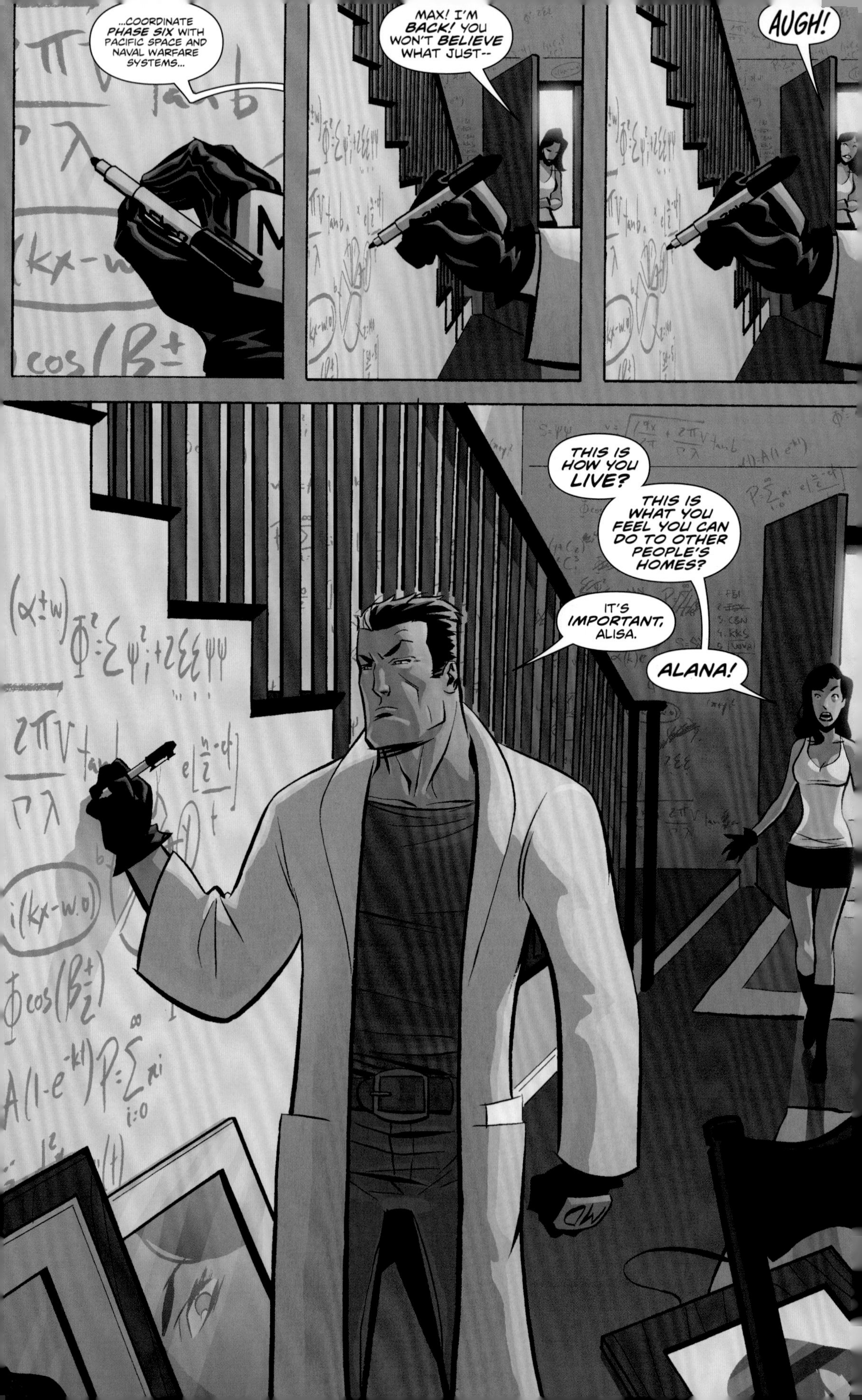
...COORDINATE PHASE SIX WITH PACIFIC SPACE AND NAVAL WARFARE SYSTEMS...
MAX! I'M BACK! YOU WON'T BELIEVE WHAT JUST--
AUGH!
THIS IS HOW YOU LIVE?
THIS IS WHAT YOU FEEL YOU CAN DO TO OTHER PEOPLE'S HOMES?
IT'S IMPORTANT, ALISA.
ALANA!

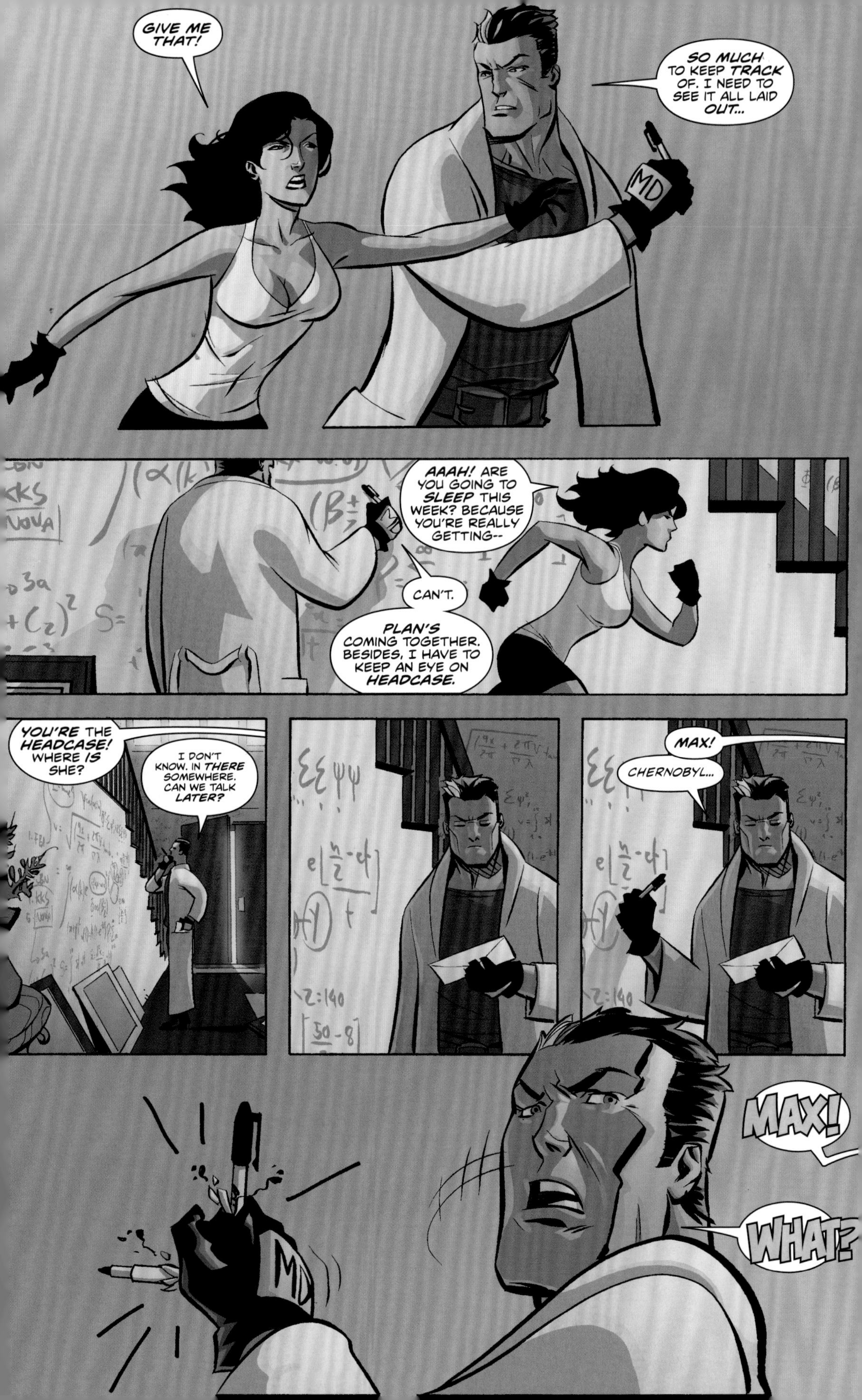
GIVE ME THAT!
SO MUCH TO KEEP TRACK OF. I NEED TO SEE IT ALL LAID OUT...
AAAH! ARE YOU GOING TO SLEEP THIS WEEK? BECAUSE YOU'RE REALLY GETTING--
CAN'T.
PLAN'S COMING TOGETHER. BESIDES, I HAVE TO KEEP AN EYE ON HEADCASE.
YOU'RE THE HEADCASE! WHERE IS SHE?
I DON'T KNOW. IN THERE SOMEWHERE. CAN WE TALK LATER?
MAX!
CHERNOBYL...
MAX!
WHAT?

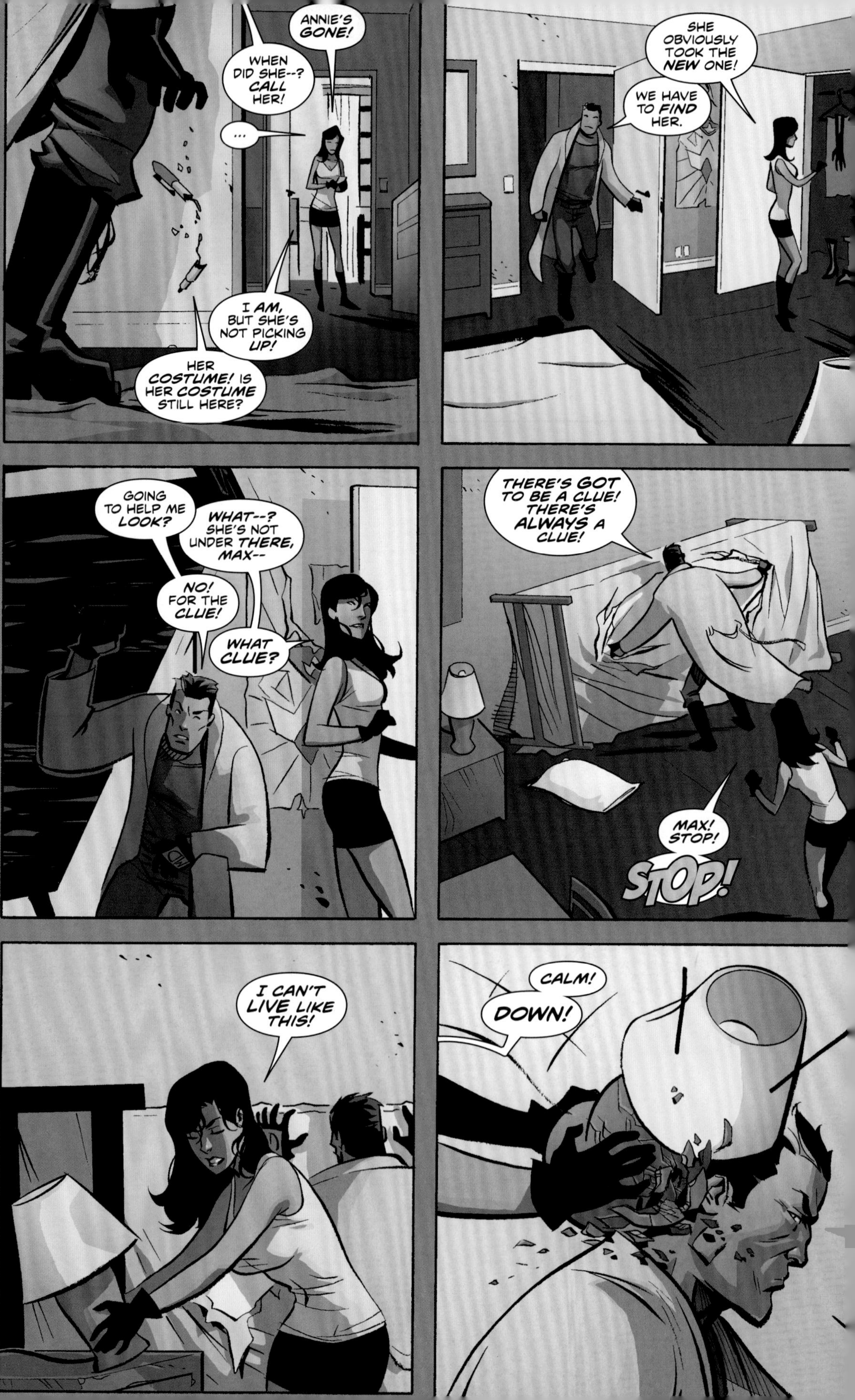
ANNIE'S GONE!
WHEN DID SHE--? CALL HER!
...
I AM, BUT SHE'S NOT PICKING UP!
HER COSTUME! IS HER COSTUME STILL HERE?
SHE OBVIOUSLY TOOK THE NEW ONE!
WE HAVE TO FIND HER.
GOING TO HELP ME LOOK?
WHAT--? SHE'S NOT UNDER THERE, MAX--
NO! FOR THE CLUE!
WHAT CLUE?
THERE'S GOT TO BE A CLUE! THERE'S ALWAYS A CLUE!
MAX! STOP!
STOP!
I CAN'T LIVE LIKE THIS!
CALM!
DOWN!

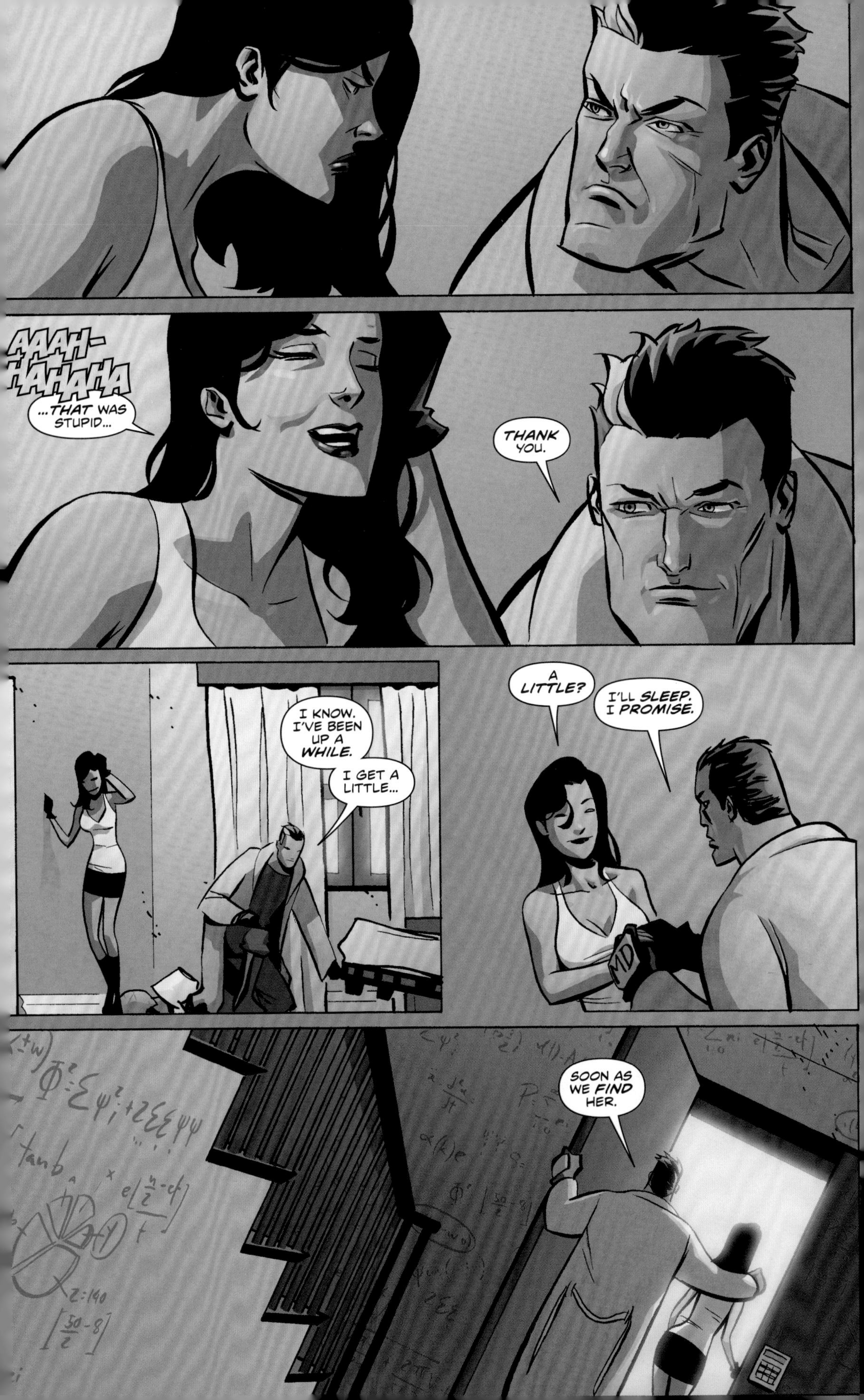
AAAH-HAHAHA
...THAT WAS STUPID...
THANK YOU.
I KNOW. I'VE BEEN UP A WHILE.
I GET A LITTLE...
A LITTLE?
I'LL SLEEP. I PROMISE.
SOON AS WE FIND HER.

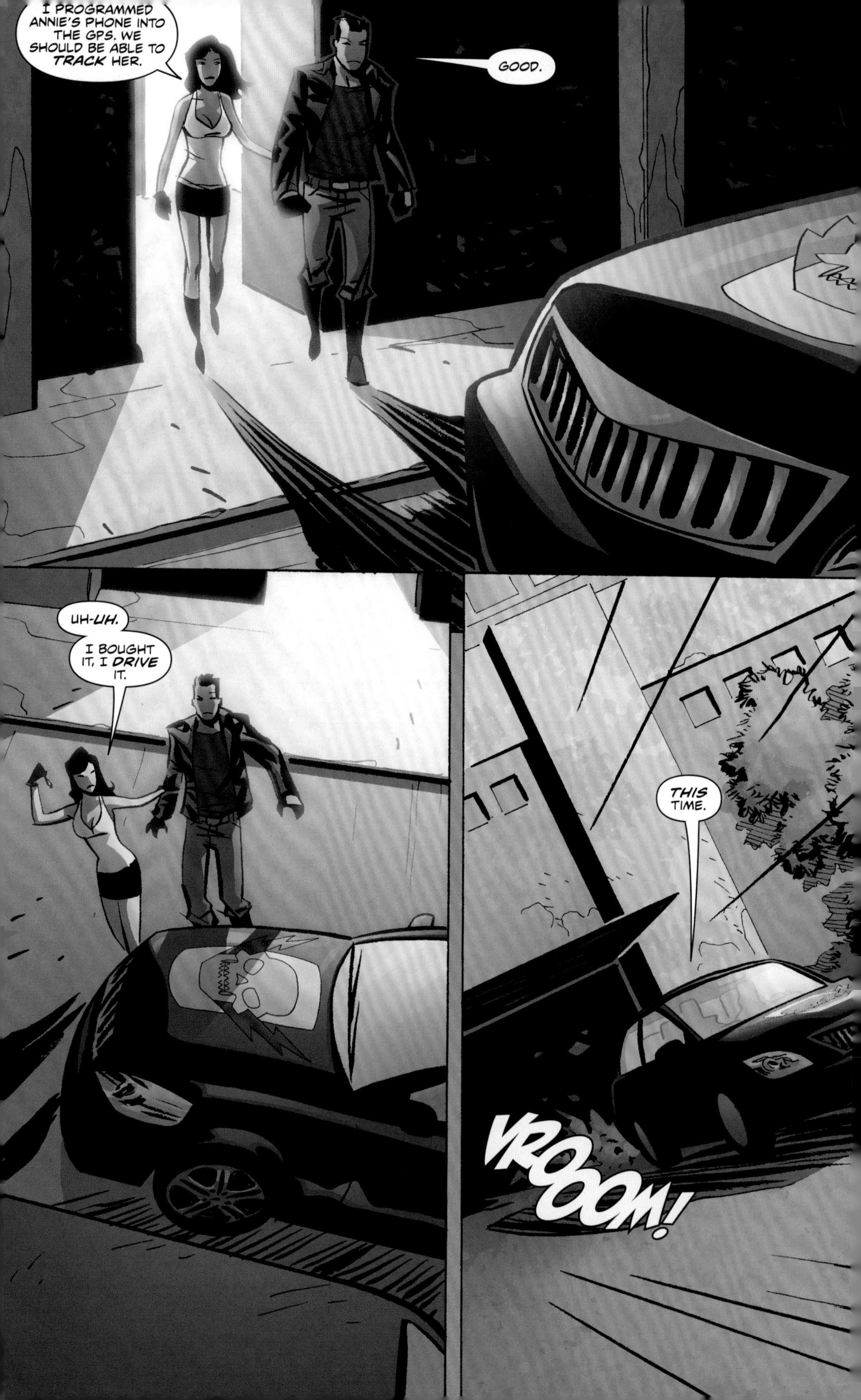
I PROGRAMMED ANNIE'S PHONE INTO THE GPS. WE SHOULD BE ABLE TO TRACK HER.
GOOD.
UH-UH.
I BOUGHT IT, I DRIVE IT.
THIS TIME.
VROOOM!

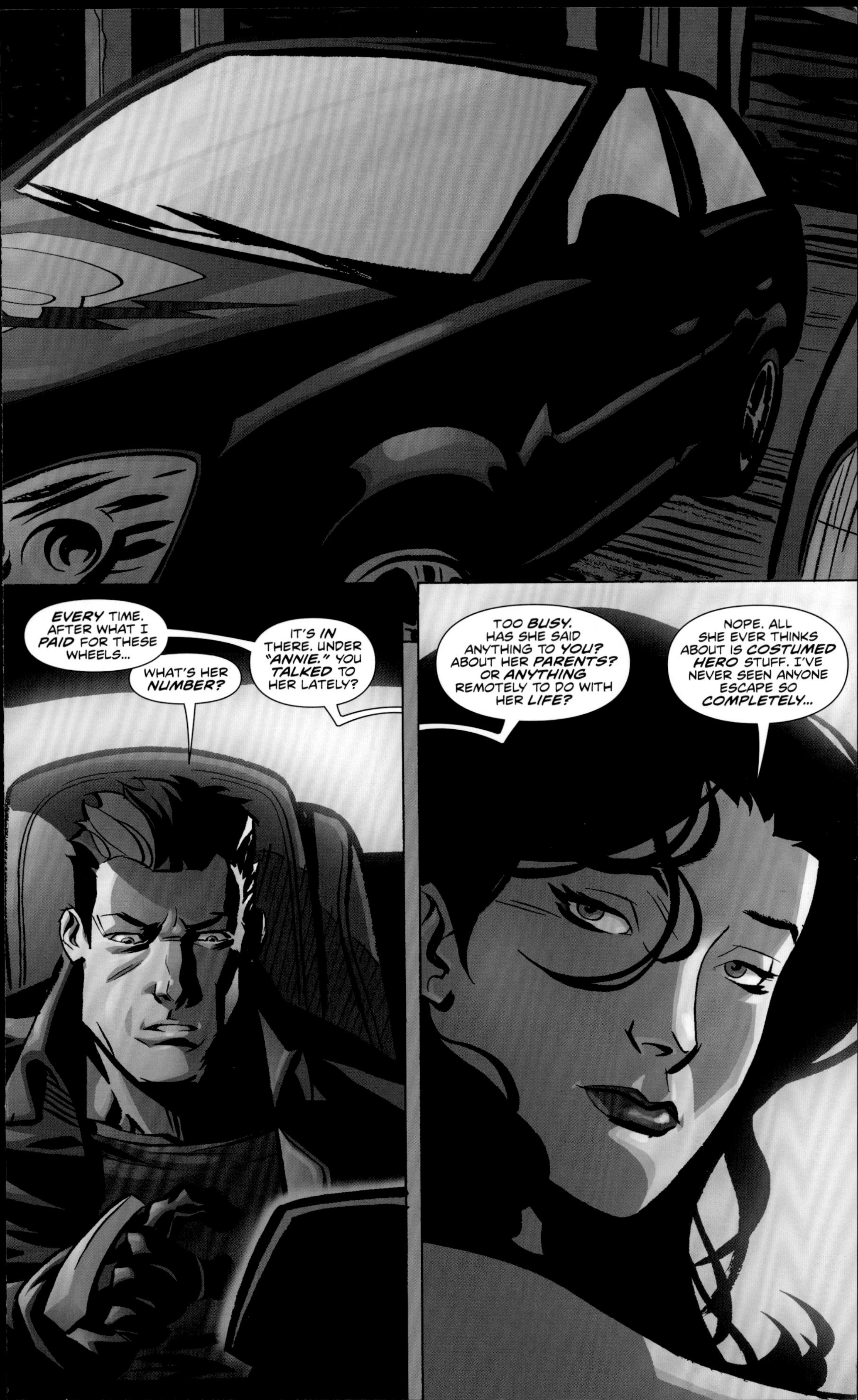
EVERY TIME. AFTER WHAT I PAID FOR THESE WHEELS...
WHAT'S HER NUMBER?
IT'S IN THERE. UNDER "ANNIE." YOU TALKED TO HER LATELY?
TOO BUSY. HAS SHE SAID ANYTHING TO YOU? ABOUT HER PARENTS? OR ANYTHING REMOTELY TO DO WITH HER LIFE?
NOPE. ALL SHE EVER THINKS ABOUT IS COSTUMED HERO STUFF. I'VE NEVER SEEN ANYONE ESCAPE SO COMPLETELY...

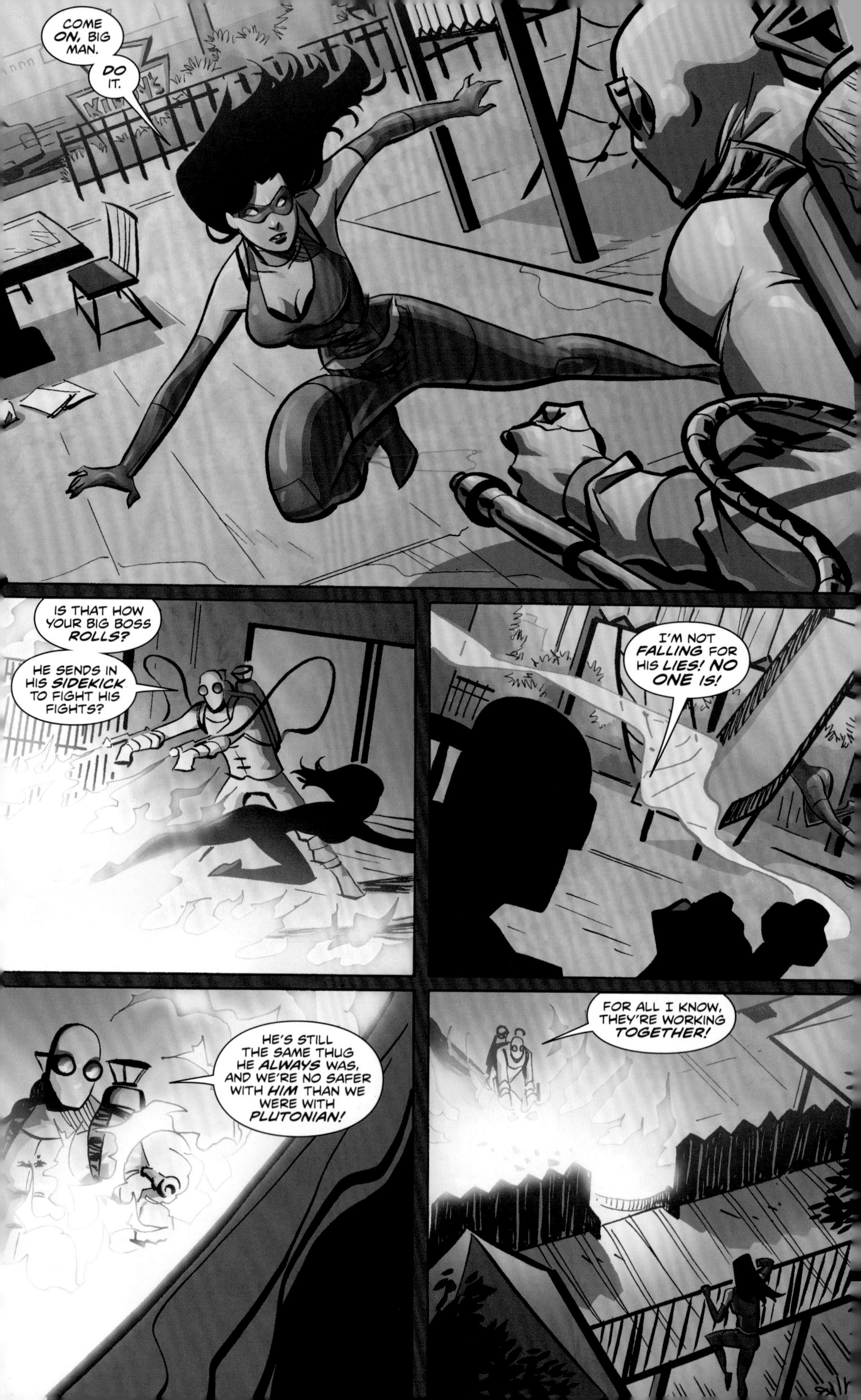
COME ON, BIG MAN.
DO IT.
IS THAT HOW YOUR BIG BOSS ROLLS?
HE SENDS IN HIS SIDEKICK TO FIGHT HIS FIGHTS?
I'M NOT FALLING FOR HIS LIES! NO ONE IS!
HE'S STILL THE SAME THUG HE ALWAYS WAS, AND WE'RE NO SAFER WITH HIM THAN WE WERE WITH PLUTONIAN!
FOR ALL I KNOW, THEY'RE WORKING TOGETHER!

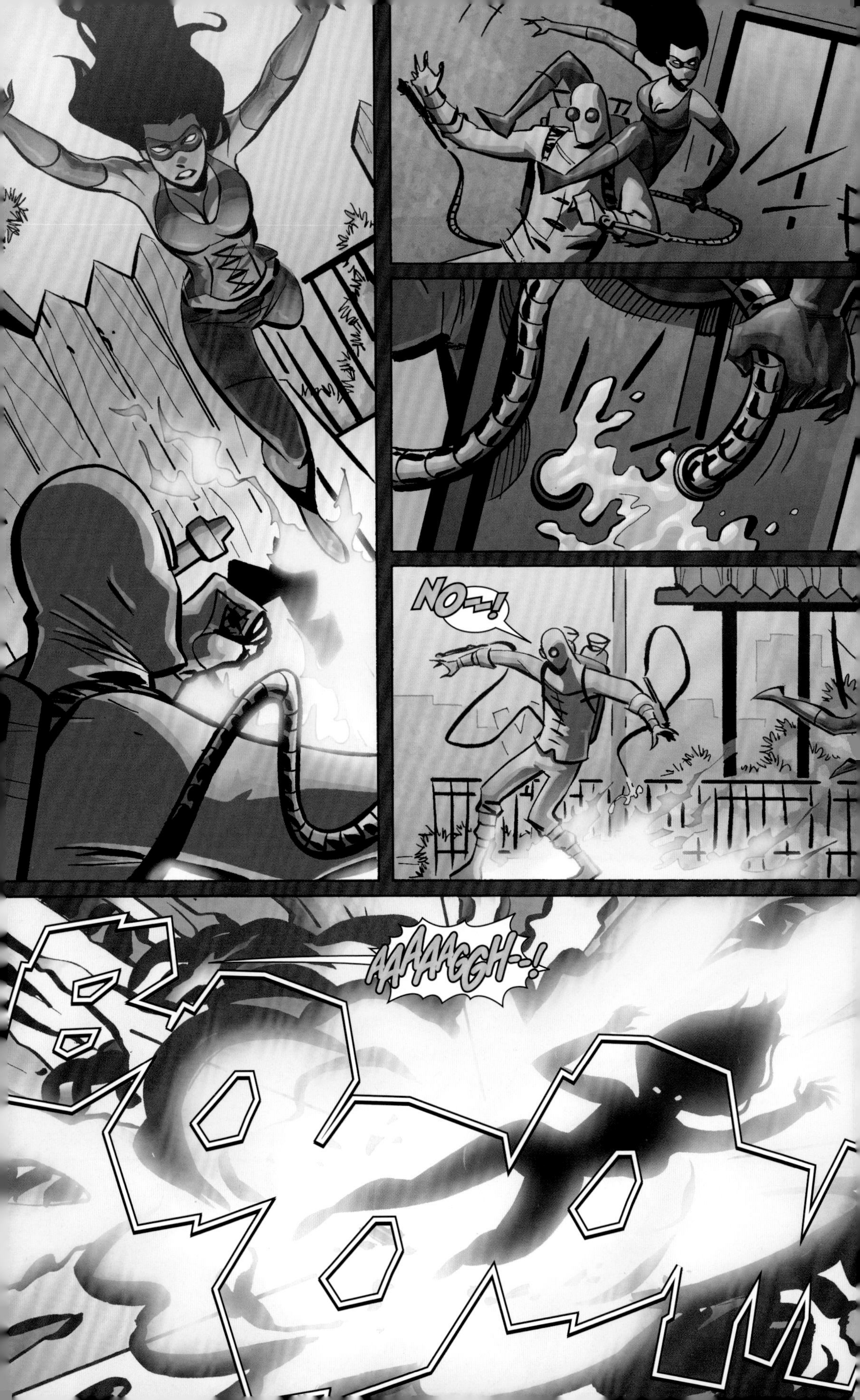
NO--!
AAAAAGGH--!

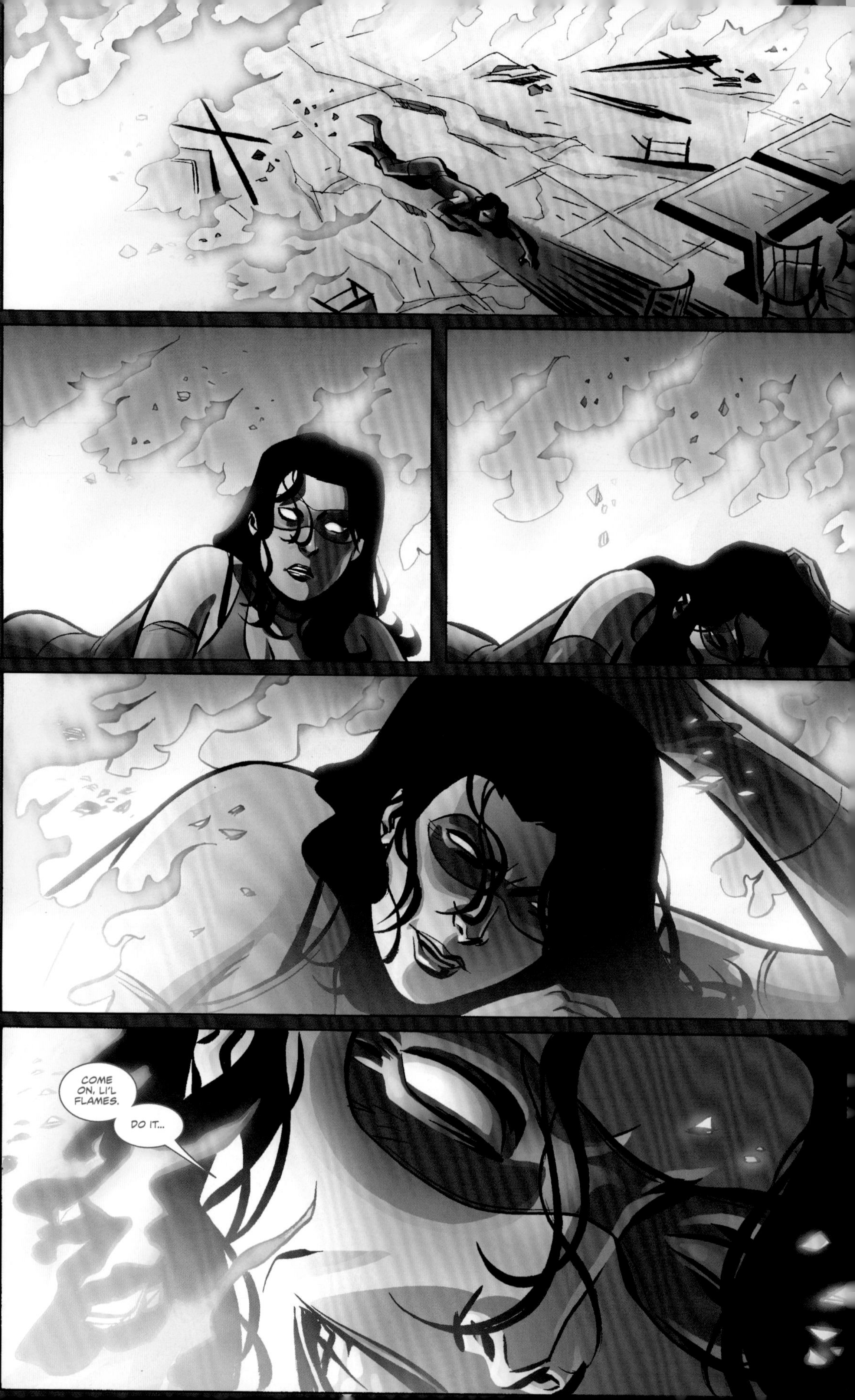
COME ON, LI'L FLAMES.
DO IT...

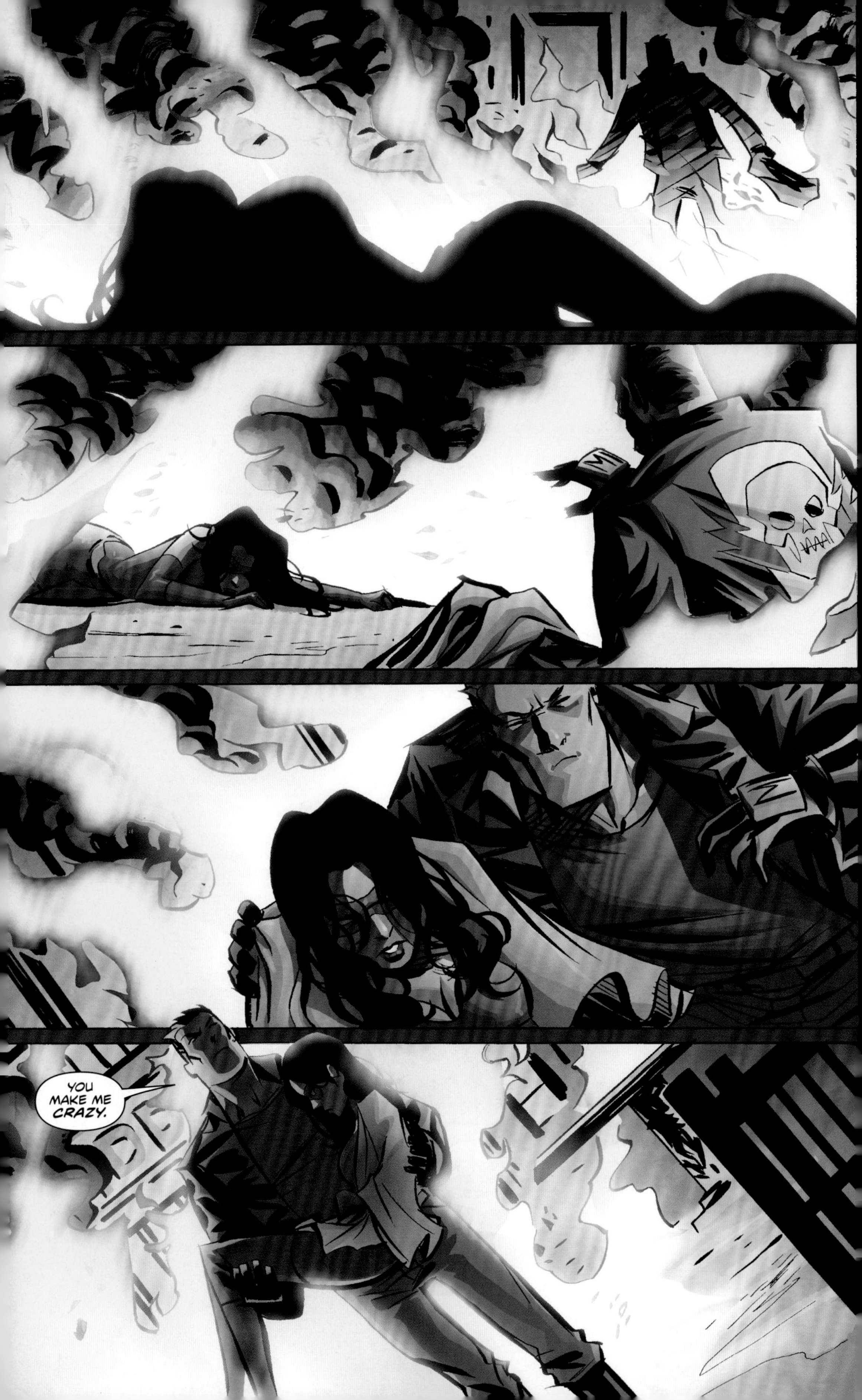
YOU MAKE ME CRAZY.

ARMADALE, WHAT THE HELL HAPPENED HERE?

JEESH, MAX, KEEP IT DOWN, OKAY? YOU'RE MORE RADIOACTIVE THAN EVER NOW.

THE WHOLE DEPARTMENT'S ON A MAXHUNT. YOU AND I CANNOT BE SEEN TOGETHER, ALL RIGHT?

YOUR GIRL JUST SAVED THAT FAST-FOOD PLACE FROM ARSONAL. THEY WERE ABLE TO EVACUATE WHILE SHE KEPT HIM DANCING.

ARSONAL? I HAVEN'T HEARD THAT NAME IN YEARS. REAL SMALL-TIMER.

HE WAS YELLING FOR YOUR HEAD ALL MORNING. IT WAS ALL OVER TV. DIDN'T YOU SEE IT?

I DON'T WATCH TV.

MAYBE YOU SHOULD START.

KEPT SAYING YOUR NEWFOUND MORALITY'S A TRICK. SAID HE HAD A PLAN TO APPREHEND YOU.

IF IT HADN'T INVOLVED TORCHING A KIDDIE RESTAURANT, I'D HAVE BEEN HAPPY TO HEAR HIM OUT.

WHY DIDN'T YOU TELL ME ABOUT THIS?

YOU WERE BUSY. WITH YOUR ANTI-PLUTONIAN PLAN.

WHAT?

LET IT GO. MEET ME LATER AT ALANA'S.

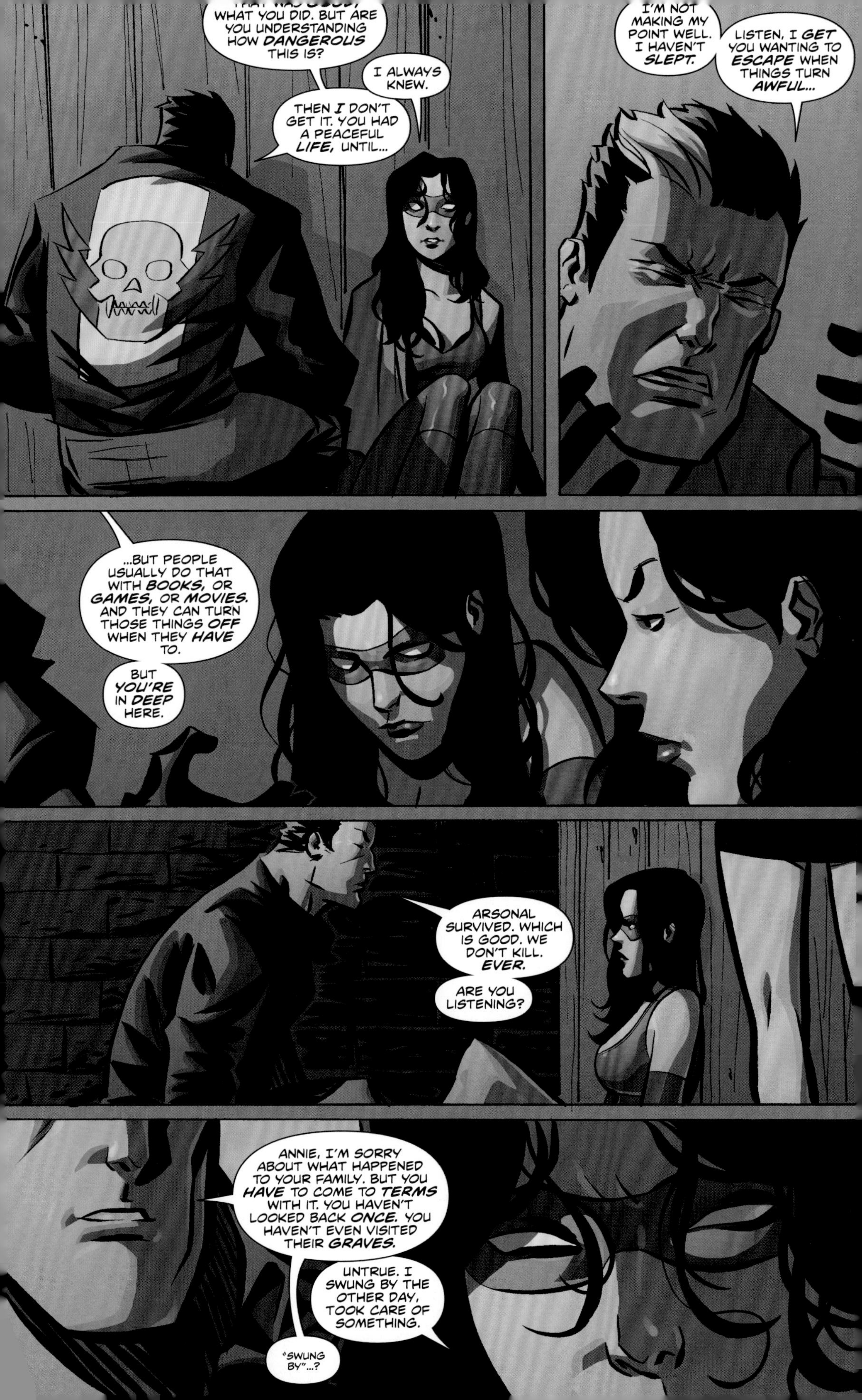

WHAT YOU DID. BUT ARE YOU UNDERSTANDING HOW DANGEROUS THIS IS?
I ALWAYS KNEW.
THEN I DON'T GET IT. YOU HAD A PEACEFUL LIFE, UNTIL...
I'M NOT MAKING MY POINT WELL. I HAVEN'T SLEPT.
LISTEN, I GET YOU WANTING TO ESCAPE WHEN THINGS TURN AWFUL...
...BUT PEOPLE USUALLY DO THAT WITH BOOKS, OR GAMES, OR MOVIES. AND THEY CAN TURN THOSE THINGS OFF WHEN THEY HAVE TO.
BUT YOU'RE IN DEEP HERE.
ARSONAL SURVIVED. WHICH IS GOOD. WE DON'T KILL. EVER.
ARE YOU LISTENING?
ANNIE, I'M SORRY ABOUT WHAT HAPPENED TO YOUR FAMILY. BUT YOU HAVE TO COME TO TERMS WITH IT. YOU HAVEN'T LOOKED BACK ONCE. YOU HAVEN'T EVEN VISITED THEIR GRAVES.
UNTRUE. I SWUNG BY THE OTHER DAY, TOOK CARE OF SOMETHING.
"SWUNG BY"...?

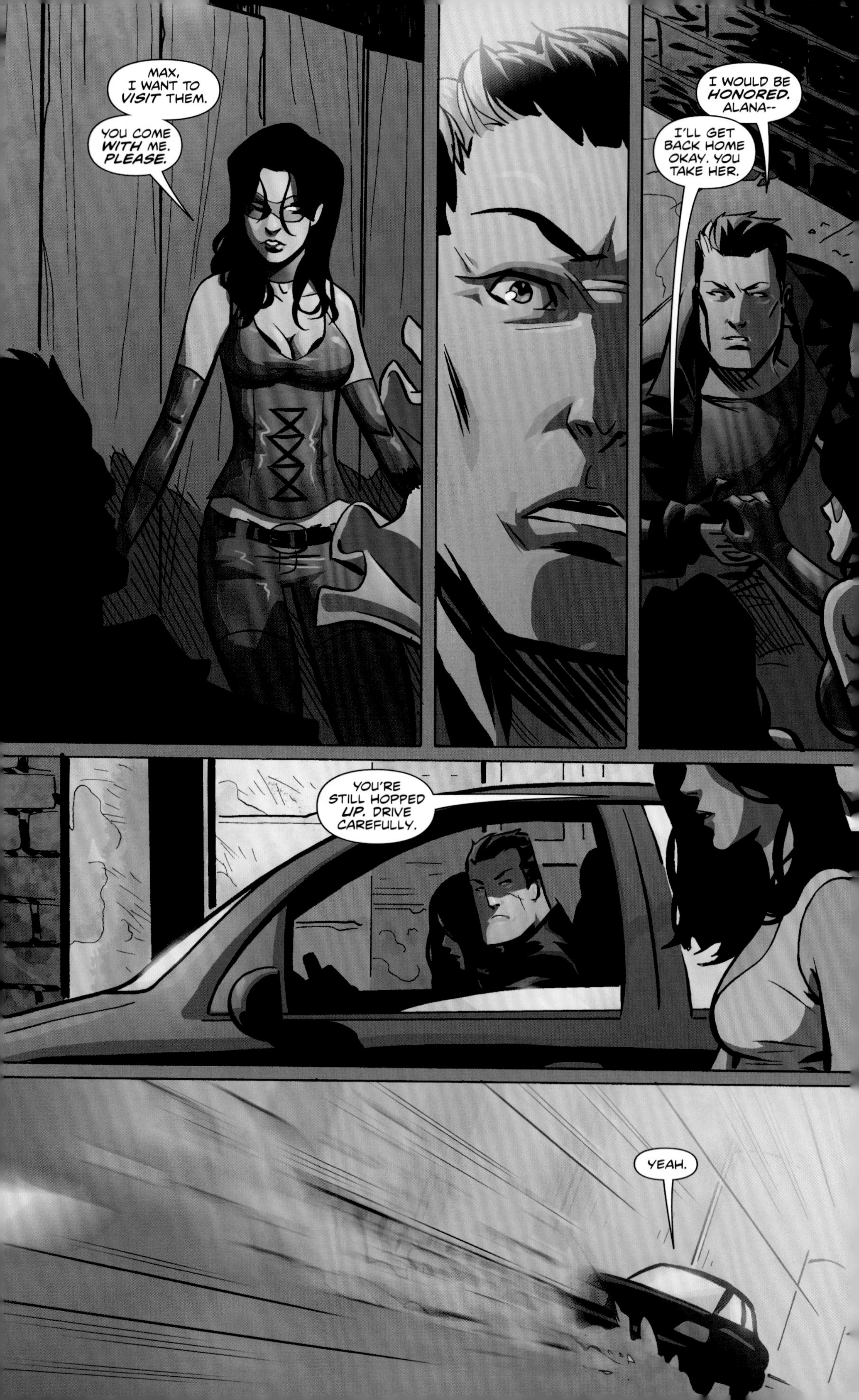
MAX, I WANT TO VISIT THEM.
YOU COME WITH ME. PLEASE.
I WOULD BE HONORED. ALANA--
I'LL GET BACK HOME OKAY. YOU TAKE HER.
YOU'RE STILL HOPPED UP. DRIVE CAREFULLY.
YEAH.

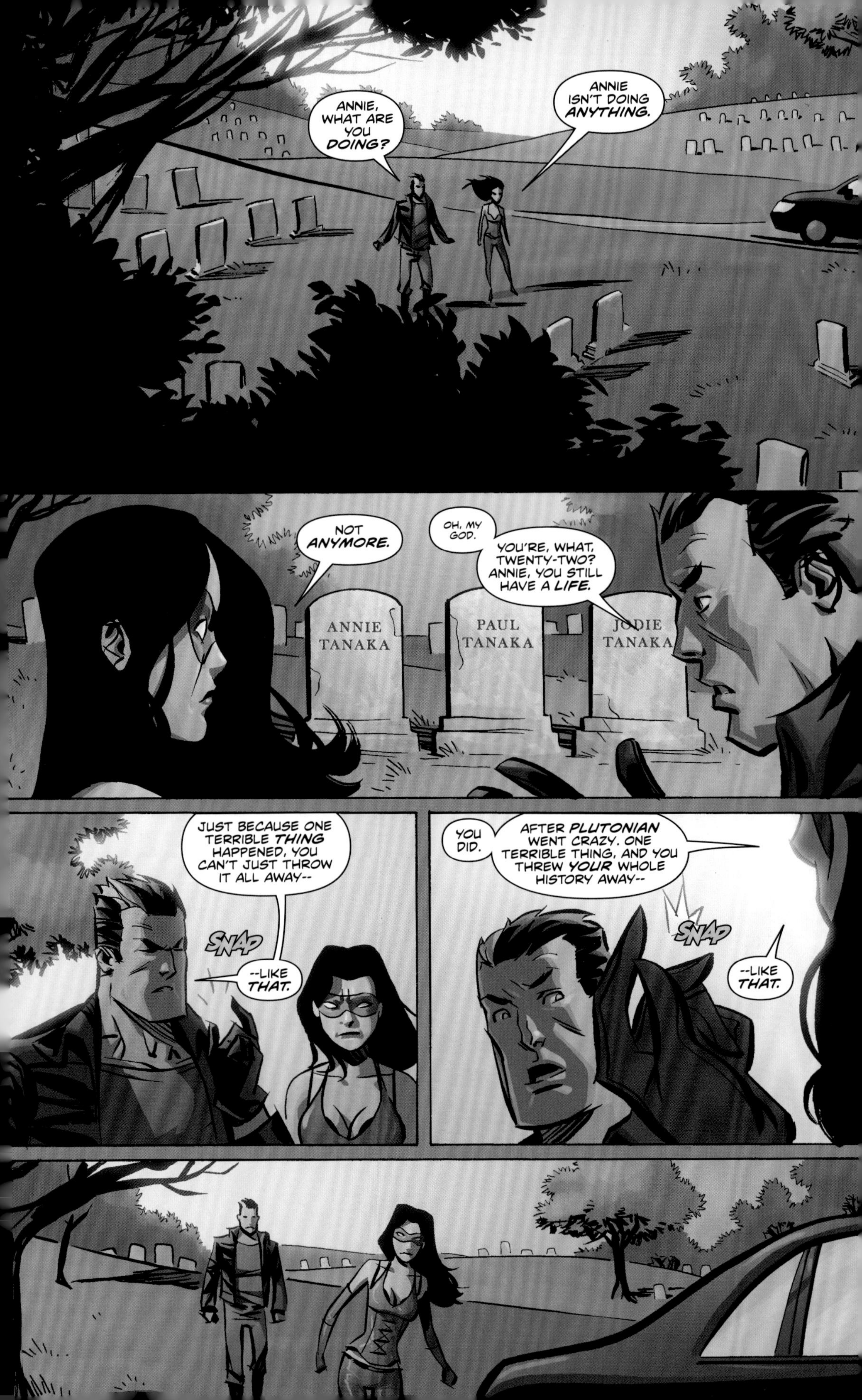
ANNIE, WHAT ARE YOU DOING?
ANNIE ISN'T DOING ANYTHING.
NOT ANYMORE.
OH, MY GOD.
YOU'RE, WHAT, TWENTY-TWO? ANNIE, YOU STILL HAVE A LIFE.
ANNIE TANAKA
PAUL TANAKA
JODIE TANAKA
JUST BECAUSE ONE TERRIBLE THING HAPPENED, YOU CAN'T JUST THROW IT ALL AWAY--
SNAP
--LIKE THAT.
YOU DID.
AFTER PLUTONIAN WENT CRAZY. ONE TERRIBLE THING, AND YOU THREW YOUR WHOLE HISTORY AWAY--
SNAP
--LIKE THAT.

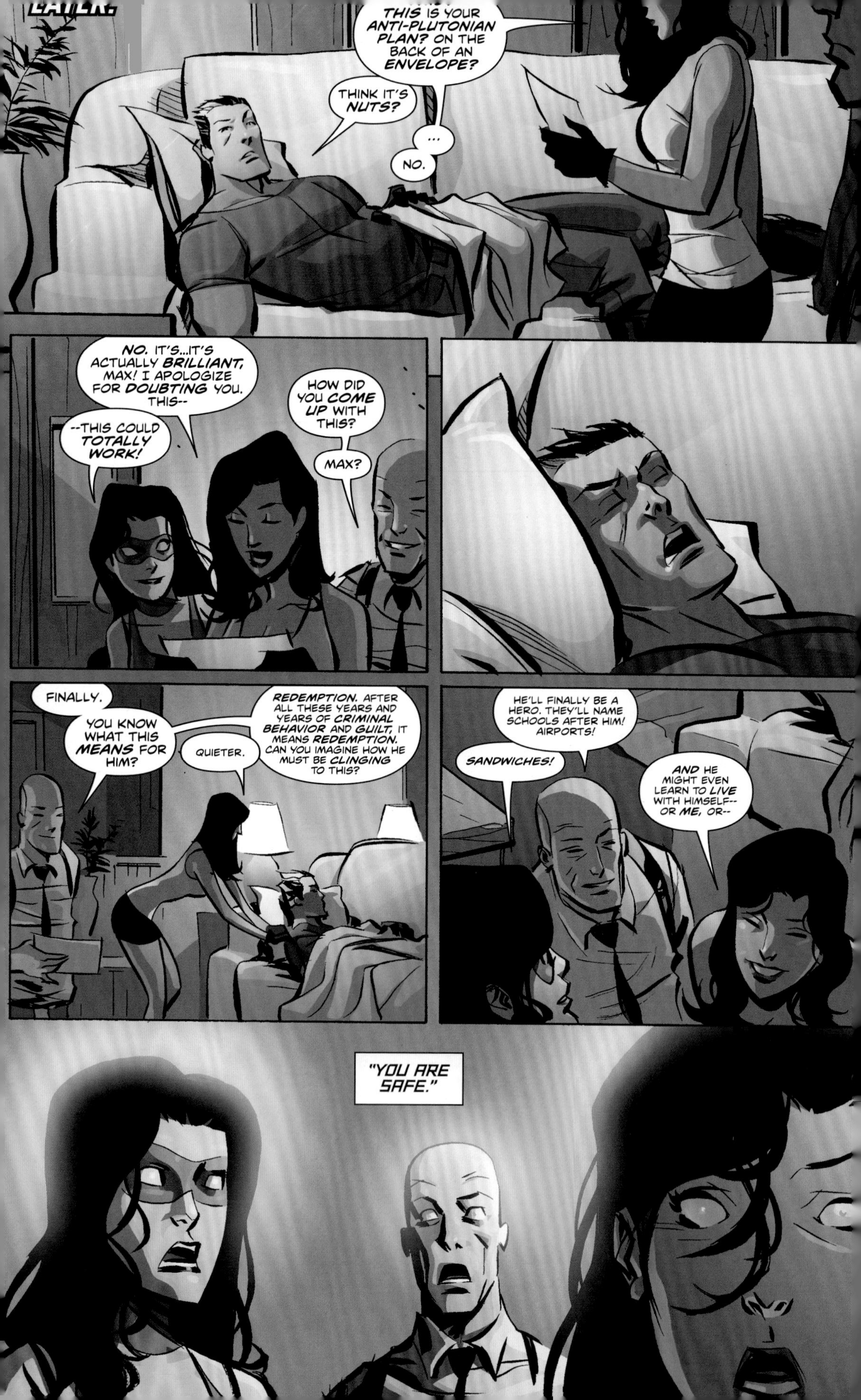

THIS IS YOUR ANTI-PLUTONIAN PLAN? ON THE BACK OF AN ENVELOPE?
THINK IT'S NUTS?
...
NO.
NO. IT'S...IT'S ACTUALLY BRILLIANT, MAX! I APOLOGIZE FOR DOUBTING YOU. THIS--
--THIS COULD TOTALLY WORK!
HOW DID YOU COME UP WITH THIS?
MAX?
FINALLY.
YOU KNOW WHAT THIS MEANS FOR HIM?
REDEMPTION. AFTER ALL THESE YEARS AND YEARS OF CRIMINAL BEHAVIOR AND GUILT, IT MEANS REDEMPTION. CAN YOU IMAGINE HOW HE MUST BE CLINGING TO THIS?
QUIETER.
HE'LL FINALLY BE A HERO. THEY'LL NAME SCHOOLS AFTER HIM! AIRPORTS!
SANDWICHES!
AND HE MIGHT EVEN LEARN TO LIVE WITH HIMSELF-- OR ME, OR--
"YOU ARE SAFE."

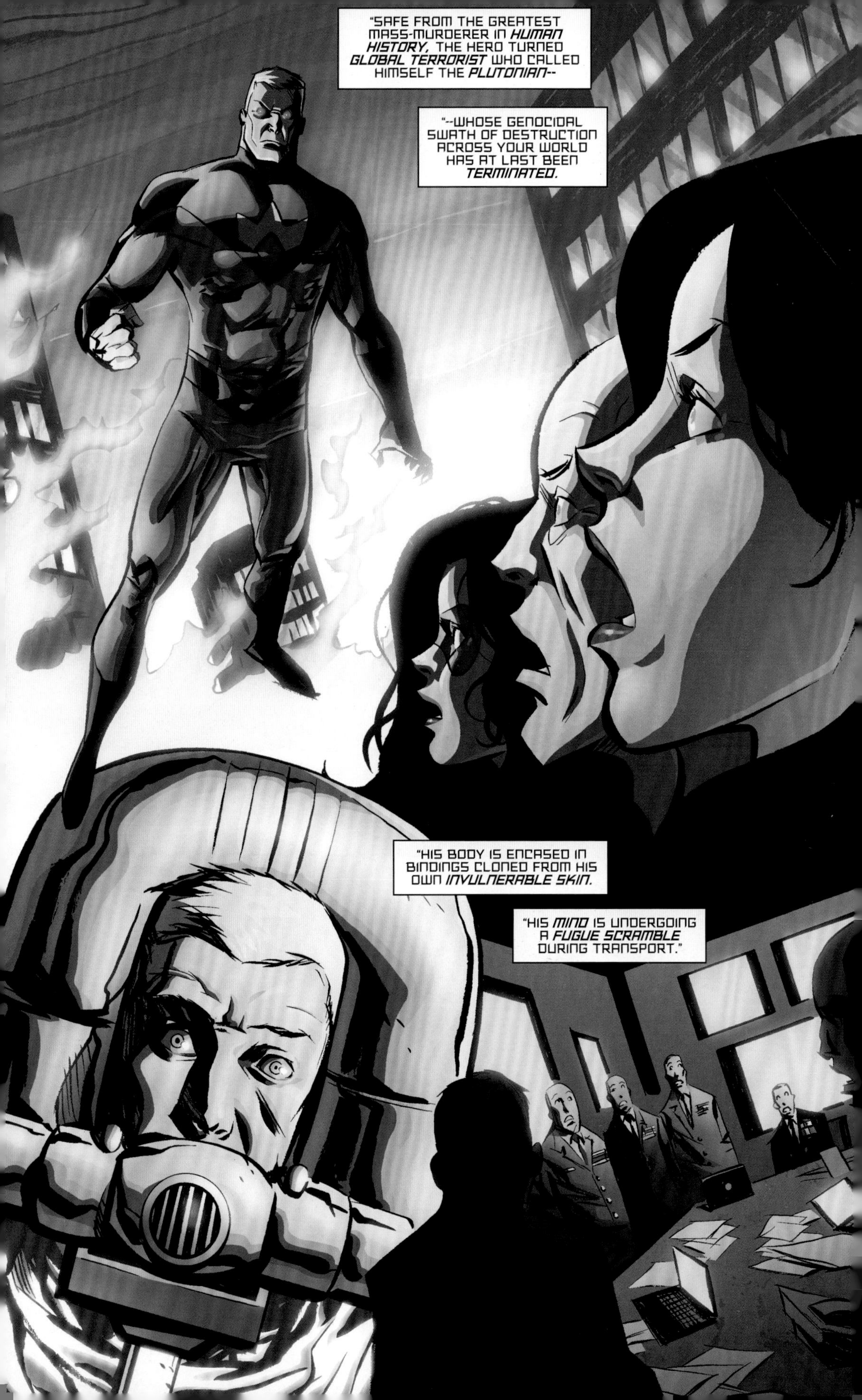
"SAFE FROM THE GREATEST MASS-MURDERER IN HUMAN HISTORY, THE HERO TURNED GLOBAL TERRORIST WHO CALLED HIMSELF THE PLUTONIAN--
"--WHOSE GENOCIDAL SWATH OF DESTRUCTION ACROSS YOUR WORLD HAS AT LAST BEEN TERMINATED.
"HIS BODY IS ENCASED IN BINDINGS CLONED FROM HIS OWN INVULNERABLE SKIN.
"HIS MIND IS UNDERGOING A FUGUE SCRAMBLE DURING TRANSPORT."

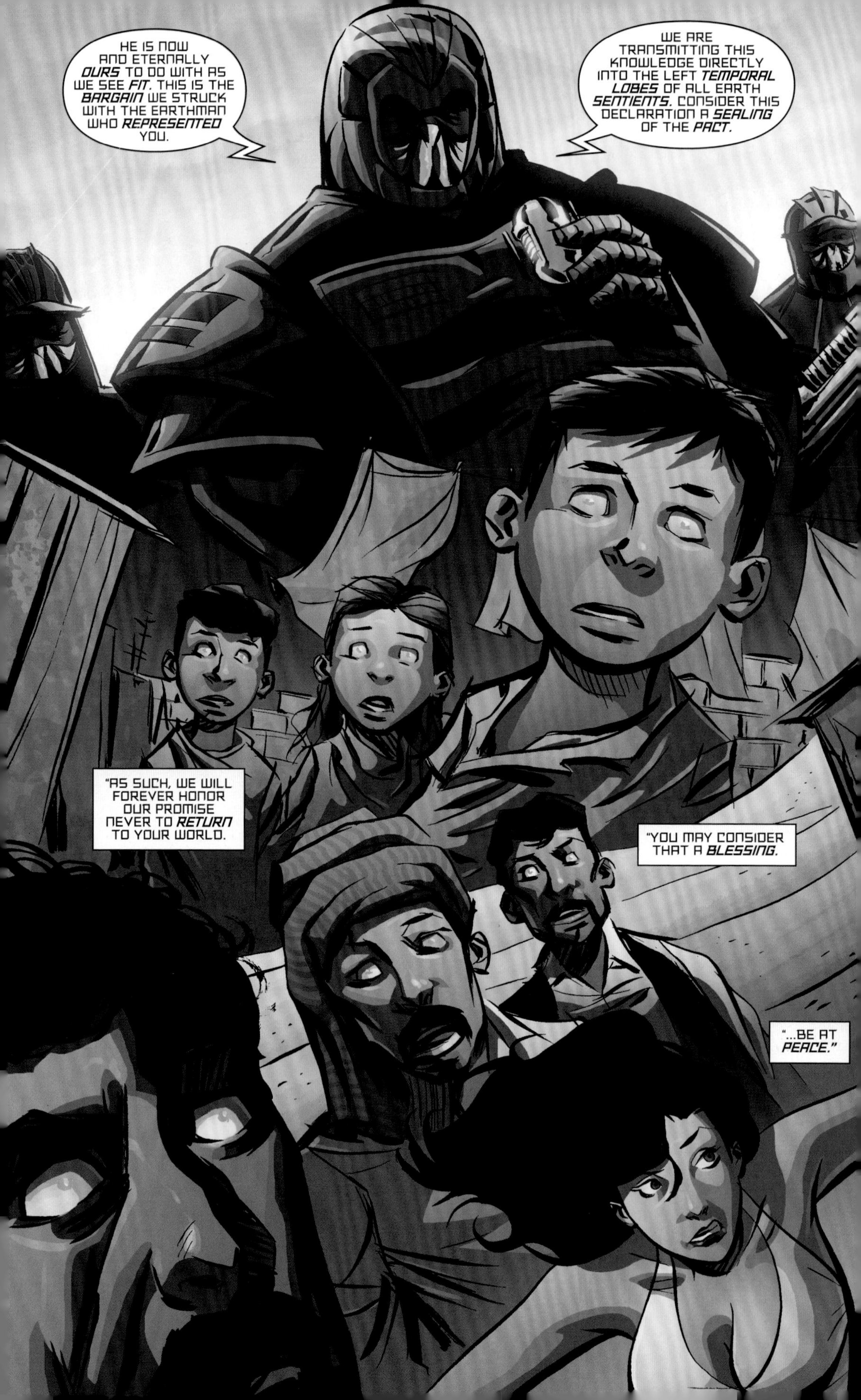
HE IS NOW AND ETERNALLY *OURS* TO DO WITH AS WE SEE *FIT*. THIS IS THE *BARGAIN* WE STRUCK WITH THE EARTHMAN WHO *REPRESENTED* YOU.
WE ARE TRANSMITTING THIS KNOWLEDGE DIRECTLY INTO THE LEFT *TEMPORAL LOBES* OF ALL EARTH *SENTIENTS*. CONSIDER THIS DECLARATION A *SEALING* OF THE *PACT*.
"AS SUCH, WE WILL FOREVER HONOR OUR PROMISE NEVER TO *RETURN* TO YOUR WORLD.
"YOU MAY CONSIDER THAT A *BLESSING*.
"...BE AT *PEACE*."

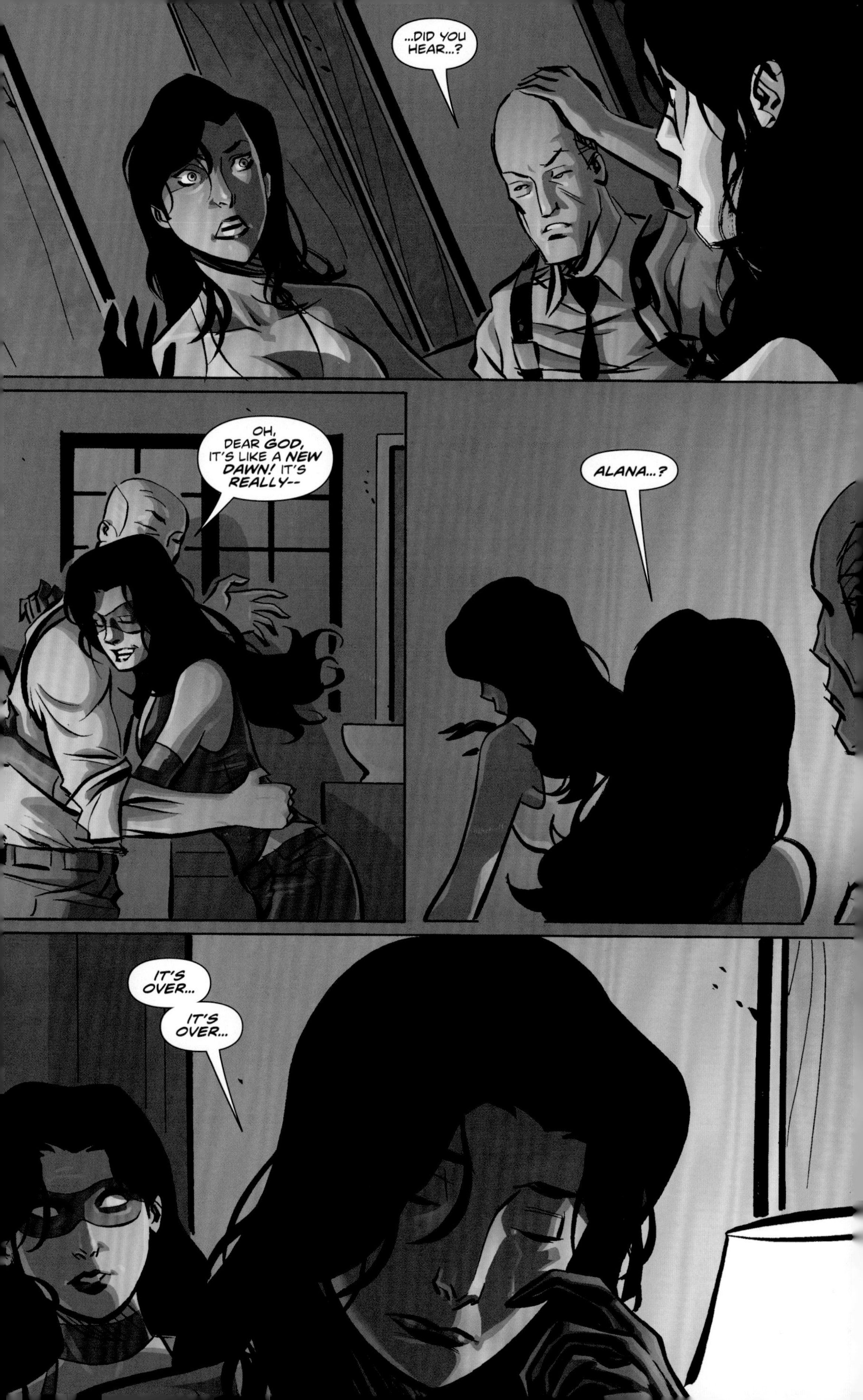
...DID YOU HEAR...?
OH, DEAR GOD, IT'S LIKE A NEW DAWN! IT'S REALLY--
ALANA...?
IT'S OVER...
IT'S OVER...

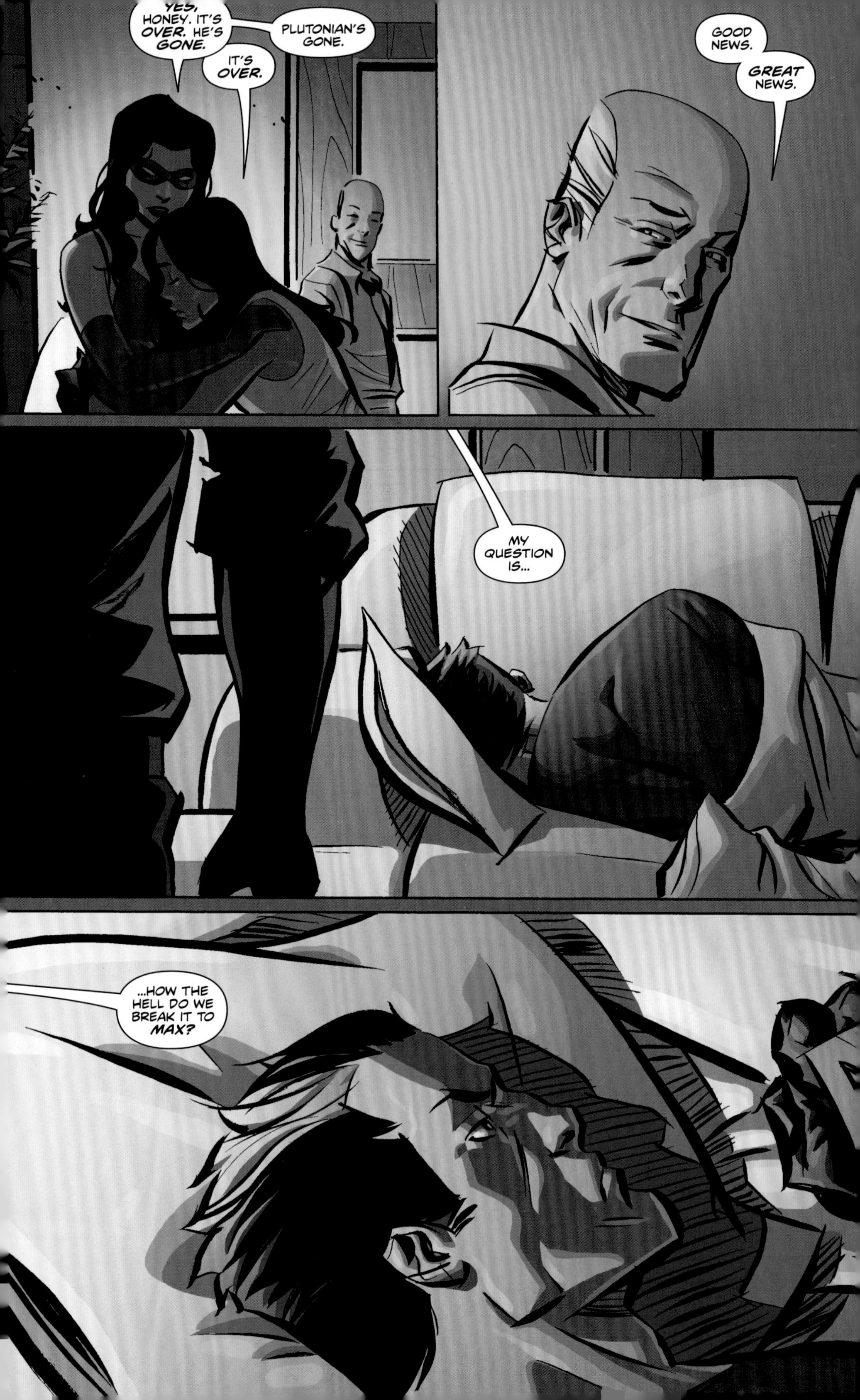
YES, HONEY. IT'S OVER. HE'S GONE.
IT'S OVER.
PLUTONIAN'S GONE.
GOOD NEWS.
GREAT NEWS.
MY QUESTION IS...
...HOW THE HELL DO WE BREAK IT TO MAX?

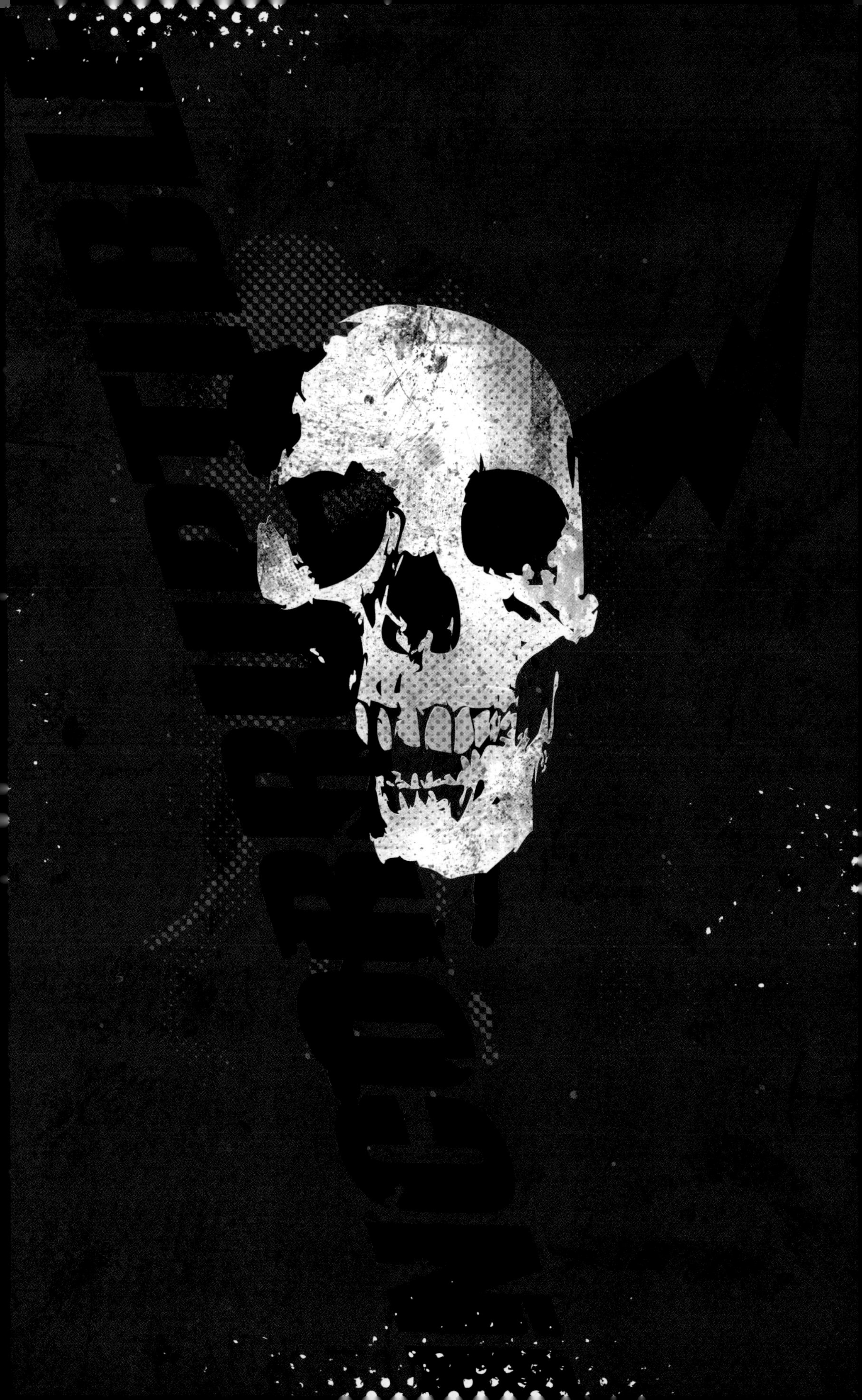

# CHAPTER 14

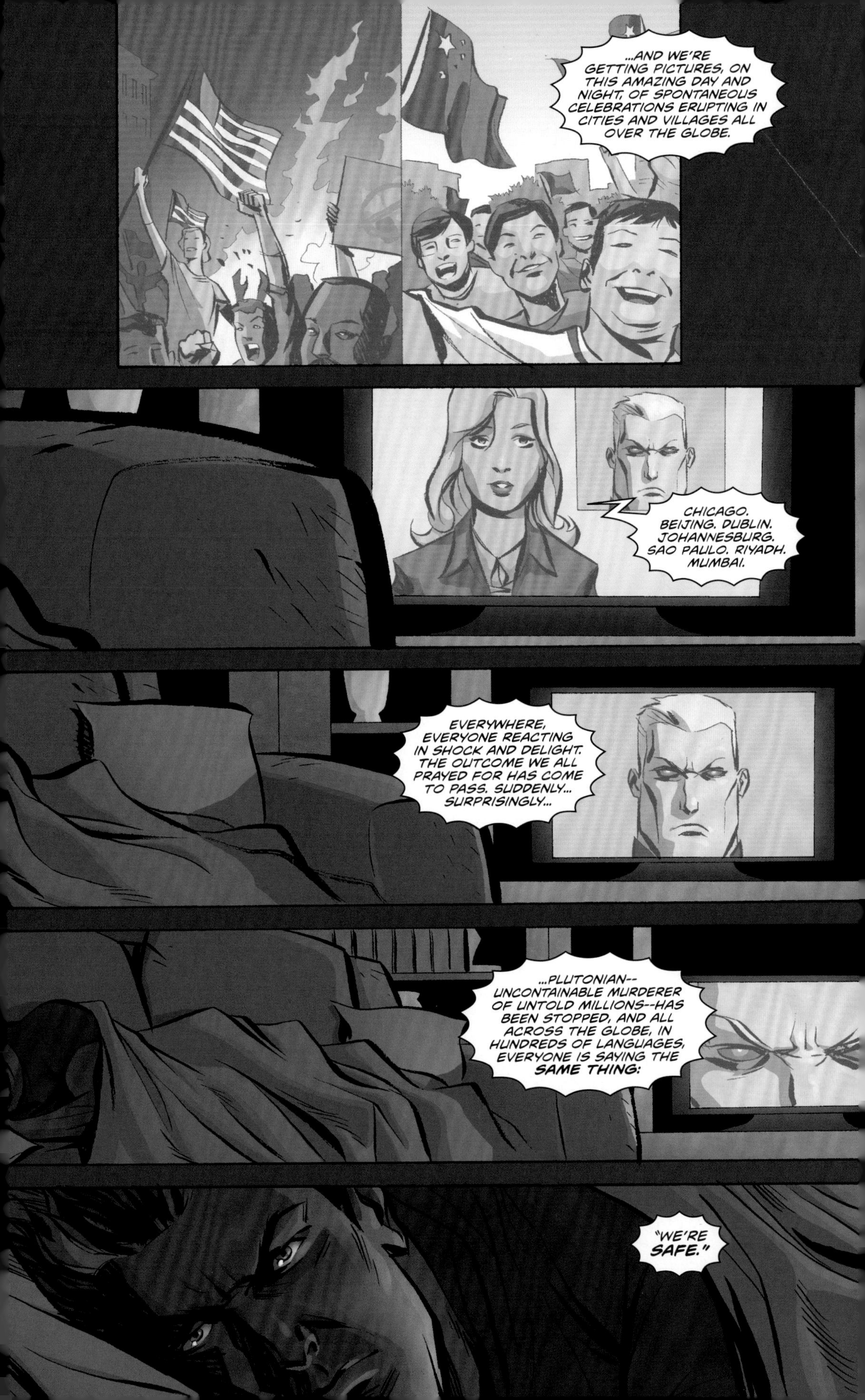
...AND WE'RE GETTING PICTURES, ON THIS AMAZING DAY AND NIGHT, OF SPONTANEOUS CELEBRATIONS ERUPTING IN CITIES AND VILLAGES ALL OVER THE GLOBE.
CHICAGO. BEIJING. DUBLIN. JOHANNESBURG. SAO PAULO. RIYADH. MUMBAI.
EVERYWHERE, EVERYONE REACTING IN SHOCK AND DELIGHT. THE OUTCOME WE ALL PRAYED FOR HAS COME TO PASS. SUDDENLY... SURPRISINGLY...
...PLUTONIAN-- UNCONTAINABLE MURDERER OF UNTOLD MILLIONS--HAS BEEN STOPPED, AND ALL ACROSS THE GLOBE, IN HUNDREDS OF LANGUAGES, EVERYONE IS SAYING THE **SAME THING:**
"WE'RE **SAFE.**"

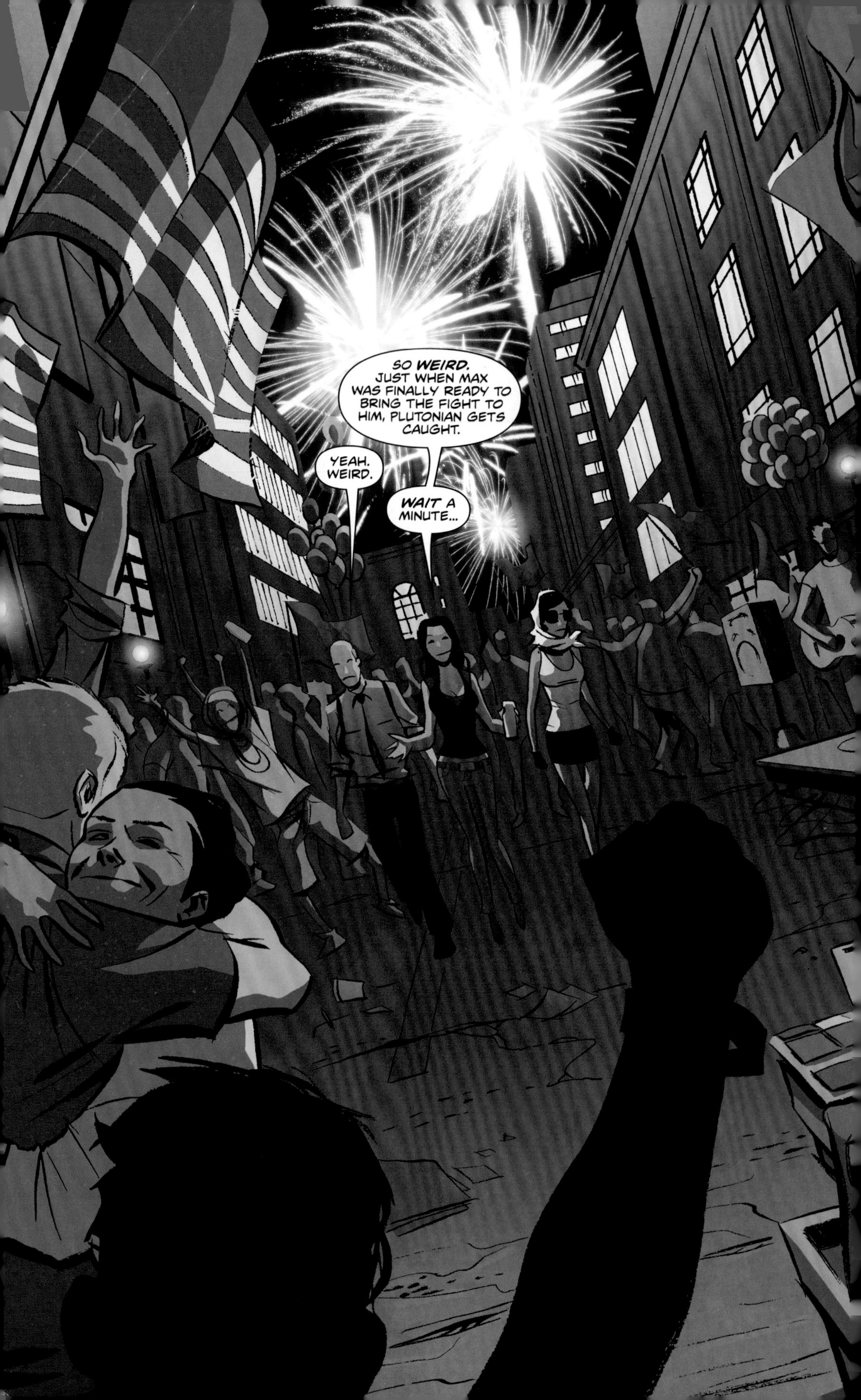
SO **WEIRD.** JUST WHEN MAX WAS FINALLY READY TO BRING THE FIGHT TO HIM, PLUTONIAN GETS CAUGHT.
YEAH. WEIRD.
**WAIT** A MINUTE...

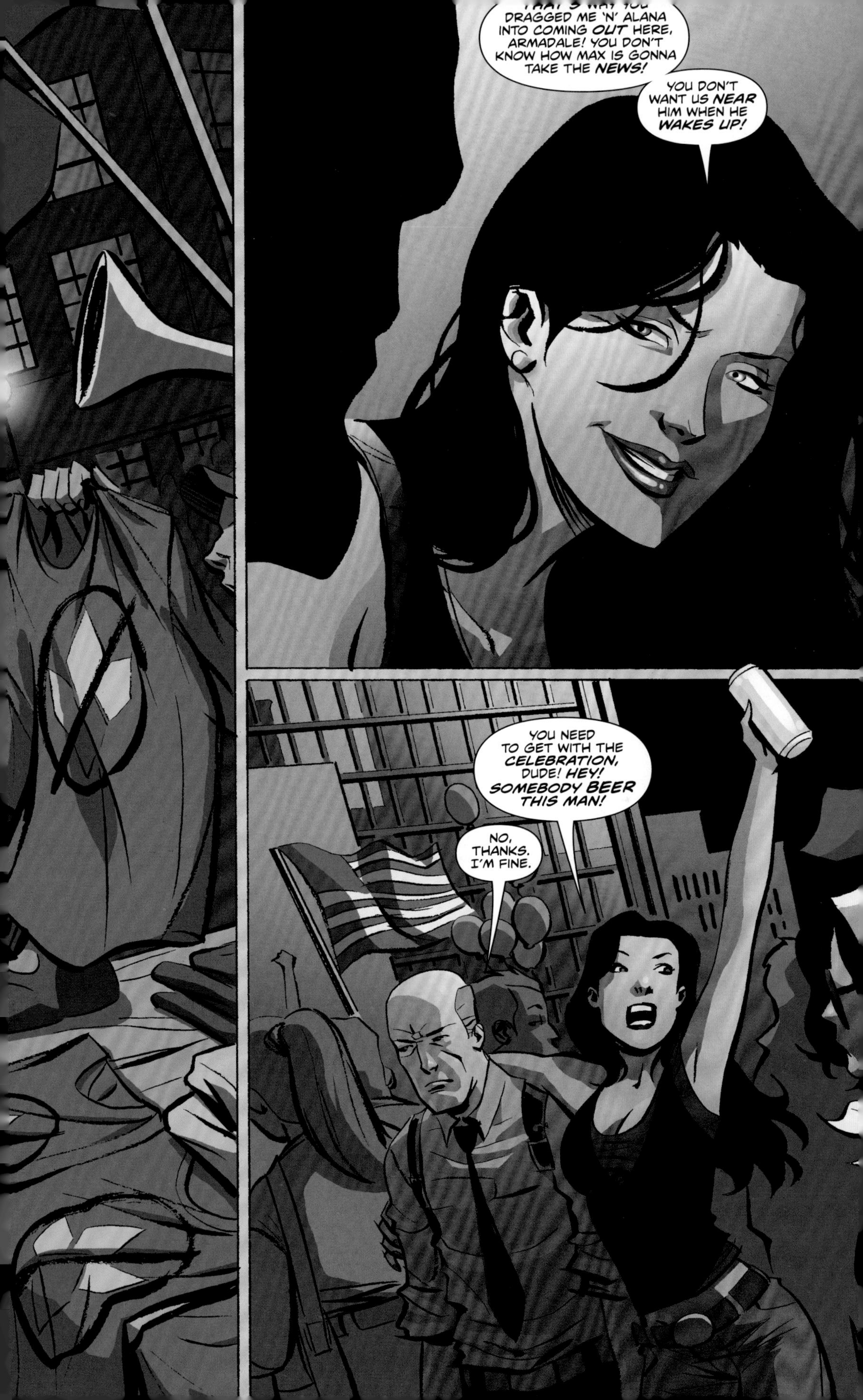
DRAGGED ME 'N' ALANA INTO COMING OUT HERE, ARMADALE! YOU DON'T KNOW HOW MAX IS GONNA TAKE THE NEWS!
YOU DON'T WANT US NEAR HIM WHEN HE WAKES UP!
YOU NEED TO GET WITH THE CELEBRATION, DUDE! HEY! SOMEBODY BEER THIS MAN!
NO, THANKS. I'M FINE.

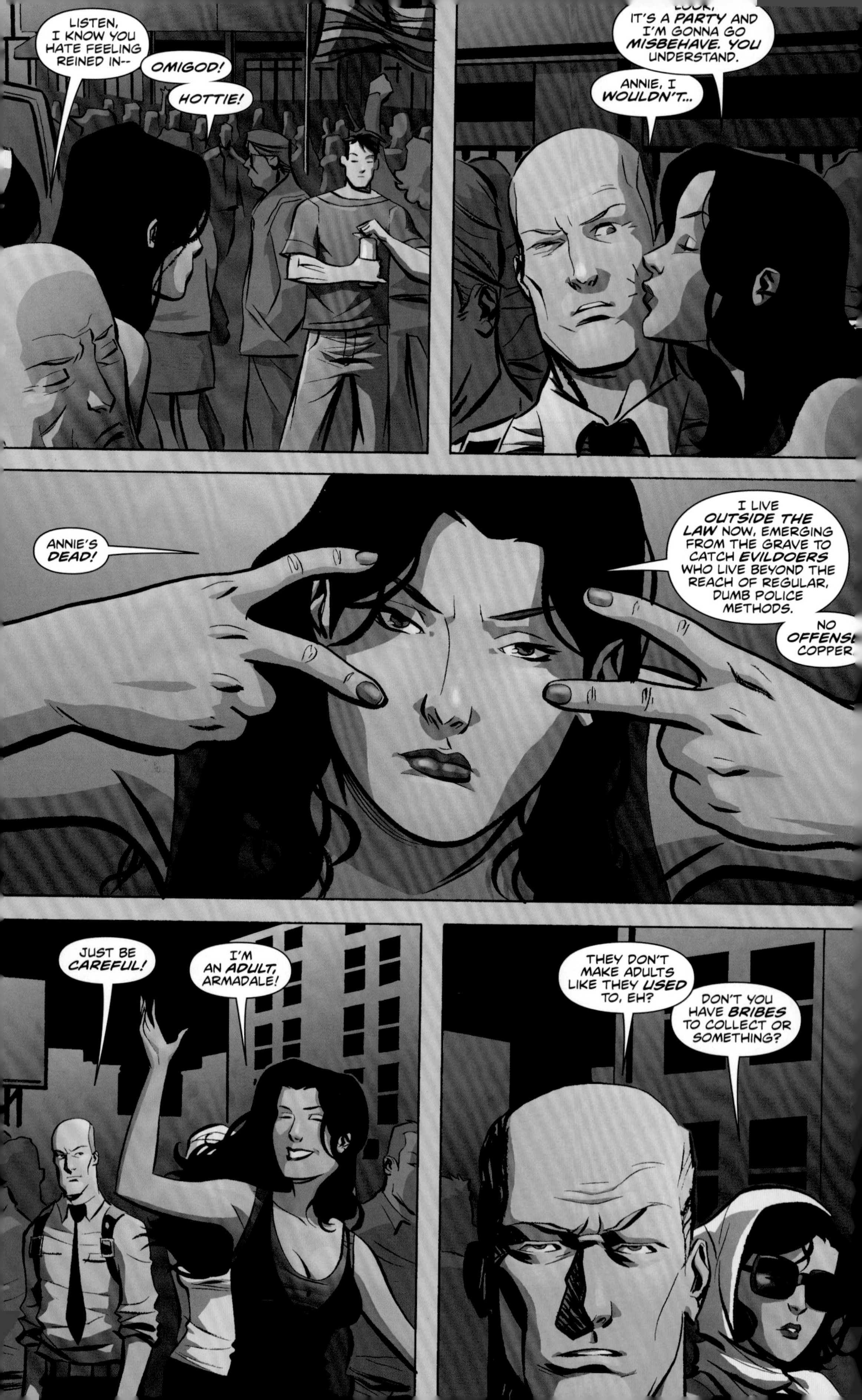
LISTEN, I KNOW YOU HATE FEELING REINED IN--
OMIGOD!
HOTTIE!
IT'S A PARTY AND I'M GONNA GO MISBEHAVE. YOU UNDERSTAND.
ANNIE, I WOULDN'T...
ANNIE'S DEAD!
I LIVE OUTSIDE THE LAW NOW, EMERGING FROM THE GRAVE TO CATCH EVILDOERS WHO LIVE BEYOND THE REACH OF REGULAR, DUMB POLICE METHODS.
NO OFFENS COPPER
JUST BE CAREFUL!
I'M AN ADULT, ARMADALE!
THEY DON'T MAKE ADULTS LIKE THEY USED TO, EH?
DON'T YOU HAVE BRIBES TO COLLECT OR SOMETHING?

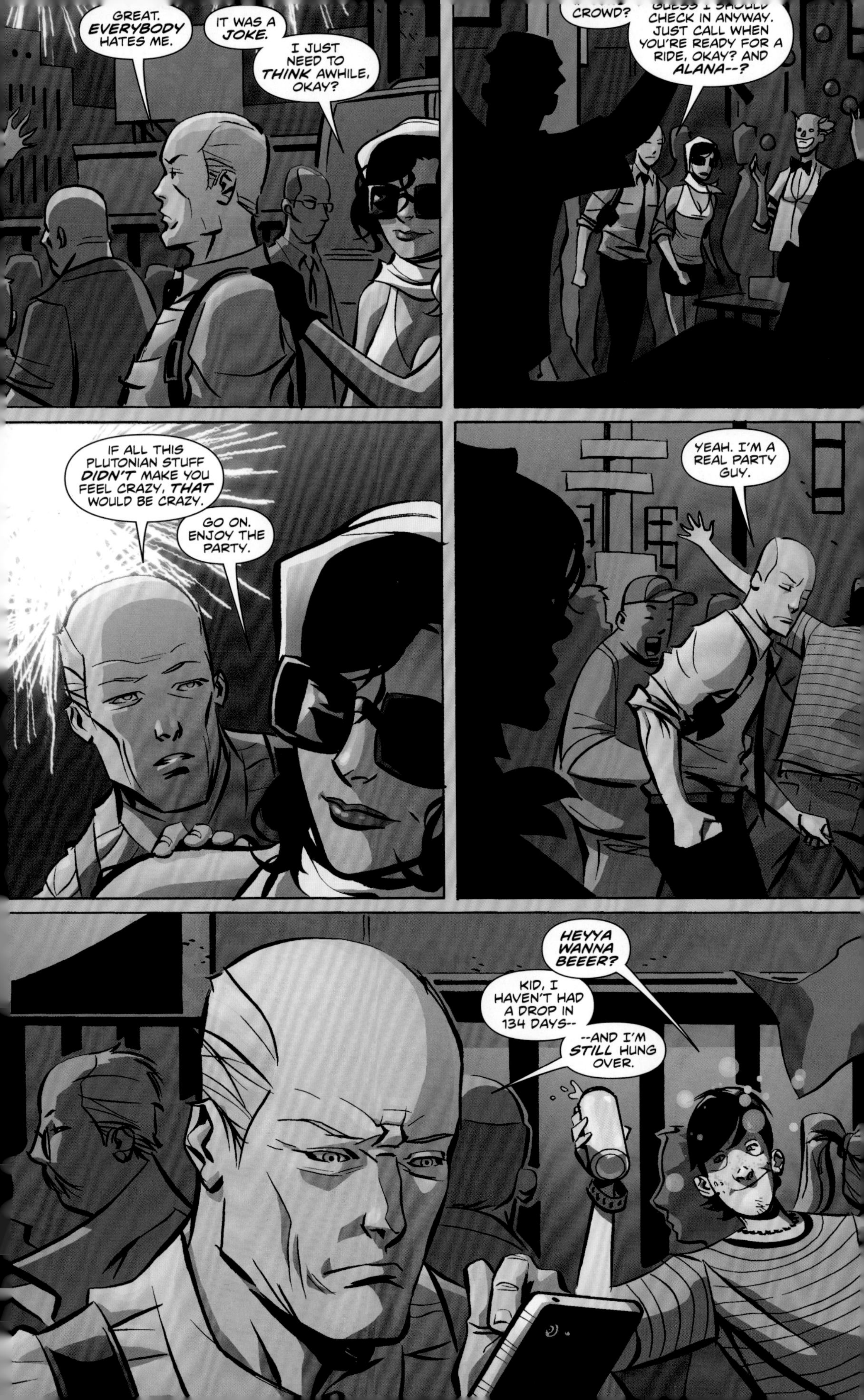
GREAT. EVERYBODY HATES ME.
IT WAS A JOKE.
I JUST NEED TO THINK AWHILE, OKAY?
CROWD?
CHECK IN ANYWAY. JUST CALL WHEN YOU'RE READY FOR A RIDE, OKAY? AND ALANA--?
IF ALL THIS PLUTONIAN STUFF DIDN'T MAKE YOU FEEL CRAZY, THAT WOULD BE CRAZY.
GO ON. ENJOY THE PARTY.
YEAH. I'M A REAL PARTY GUY.
HEYYA WANNA BEEER?
KID, I HAVEN'T HAD A DROP IN 134 DAYS--
--AND I'M STILL HUNG OVER.

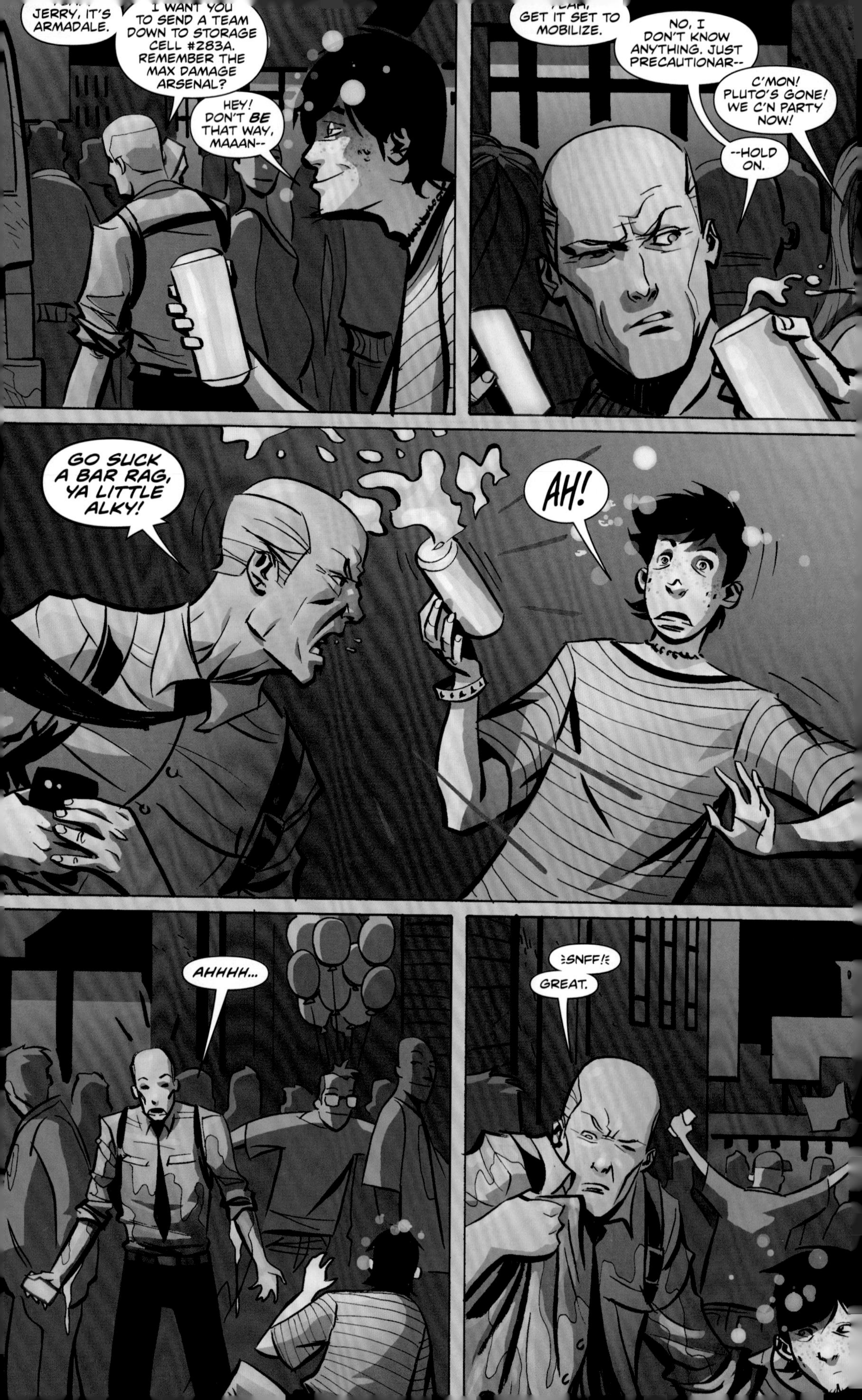

JERRY, IT'S ARMADALE.
I WANT YOU TO SEND A TEAM DOWN TO STORAGE CELL #283A. REMEMBER THE MAX DAMAGE ARSENAL?
HEY! DON'T BE THAT WAY, MAAAN--
GET IT SET TO MOBILIZE.
NO, I DON'T KNOW ANYTHING. JUST PRECAUTIONAR--
C'MON! PLUTO'S GONE! WE C'N PARTY NOW!
--HOLD ON.
GO SUCK A BAR RAG, YA LITTLE ALKY!
AH!
AHHHH...
SNFF!
GREAT.

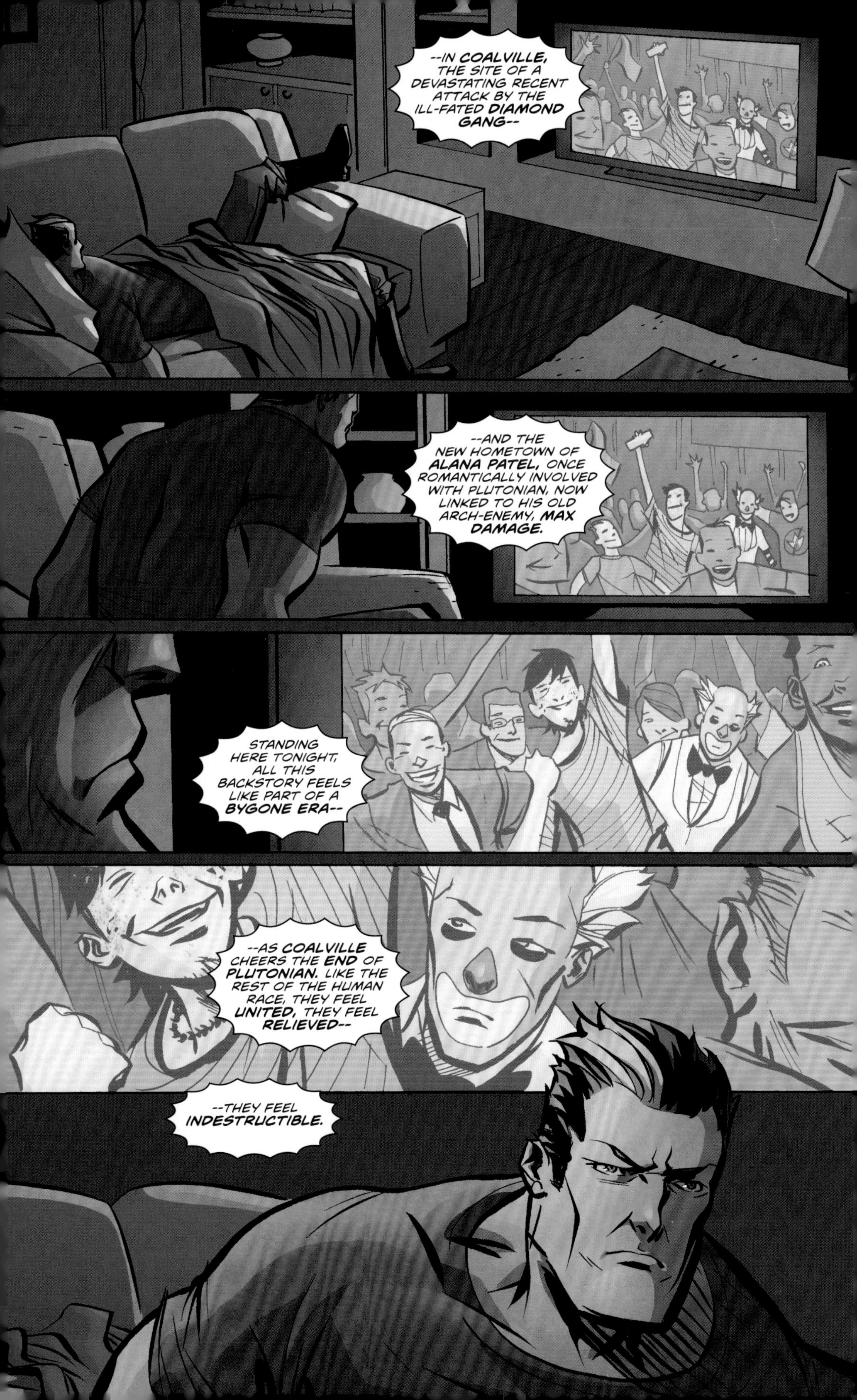
--IN COALVILLE, THE SITE OF A DEVASTATING RECENT ATTACK BY THE ILL-FATED DIAMOND GANG--
--AND THE NEW HOMETOWN OF ALANA PATEL, ONCE ROMANTICALLY INVOLVED WITH PLUTONIAN, NOW LINKED TO HIS OLD ARCH-ENEMY, MAX DAMAGE.
STANDING HERE TONIGHT, ALL THIS BACKSTORY FEELS LIKE PART OF A BYGONE ERA--
--AS COALVILLE CHEERS THE END OF PLUTONIAN. LIKE THE REST OF THE HUMAN RACE, THEY FEEL UNITED, THEY FEEL RELIEVED--
--THEY FEEL INDESTRUCTIBLE.

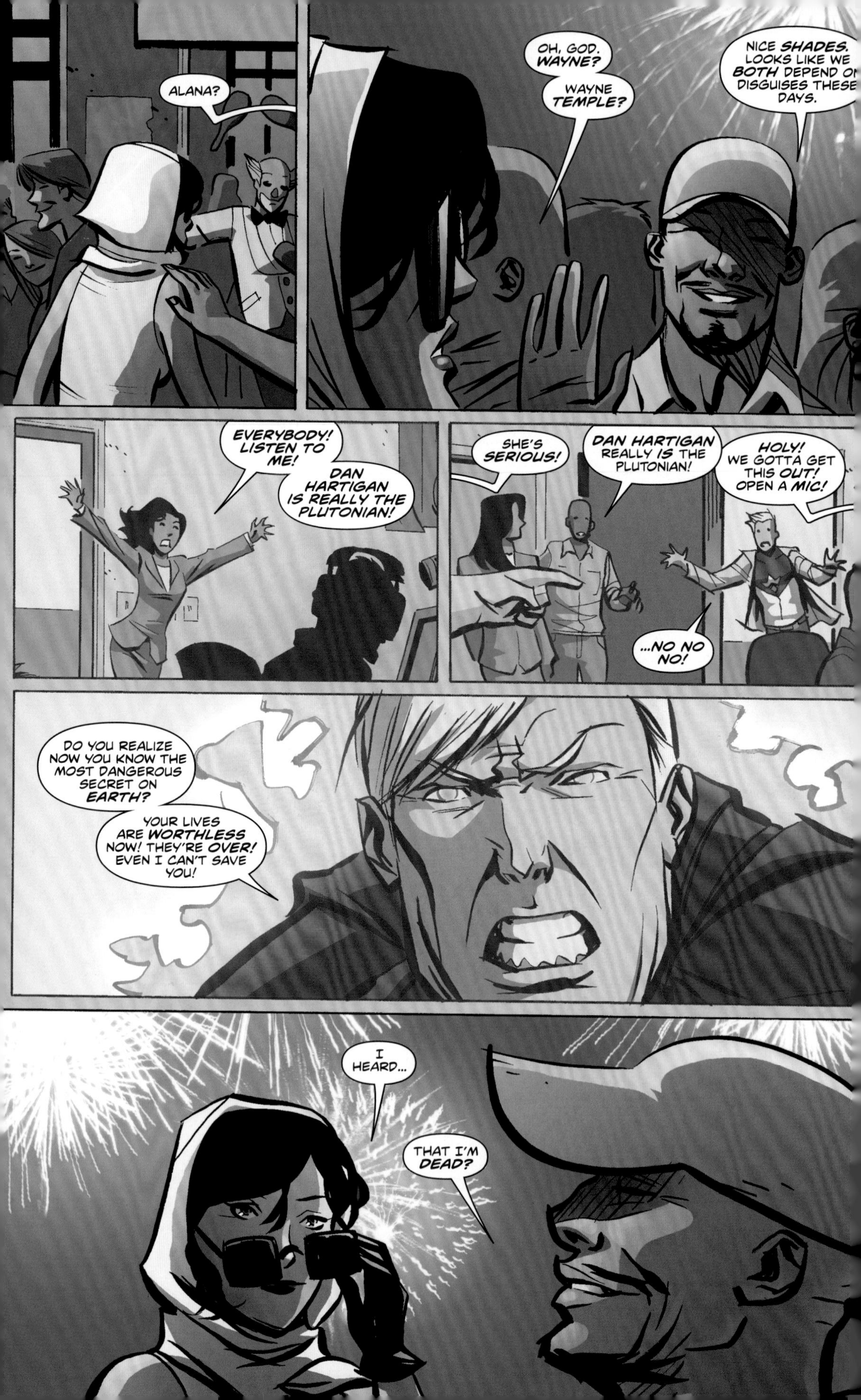
ALANA?
OH, GOD. WAYNE?
WAYNE TEMPLE?
NICE SHADES. LOOKS LIKE WE BOTH DEPEND ON DISGUISES THESE DAYS.
EVERYBODY! LISTEN TO ME!
DAN HARTIGAN IS REALLY THE PLUTONIAN!
SHE'S SERIOUS!
DAN HARTIGAN REALLY IS THE PLUTONIAN!
HOLY! WE GOTTA GET THIS OUT! OPEN A MIC!
...NO NO NO!
DO YOU REALIZE NOW YOU KNOW THE MOST DANGEROUS SECRET ON EARTH?
YOUR LIVES ARE WORTHLESS NOW! THEY'RE OVER! EVEN I CAN'T SAVE YOU!
I HEARD...
THAT I'M DEAD?

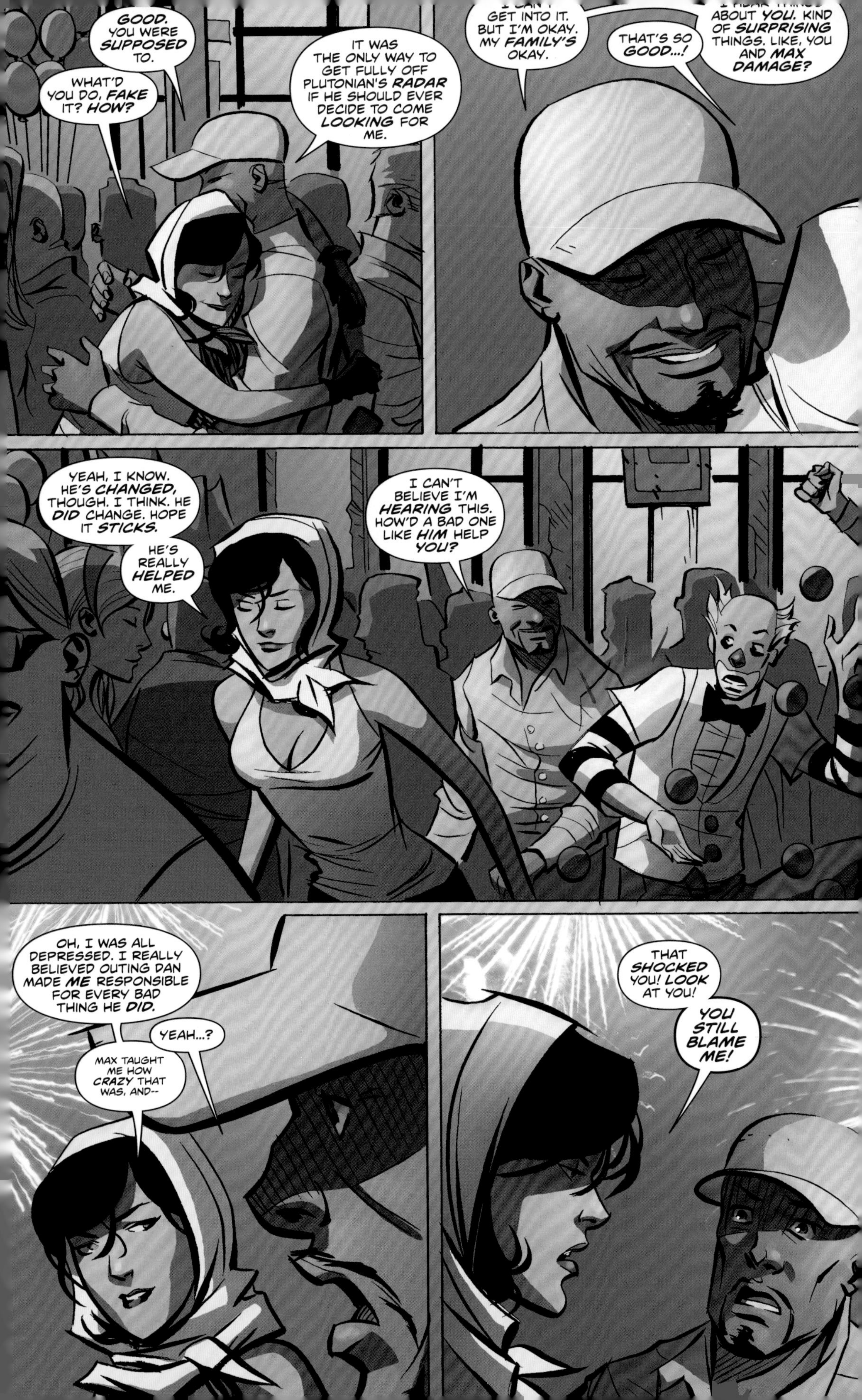
GOOD. YOU WERE SUPPOSED TO.
WHAT'D YOU DO, FAKE IT? HOW?
IT WAS THE ONLY WAY TO GET FULLY OFF PLUTONIAN'S RADAR IF HE SHOULD EVER DECIDE TO COME LOOKING FOR ME.
GET INTO IT. BUT I'M OKAY. MY FAMILY'S OKAY.
THAT'S SO GOOD...!
ABOUT YOU. KIND OF SURPRISING THINGS. LIKE, YOU AND MAX DAMAGE?
YEAH, I KNOW. HE'S CHANGED, THOUGH. I THINK. HE DID CHANGE. HOPE IT STICKS.
HE'S REALLY HELPED ME.
I CAN'T BELIEVE I'M HEARING THIS. HOW'D A BAD ONE LIKE HIM HELP YOU?
OH, I WAS ALL DEPRESSED. I REALLY BELIEVED OUTING DAN MADE ME RESPONSIBLE FOR EVERY BAD THING HE DID.
YEAH...?
MAX TAUGHT ME HOW CRAZY THAT WAS, AND--
THAT SHOCKED YOU! LOOK AT YOU!
YOU STILL BLAME ME!

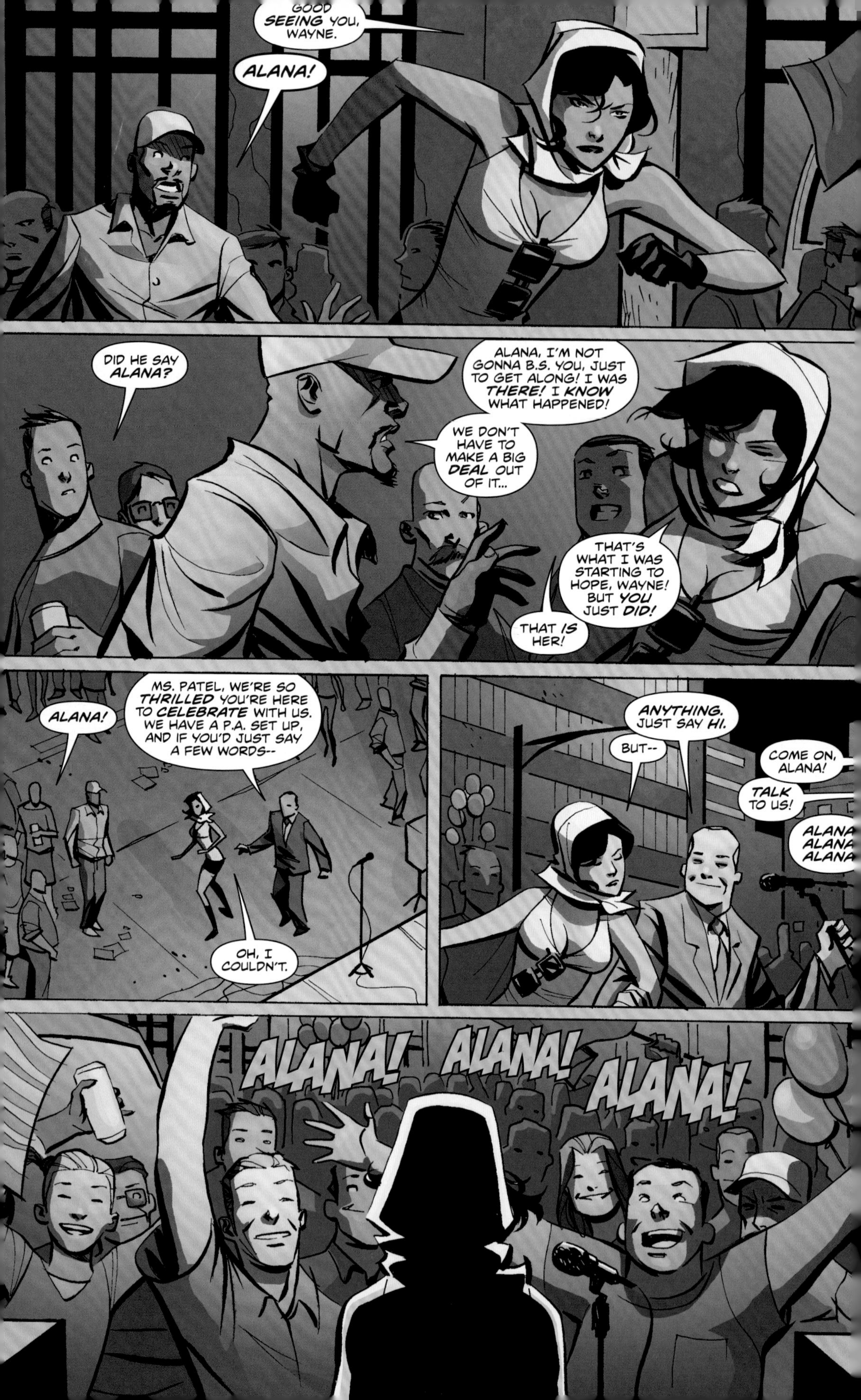
GOOD SEEING YOU, WAYNE.
ALANA!
DID HE SAY ALANA?
ALANA, I'M NOT GONNA B.S. YOU, JUST TO GET ALONG! I WAS THERE! I KNOW WHAT HAPPENED!
WE DON'T HAVE TO MAKE A BIG DEAL OUT OF IT...
THAT'S WHAT I WAS STARTING TO HOPE, WAYNE! BUT YOU JUST DID!
THAT IS HER!
ALANA!
MS. PATEL, WE'RE SO THRILLED YOU'RE HERE TO CELEBRATE WITH US. WE HAVE A P.A. SET UP, AND IF YOU'D JUST SAY A FEW WORDS--
OH, I COULDN'T.
ANYTHING. JUST SAY HI.
BUT--
COME ON, ALANA!
TALK TO US!
ALANA
ALANA
ALANA
ALANA! ALANA! ALANA!

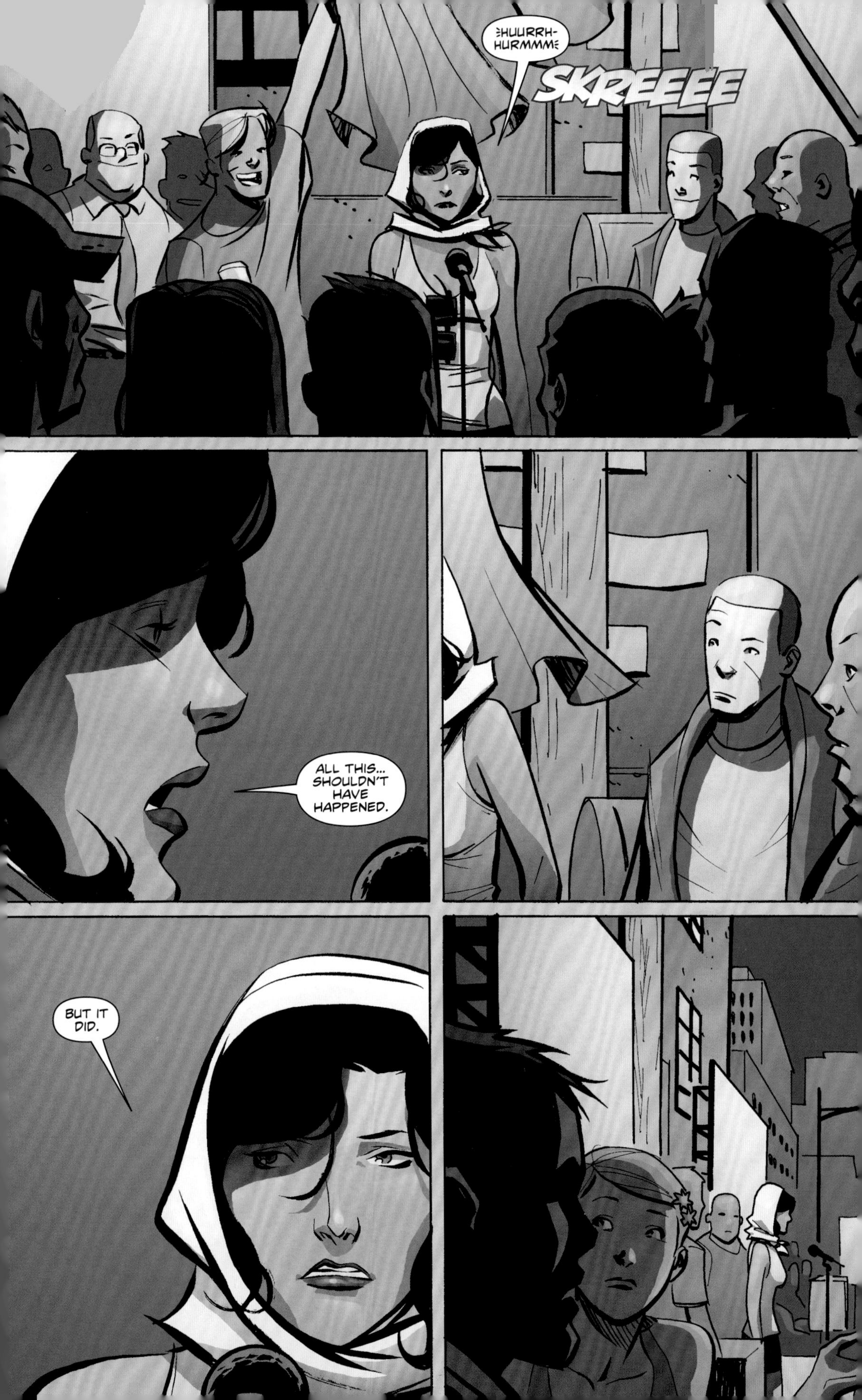
HUURRH-
HURMMM
SKREEEEE
ALL THIS... SHOULDN'T HAVE HAPPENED.
BUT IT DID.

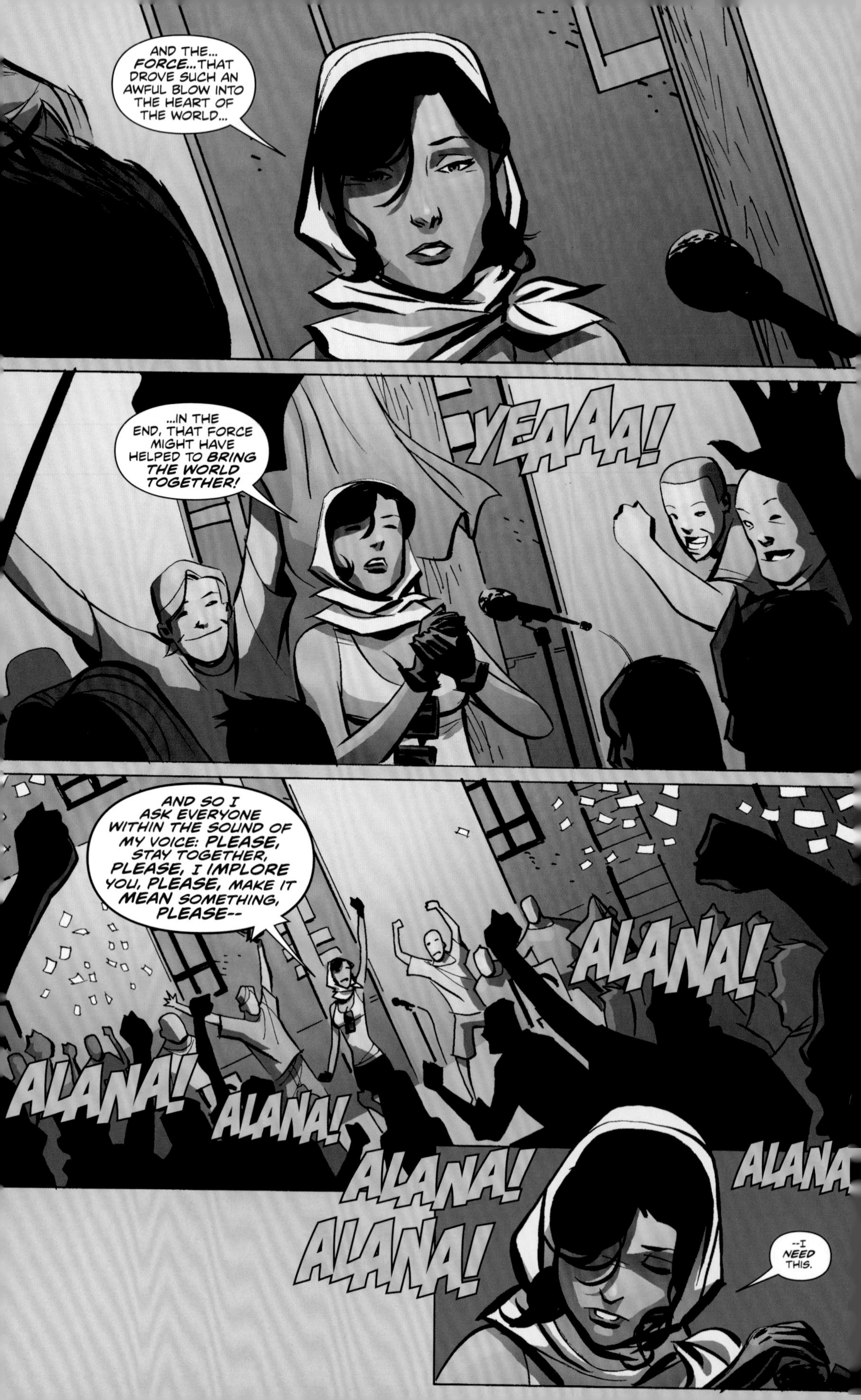
AND THE... FORCE...THAT DROVE SUCH AN AWFUL BLOW INTO THE HEART OF THE WORLD...
...IN THE END, THAT FORCE MIGHT HAVE HELPED TO BRING THE WORLD TOGETHER!
YEAAAA!
AND SO I ASK EVERYONE WITHIN THE SOUND OF MY VOICE: PLEASE, STAY TOGETHER, PLEASE, I IMPLORE YOU, PLEASE, MAKE IT MEAN SOMETHING, PLEASE--
ALANA!
ALANA!
ALANA!
ALANA!
ALANA
ALANA!
--I NEED THIS.

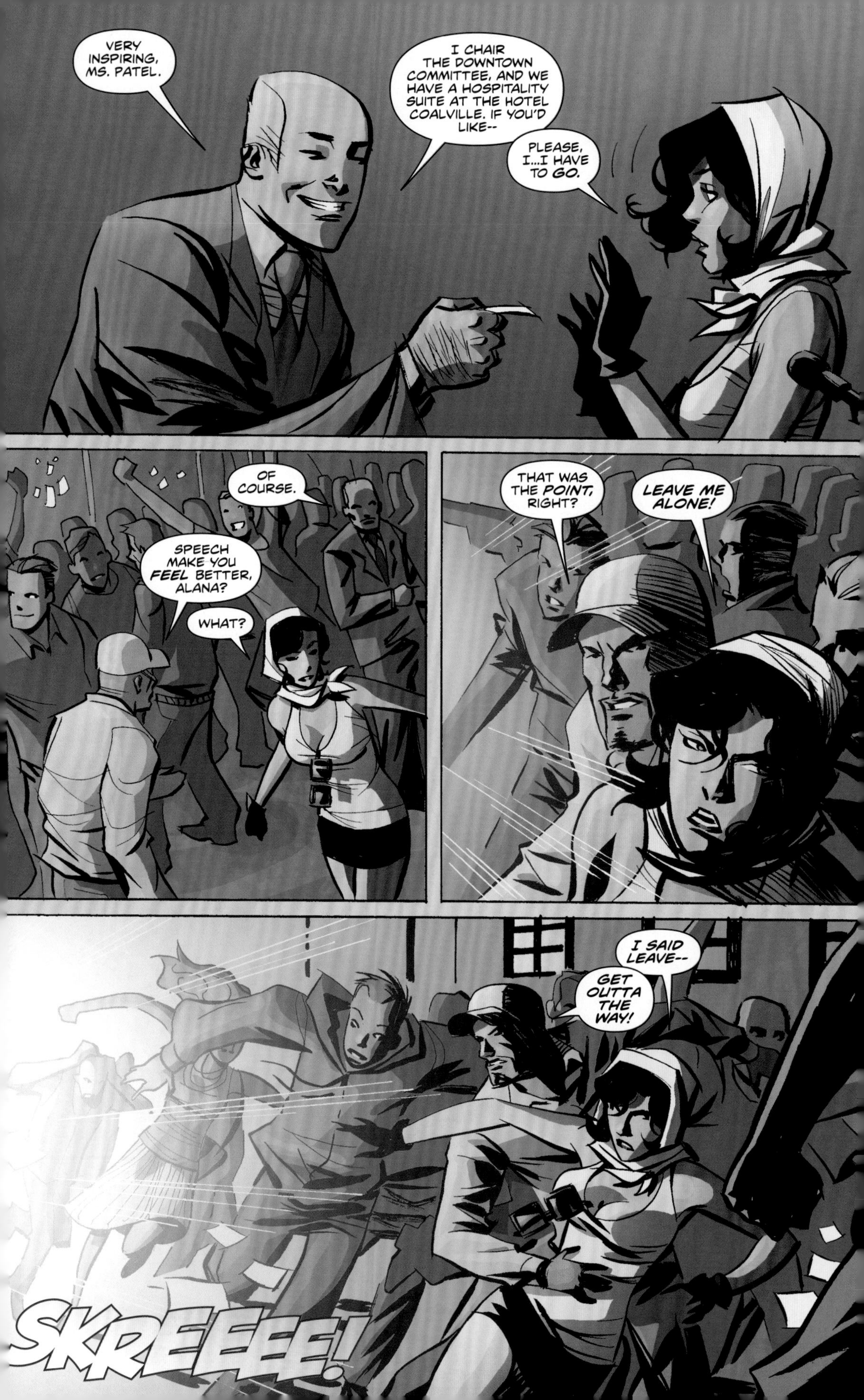
VERY INSPIRING, MS. PATEL.
I CHAIR THE DOWNTOWN COMMITTEE, AND WE HAVE A HOSPITALITY SUITE AT THE HOTEL COALVILLE. IF YOU'D LIKE--
PLEASE, I...I HAVE TO GO.
OF COURSE.
SPEECH MAKE YOU FEEL BETTER, ALANA?
WHAT?
THAT WAS THE POINT, RIGHT?
LEAVE ME ALONE!
I SAID LEAVE--
GET OUTTA THE WAY!
SKREEEEE!

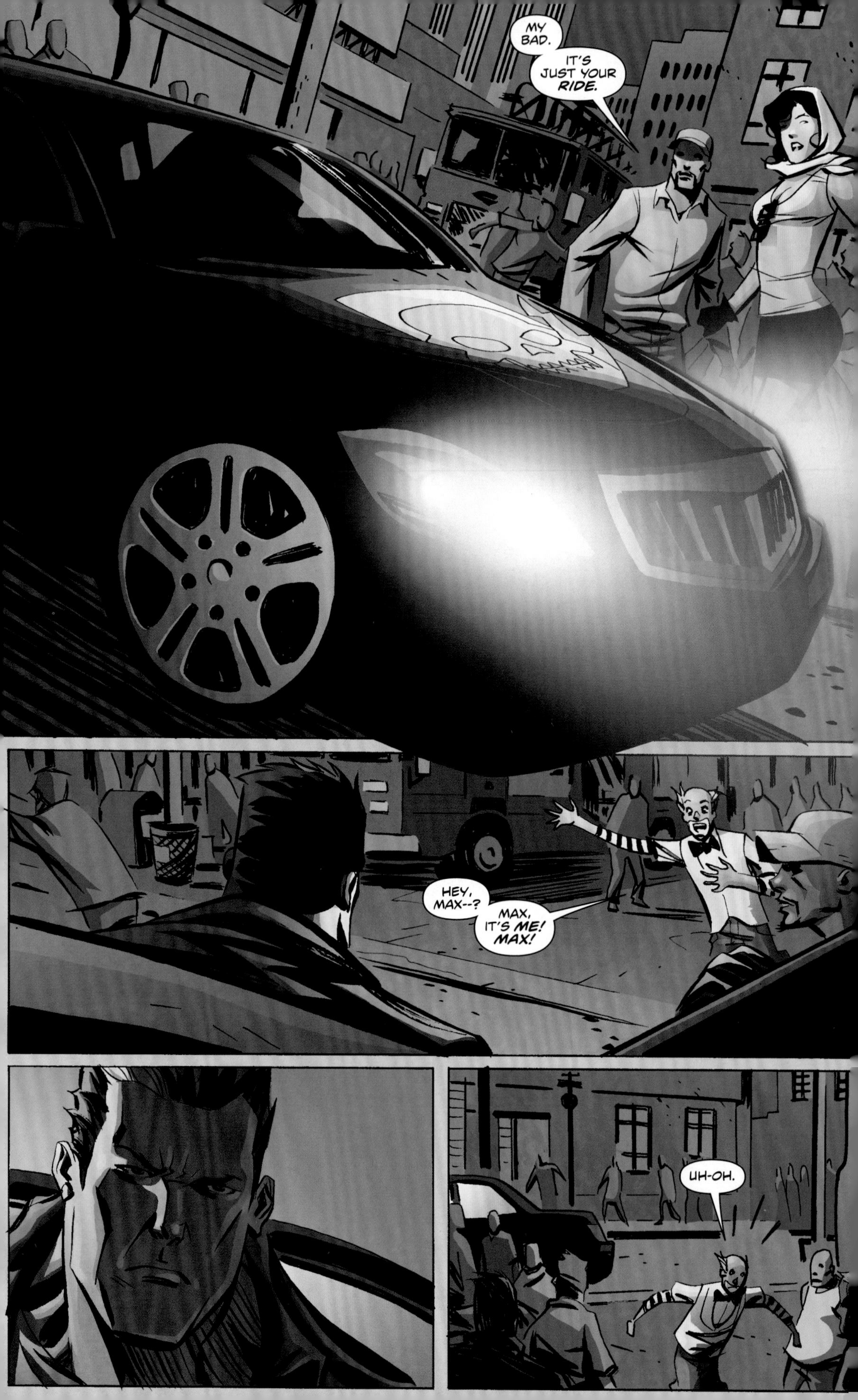
MY BAD.
IT'S JUST YOUR RIDE.
HEY, MAX--?
MAX, IT'S ME! MAX!
UH-OH.

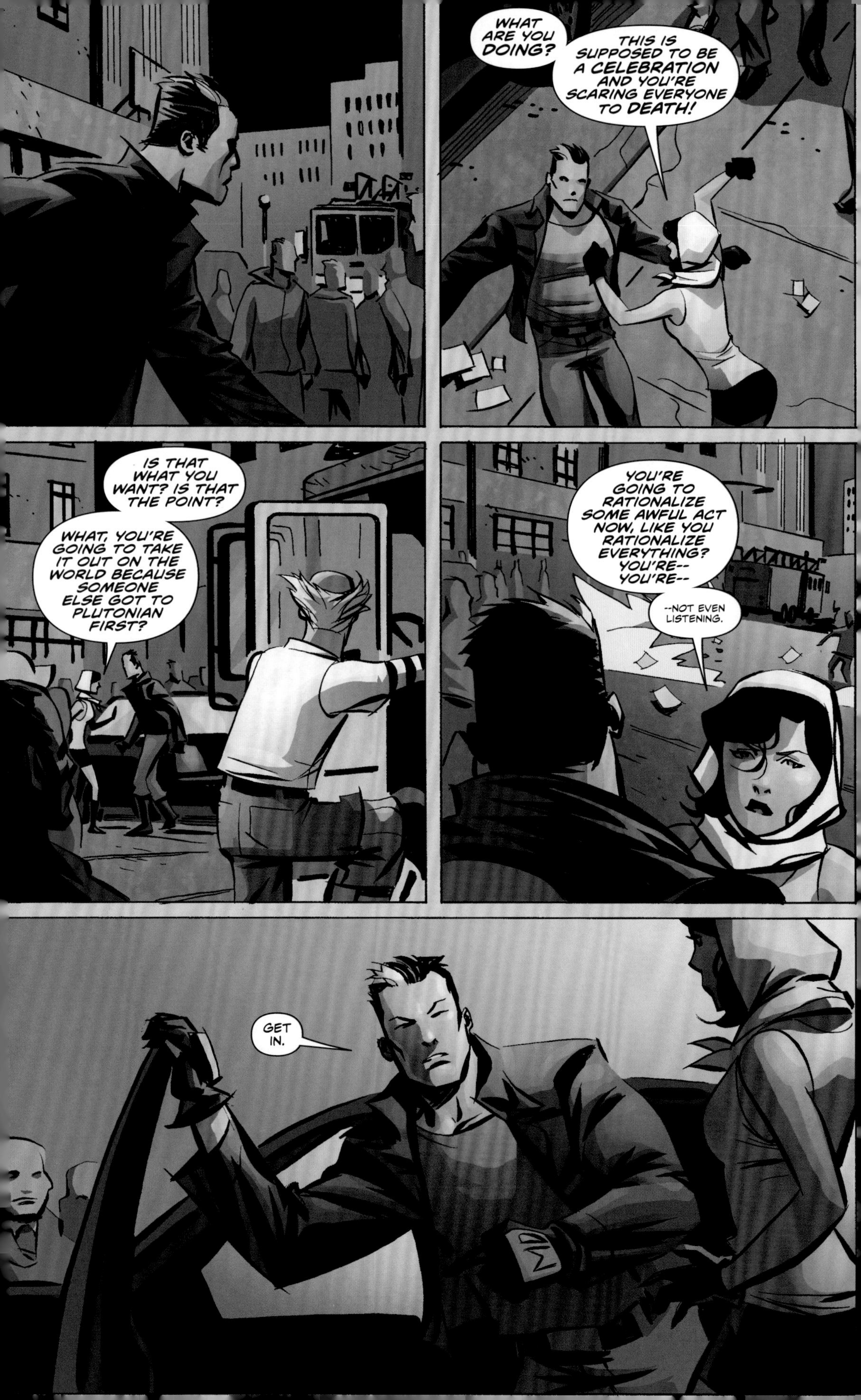
WHAT ARE YOU DOING?
THIS IS SUPPOSED TO BE A CELEBRATION AND YOU'RE SCARING EVERYONE TO DEATH!
IS THAT WHAT YOU WANT? IS THAT THE POINT?
WHAT, YOU'RE GOING TO TAKE IT OUT ON THE WORLD BECAUSE SOMEONE ELSE GOT TO PLUTONIAN FIRST?
YOU'RE GOING TO RATIONALIZE SOME AWFUL ACT NOW, LIKE YOU RATIONALIZE EVERYTHING? YOU'RE-- YOU'RE--
--NOT EVEN LISTENING.
GET IN.

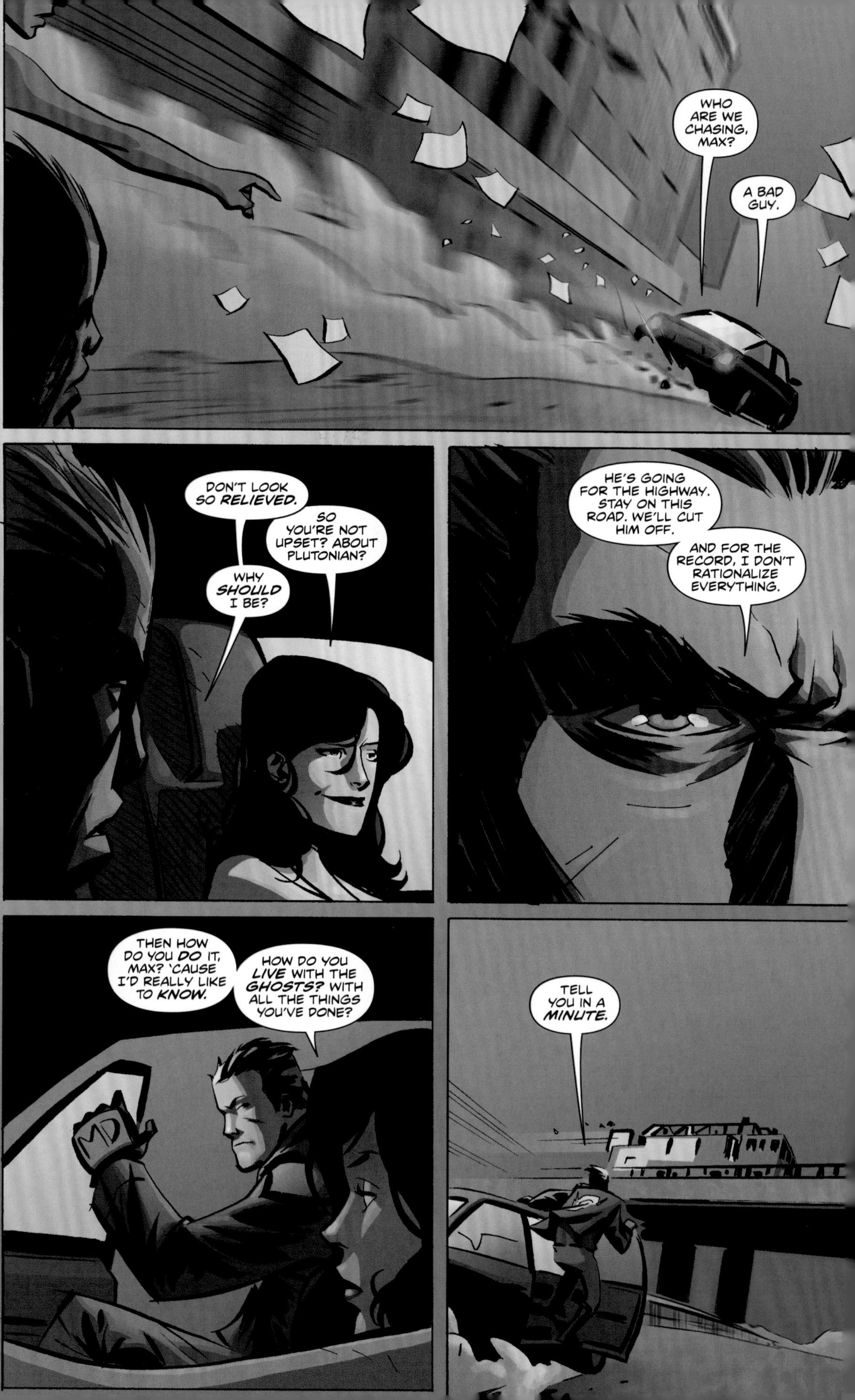
WHO ARE WE CHASING, MAX?
A BAD GUY.
DON'T LOOK SO *RELIEVED.*
SO YOU'RE NOT UPSET? ABOUT PLUTONIAN?
WHY *SHOULD* I BE?
HE'S GOING FOR THE HIGHWAY. STAY ON THIS ROAD. WE'LL CUT HIM OFF.
AND FOR THE RECORD, I DON'T RATIONALIZE EVERYTHING.
THEN HOW DO YOU *DO* IT, MAX? 'CAUSE I'D REALLY LIKE TO *KNOW.*
HOW DO YOU *LIVE* WITH THE *GHOSTS?* WITH ALL THE THINGS YOU'VE DONE?
MD
TELL YOU IN A *MINUTE.*

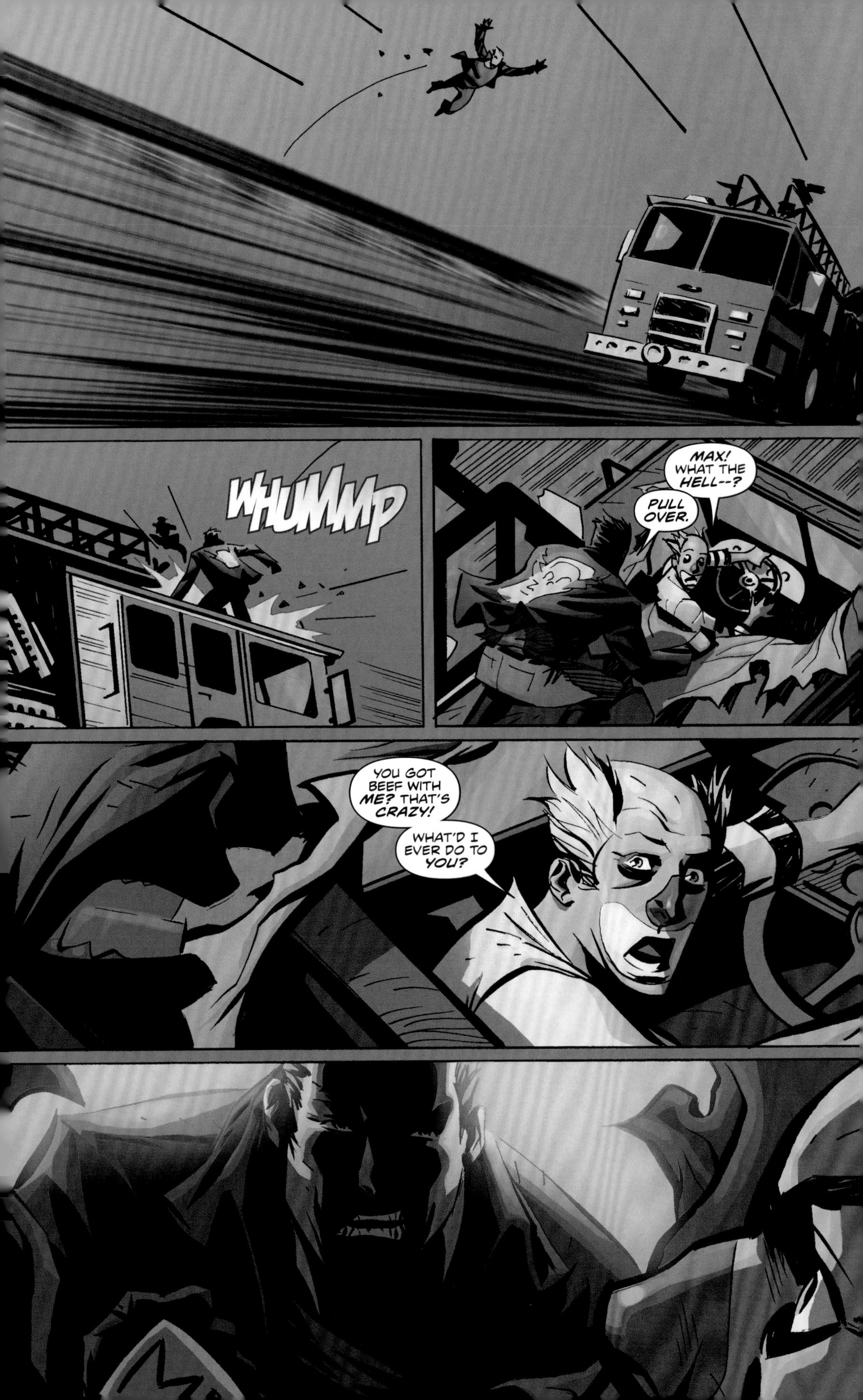
WHUMMP
MAX! WHAT THE HELL--?
PULL OVER.
YOU GOT BEEF WITH ME? THAT'S CRAZY!
WHAT'D I EVER DO TO YOU?

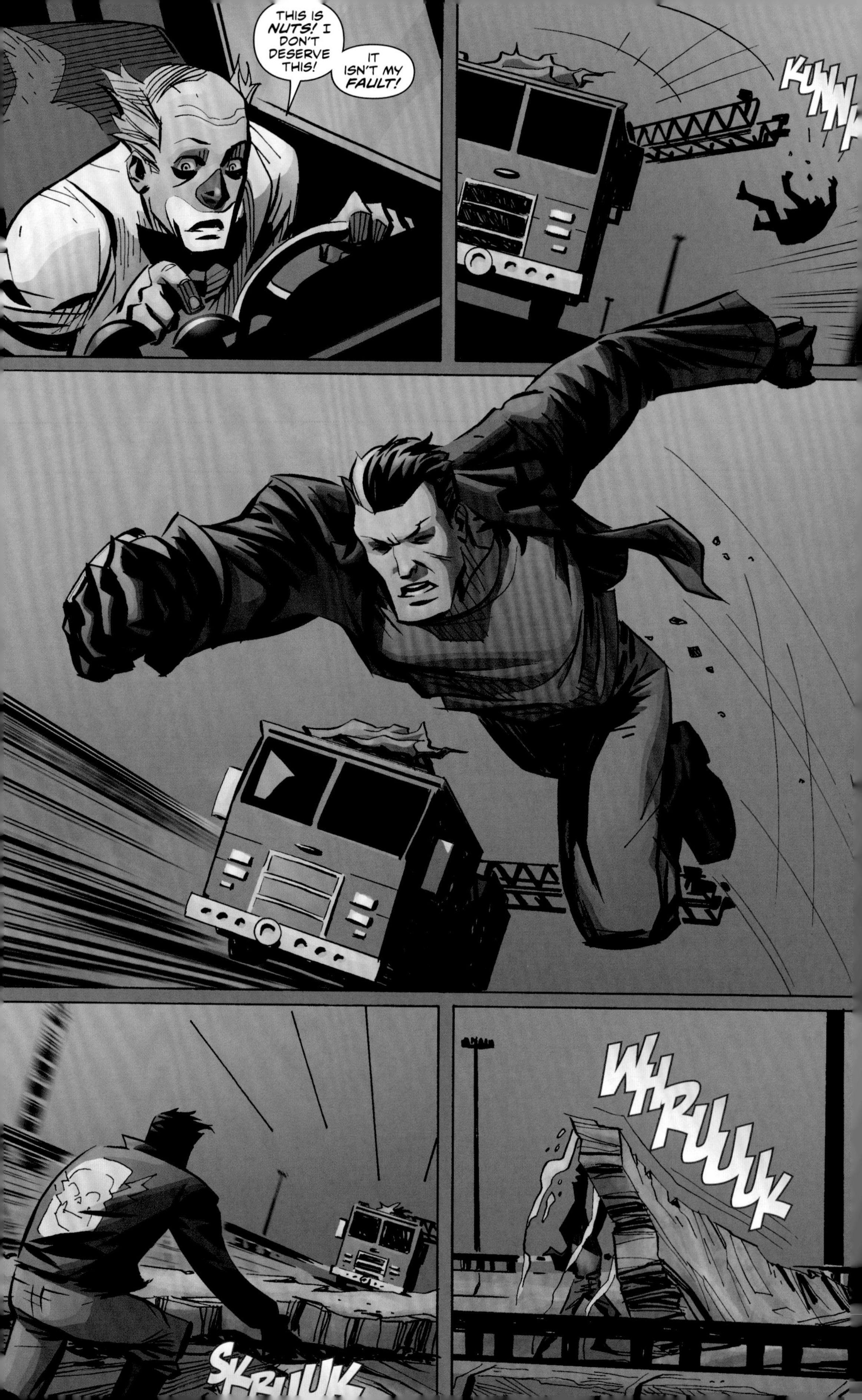
THIS IS NUTS! I DON'T DESERVE THIS!
IT ISN'T MY FAULT!
KUNNK
WHRUUUK
SKRUUK

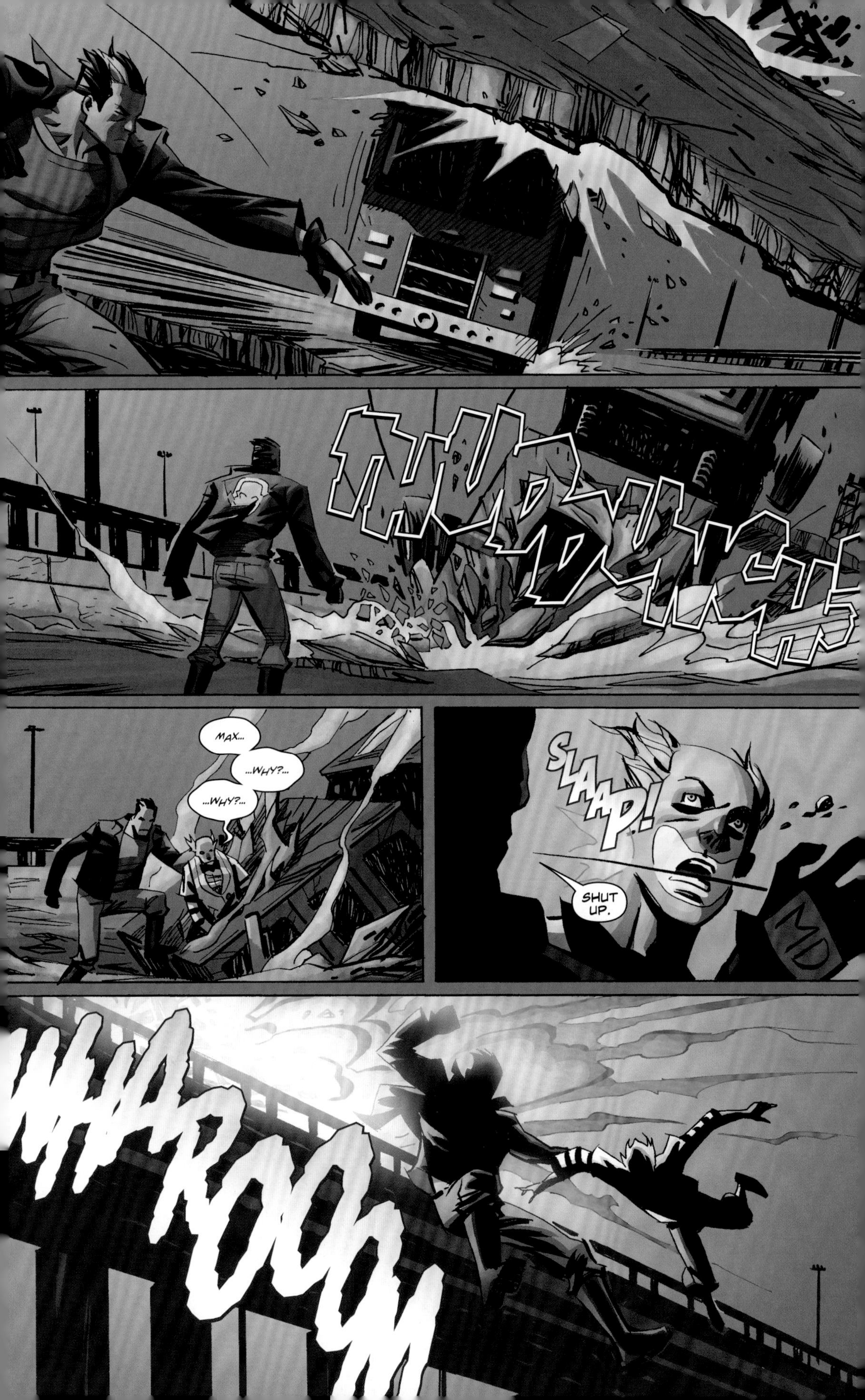
THUDUNCH
MAX...
...WHY?...
...WHY?...
SLAAAP!
SHUT UP.
WHAROOM

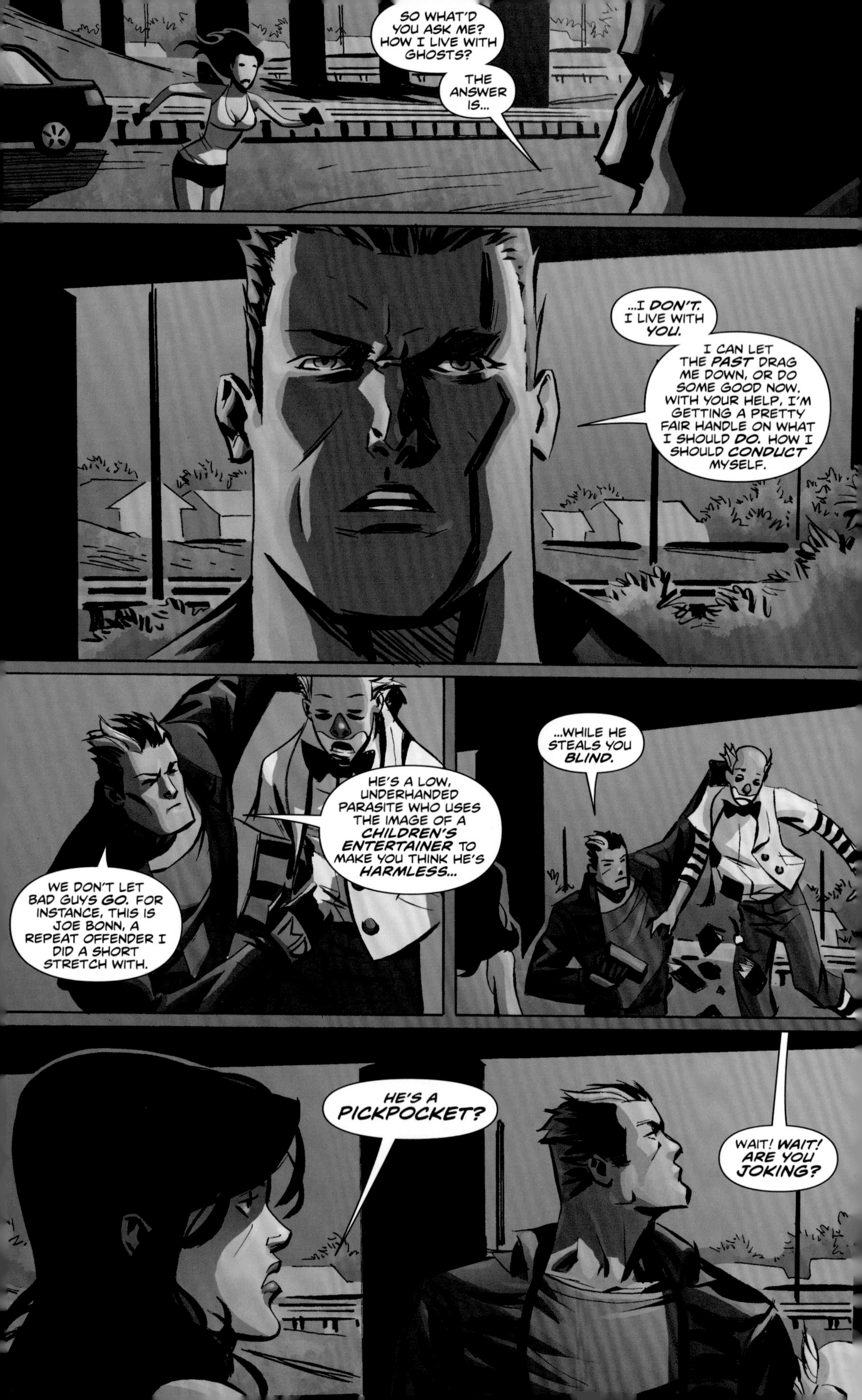
SO WHAT'D YOU ASK ME? HOW I LIVE WITH GHOSTS?
THE ANSWER IS...
...I DON'T. I LIVE WITH YOU.
I CAN LET THE PAST DRAG ME DOWN, OR DO SOME GOOD NOW. WITH YOUR HELP, I'M GETTING A PRETTY FAIR HANDLE ON WHAT I SHOULD DO. HOW I SHOULD CONDUCT MYSELF.
WE DON'T LET BAD GUYS GO. FOR INSTANCE, THIS IS JOE BONN, A REPEAT OFFENDER I DID A SHORT STRETCH WITH.
HE'S A LOW, UNDERHANDED PARASITE WHO USES THE IMAGE OF A CHILDREN'S ENTERTAINER TO MAKE YOU THINK HE'S HARMLESS...
...WHILE HE STEALS YOU BLIND.
HE'S A PICKPOCKET?
WAIT! WAIT! ARE YOU JOKING?

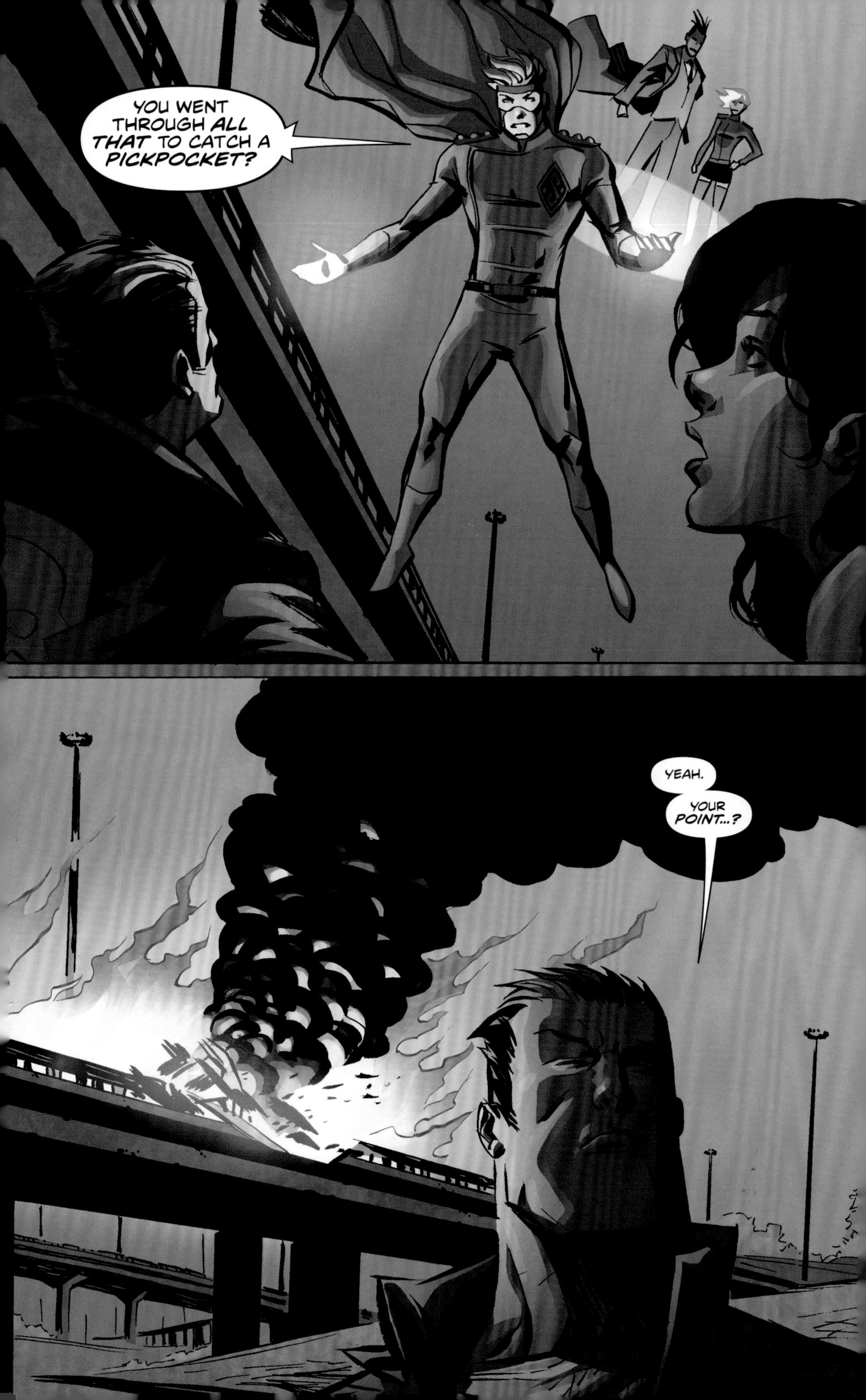
YOU WENT THROUGH ALL THAT TO CATCH A PICKPOCKET?
YEAH.
YOUR POINT...?

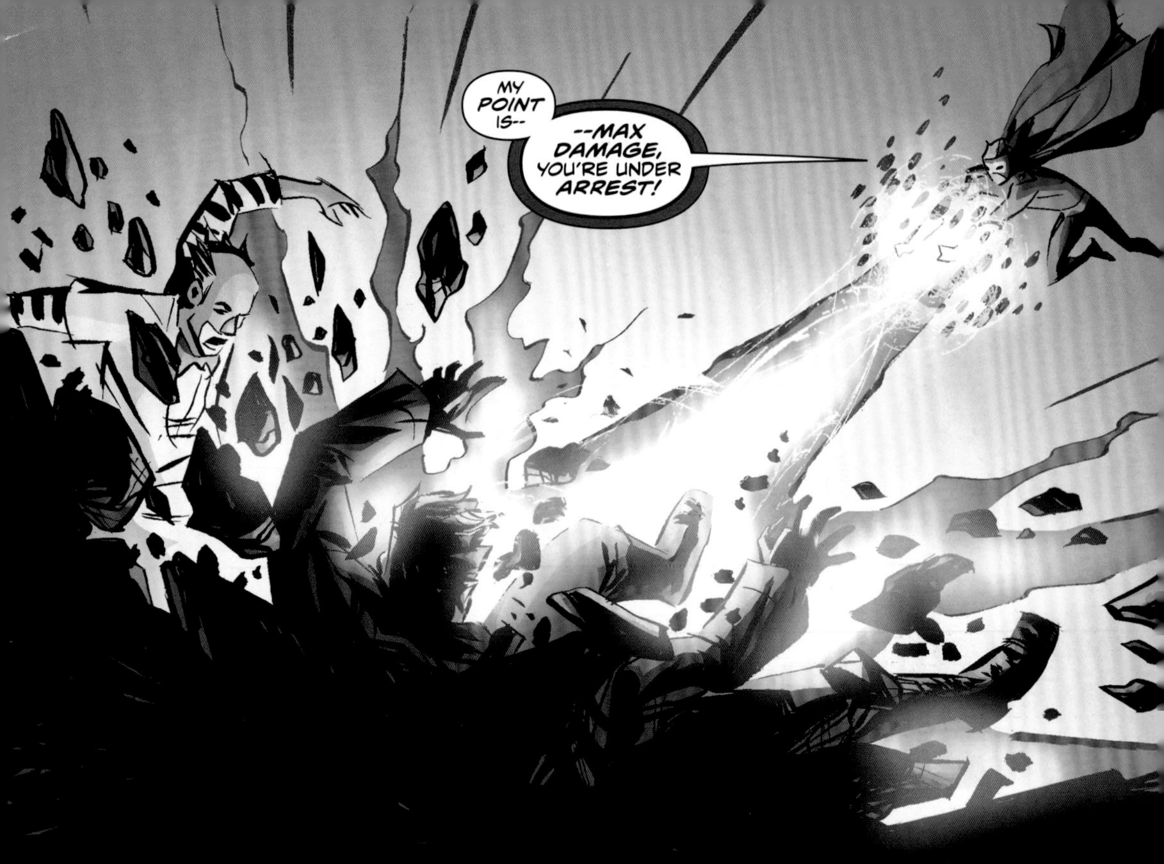
MY POINT IS--
--MAX DAMAGE, YOU'RE UNDER ARREST!

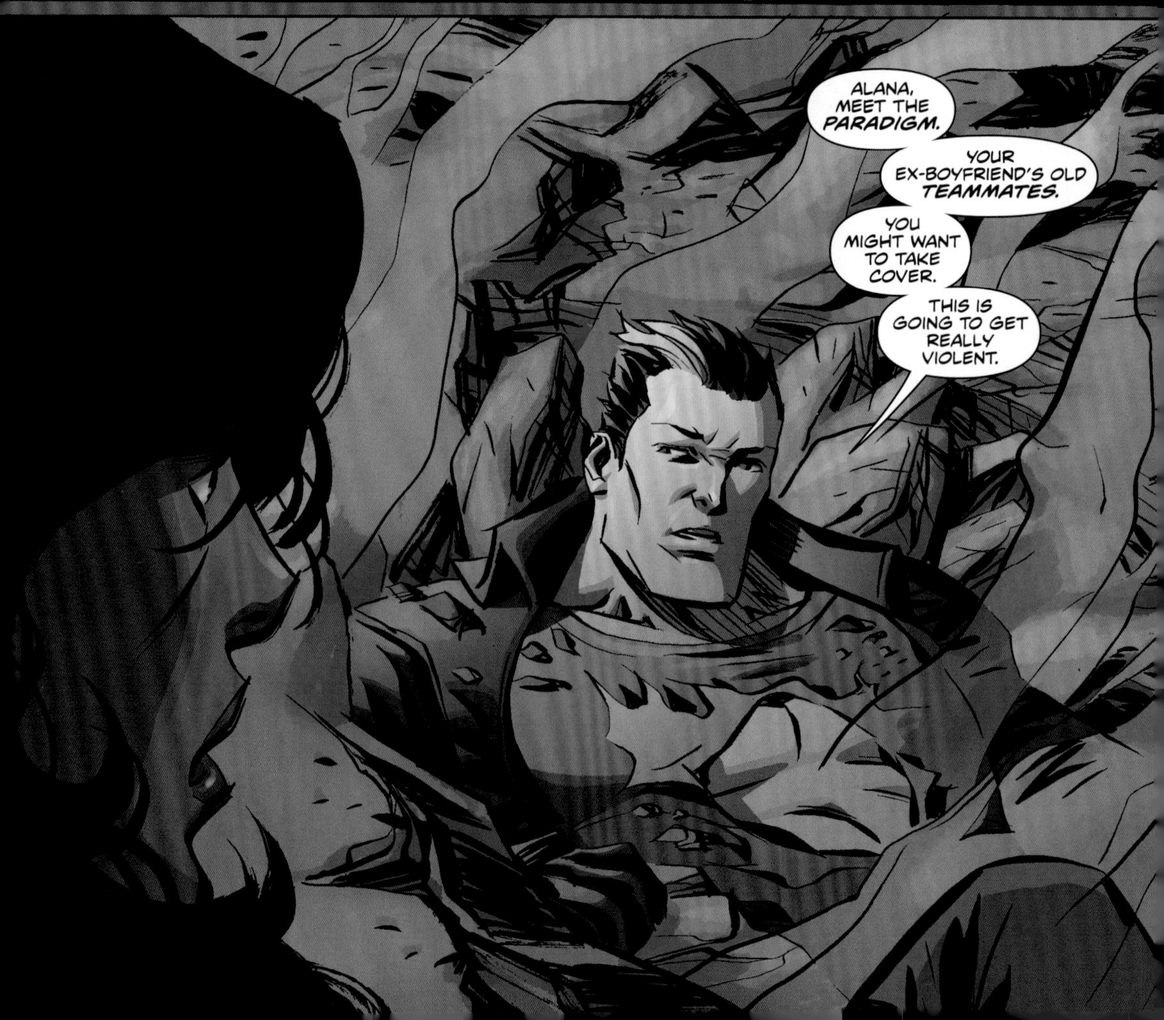
ALANA, MEET THE PARADIGM.
YOUR EX-BOYFRIEND'S OLD TEAMMATES.
YOU MIGHT WANT TO TAKE COVER.
THIS IS GOING TO GET REALLY VIOLENT.

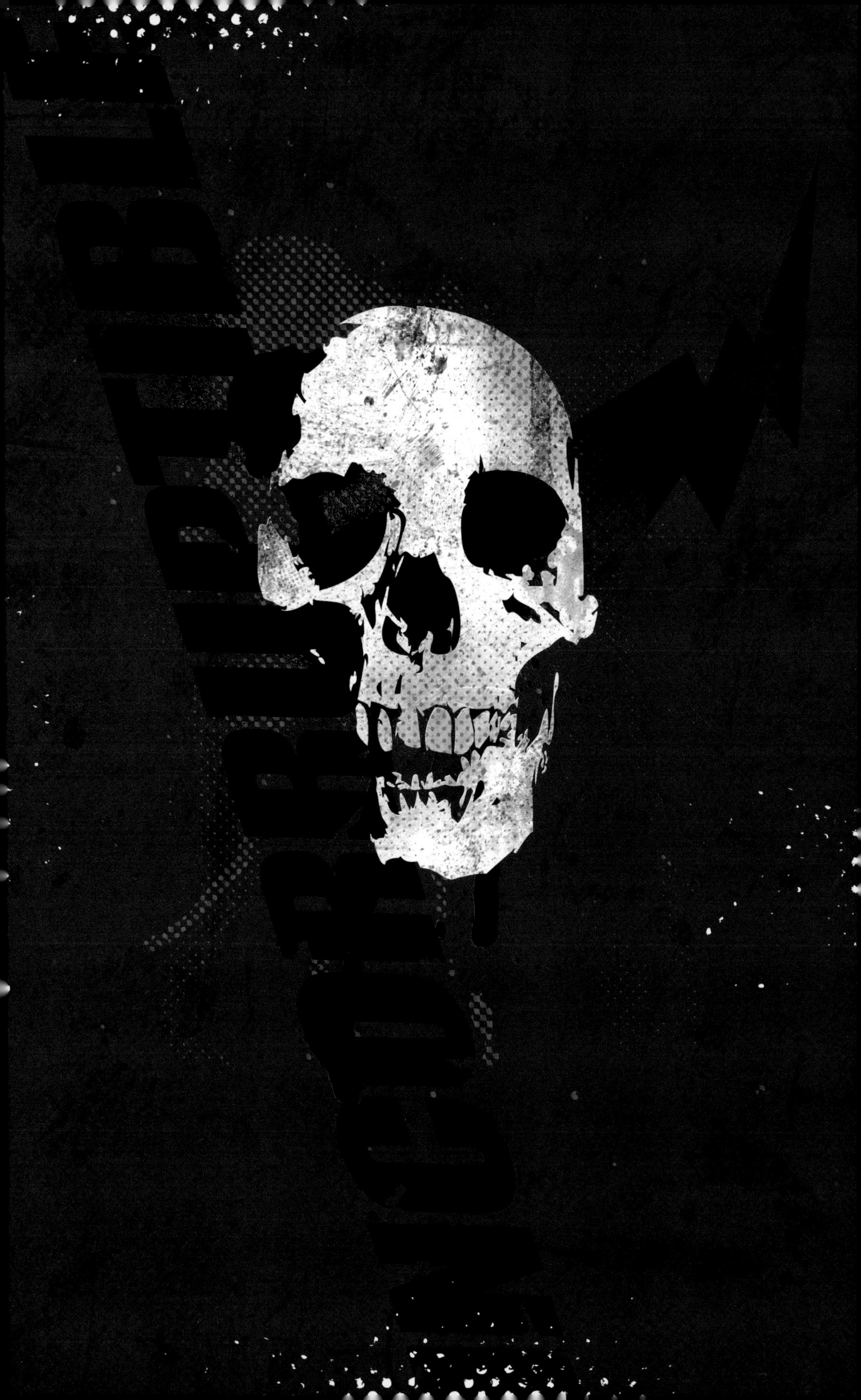

# CHAPTER 15

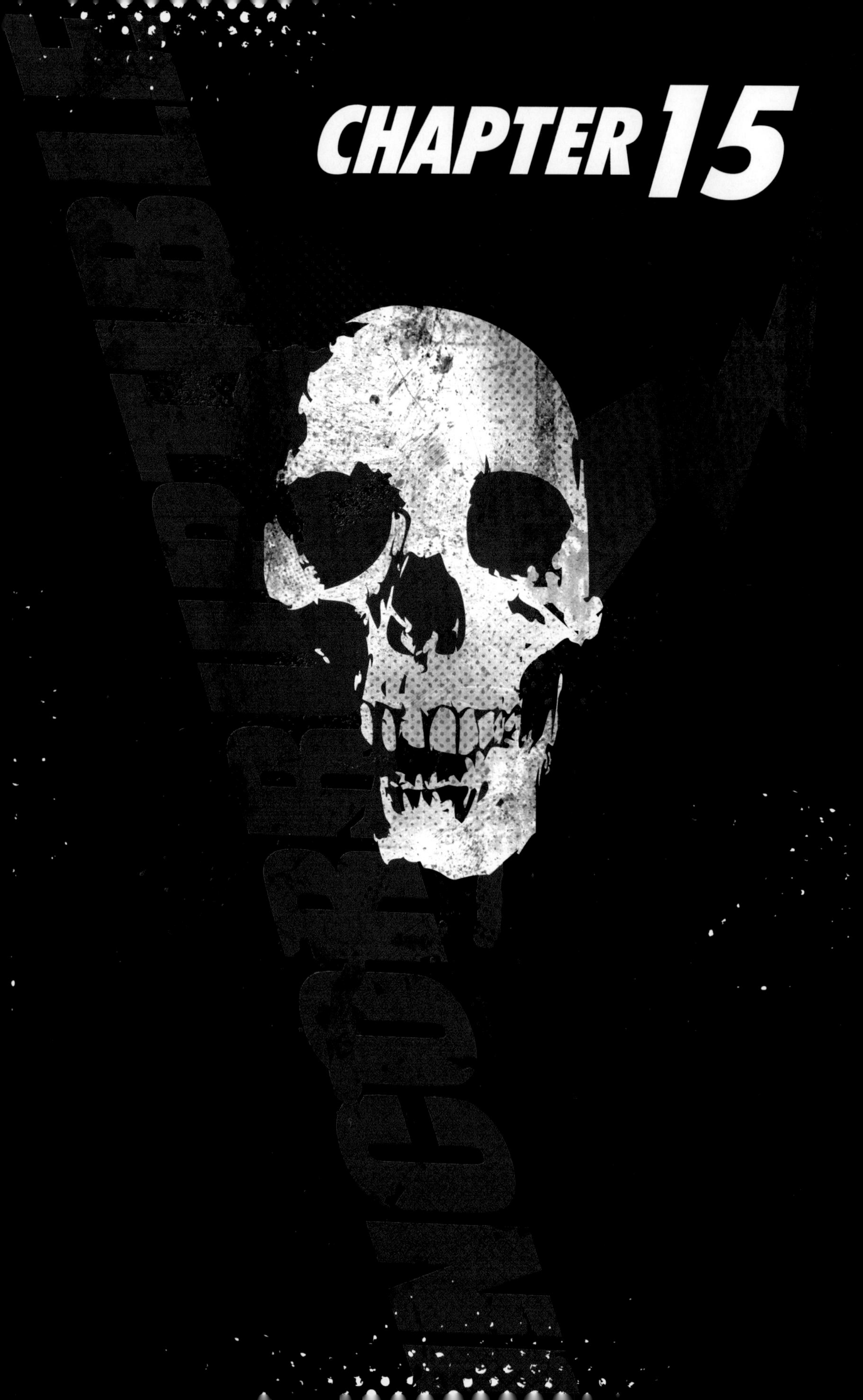

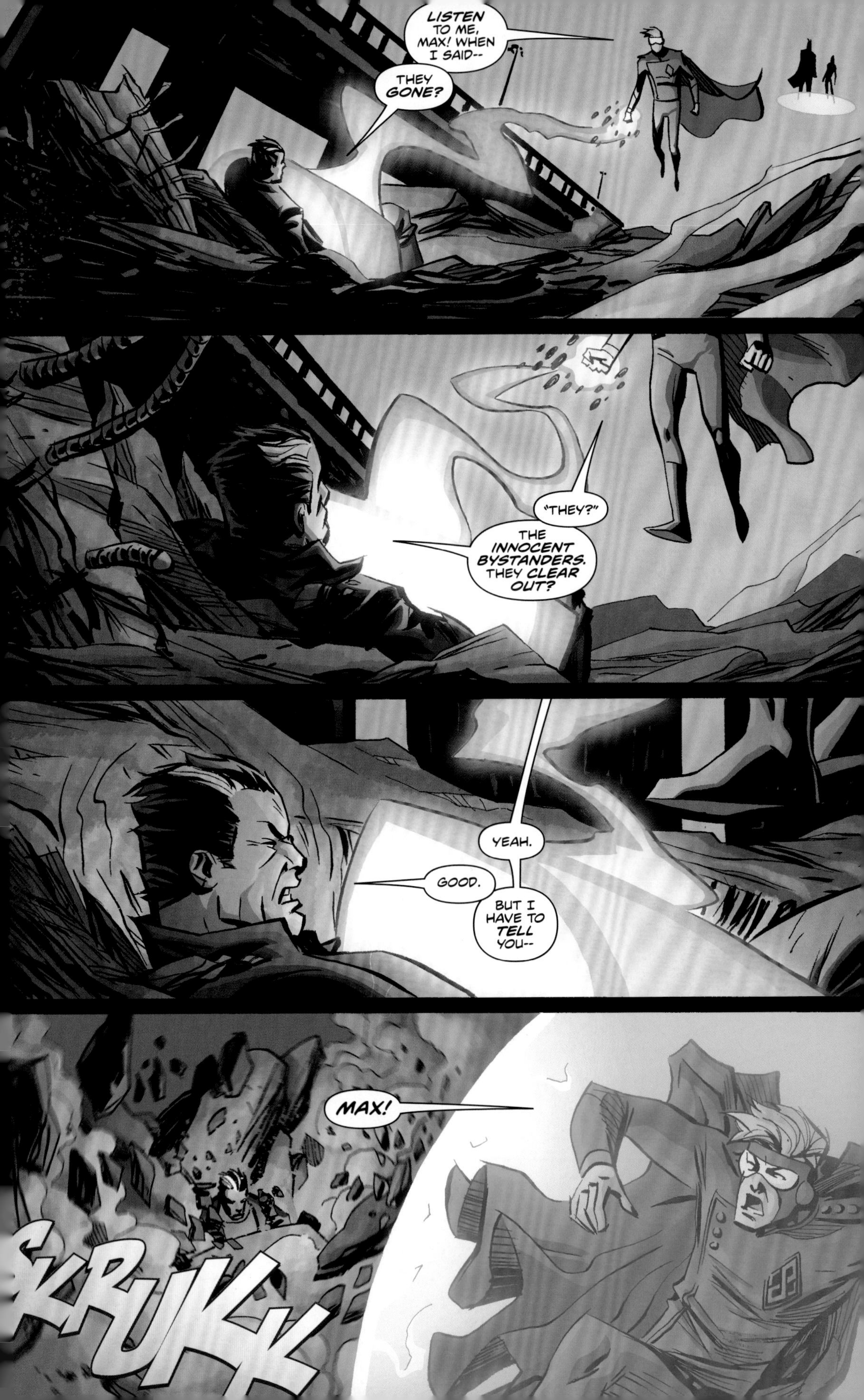

LISTEN TO ME, MAX! WHEN I SAID--
THEY GONE?
"THEY?"
THE INNOCENT BYSTANDERS. THEY CLEAR OUT?
YEAH.
GOOD.
BUT I HAVE TO TELL YOU--
MAX!
SKRUKK

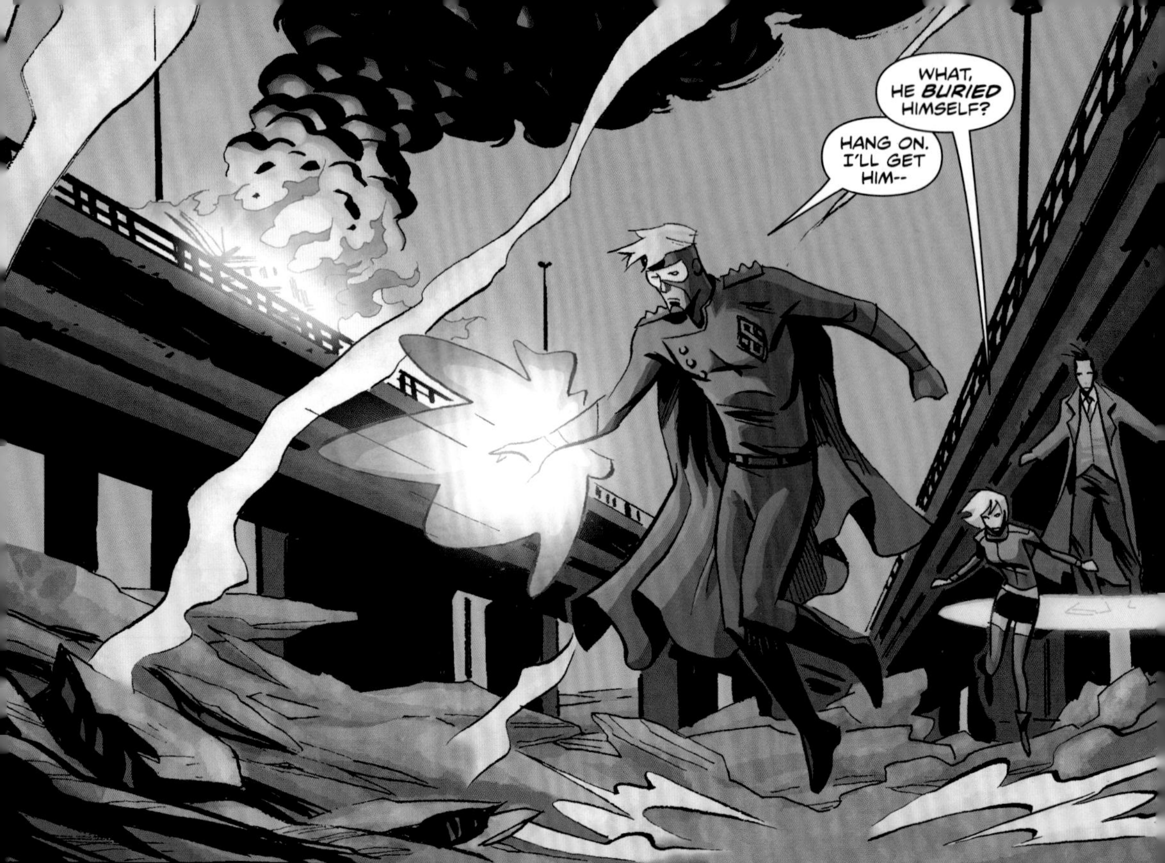
HANG ON. I'LL GET HIM--
WHAT, HE *BURIED* HIMSELF?

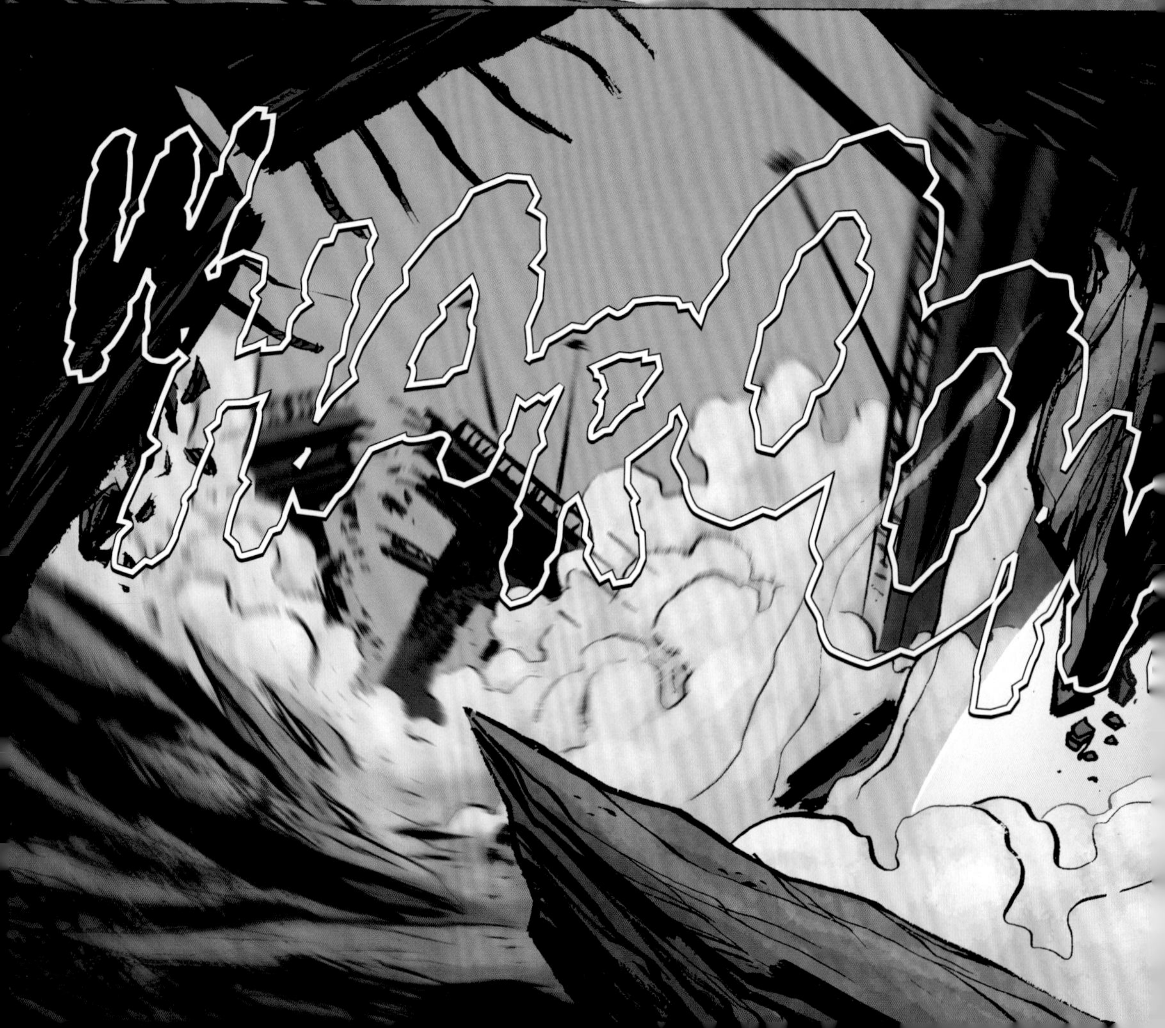
WHAAROOM

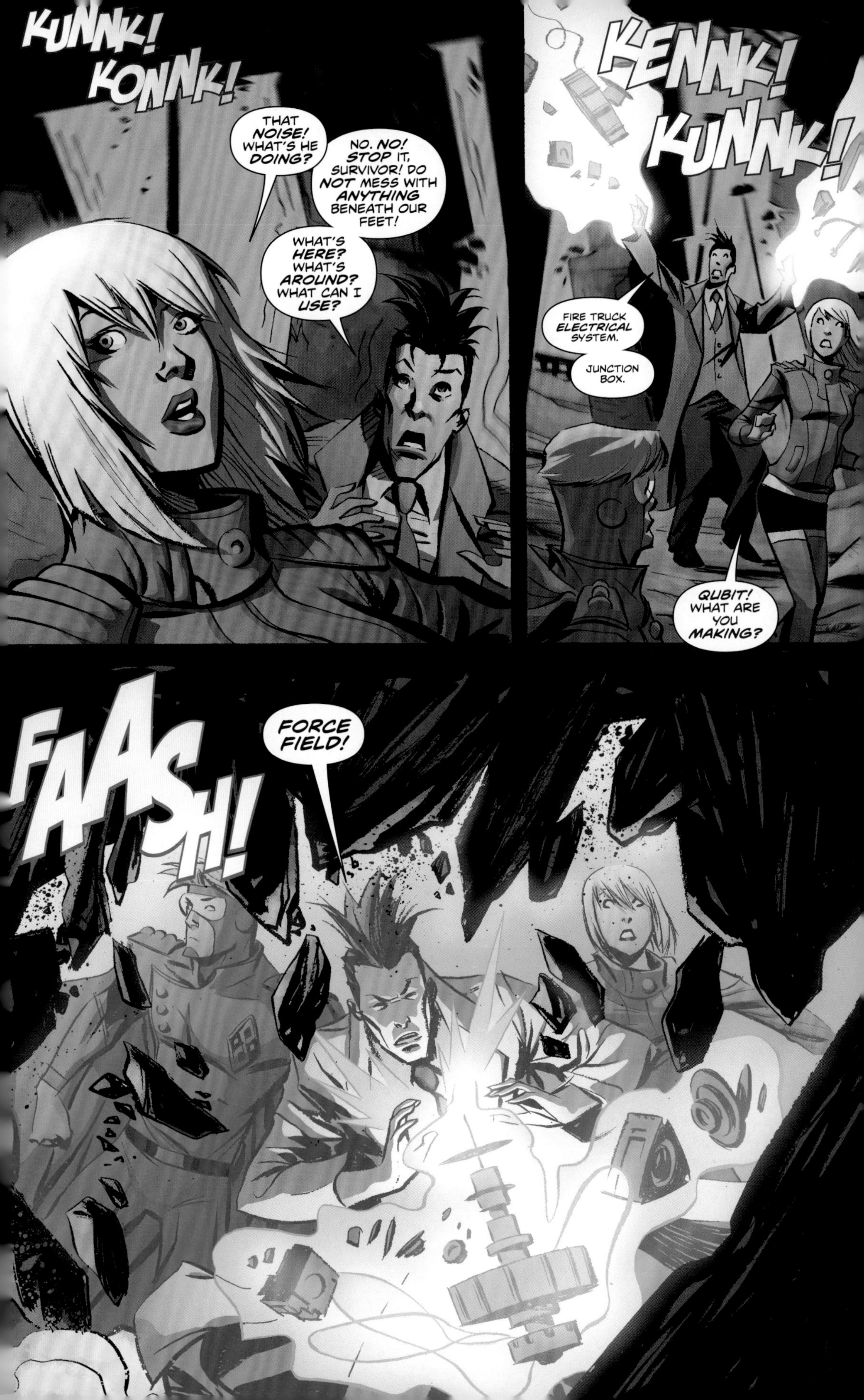
KUNNK! KONNK!
THAT NOISE! WHAT'S HE DOING?
NO. NO! STOP IT, SURVIVOR! DO NOT MESS WITH ANYTHING BENEATH OUR FEET!
WHAT'S HERE? WHAT'S AROUND? WHAT CAN I USE?
KENNK! KUNNK!
FIRE TRUCK ELECTRICAL SYSTEM.
JUNCTION BOX.
QUBIT! WHAT ARE YOU MAKING?
FAASH!
FORCE FIELD!

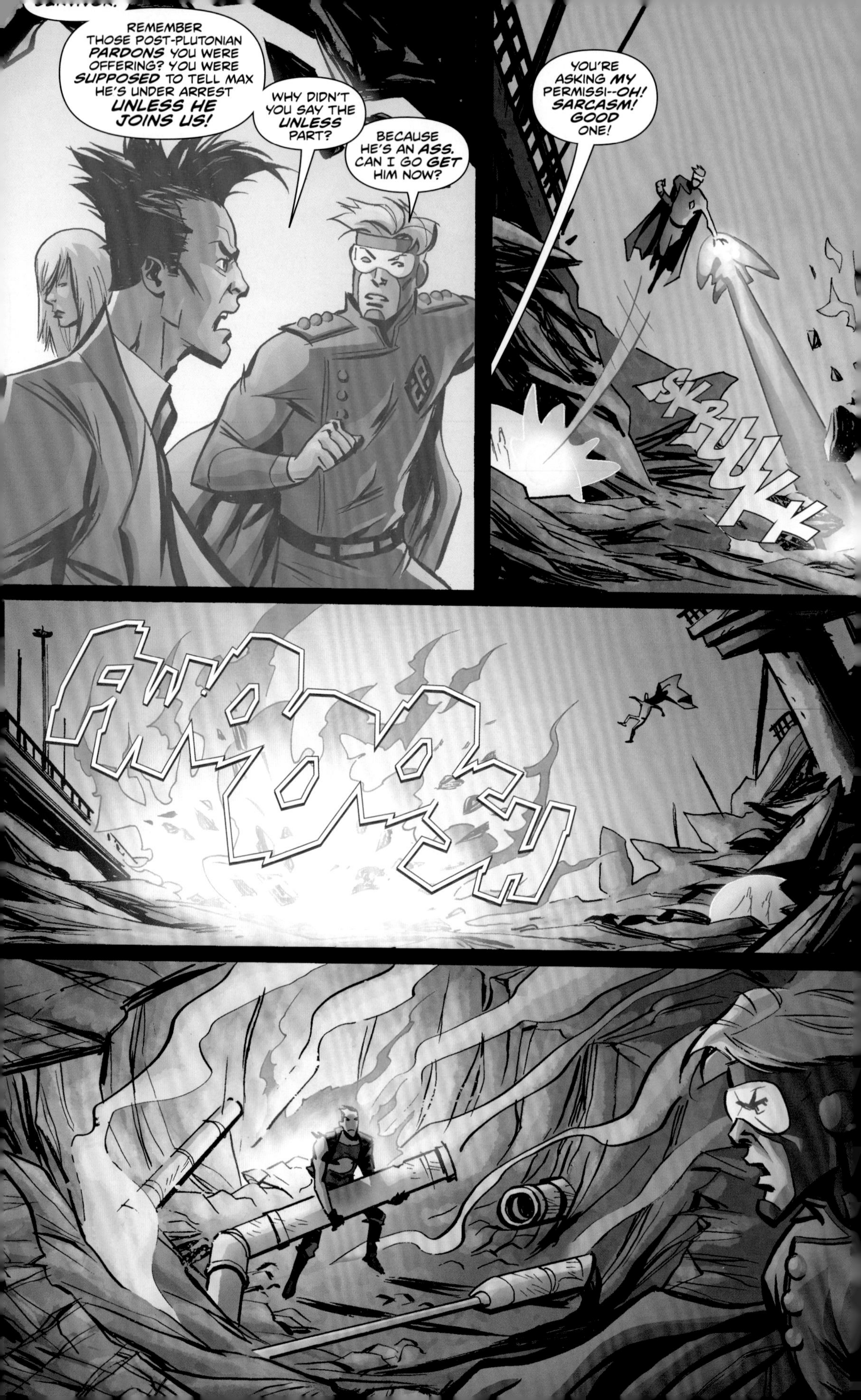
REMEMBER THOSE POST-PLUTONIAN PARDONS YOU WERE OFFERING? YOU WERE SUPPOSED TO TELL MAX HE'S UNDER ARREST UNLESS HE JOINS US!
WHY DIDN'T YOU SAY THE UNLESS PART?
BECAUSE HE'S AN ASS. CAN I GO GET HIM NOW?
YOU'RE ASKING MY PERMISSI--OH! SARCASM! GOOD ONE!

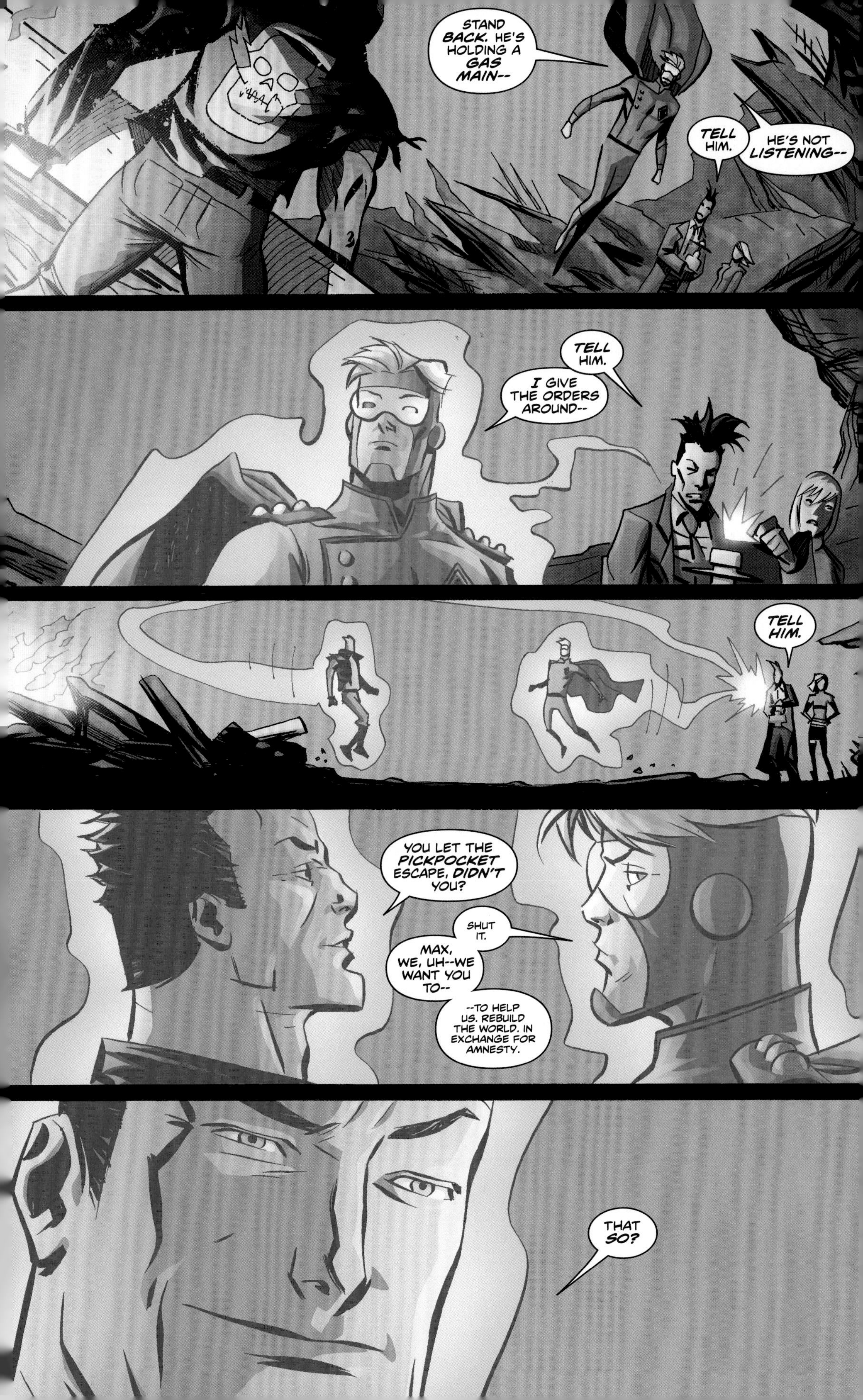
STAND BACK. HE'S HOLDING A GAS MAIN--
TELL HIM.
HE'S NOT LISTENING--
TELL HIM.
I GIVE THE ORDERS AROUND--
TELL HIM.
YOU LET THE PICKPOCKET ESCAPE, DIDN'T YOU?
SHUT IT.
MAX, WE, UH--WE WANT YOU TO--
--TO HELP US. REBUILD THE WORLD. IN EXCHANGE FOR AMNESTY.
THAT SO?

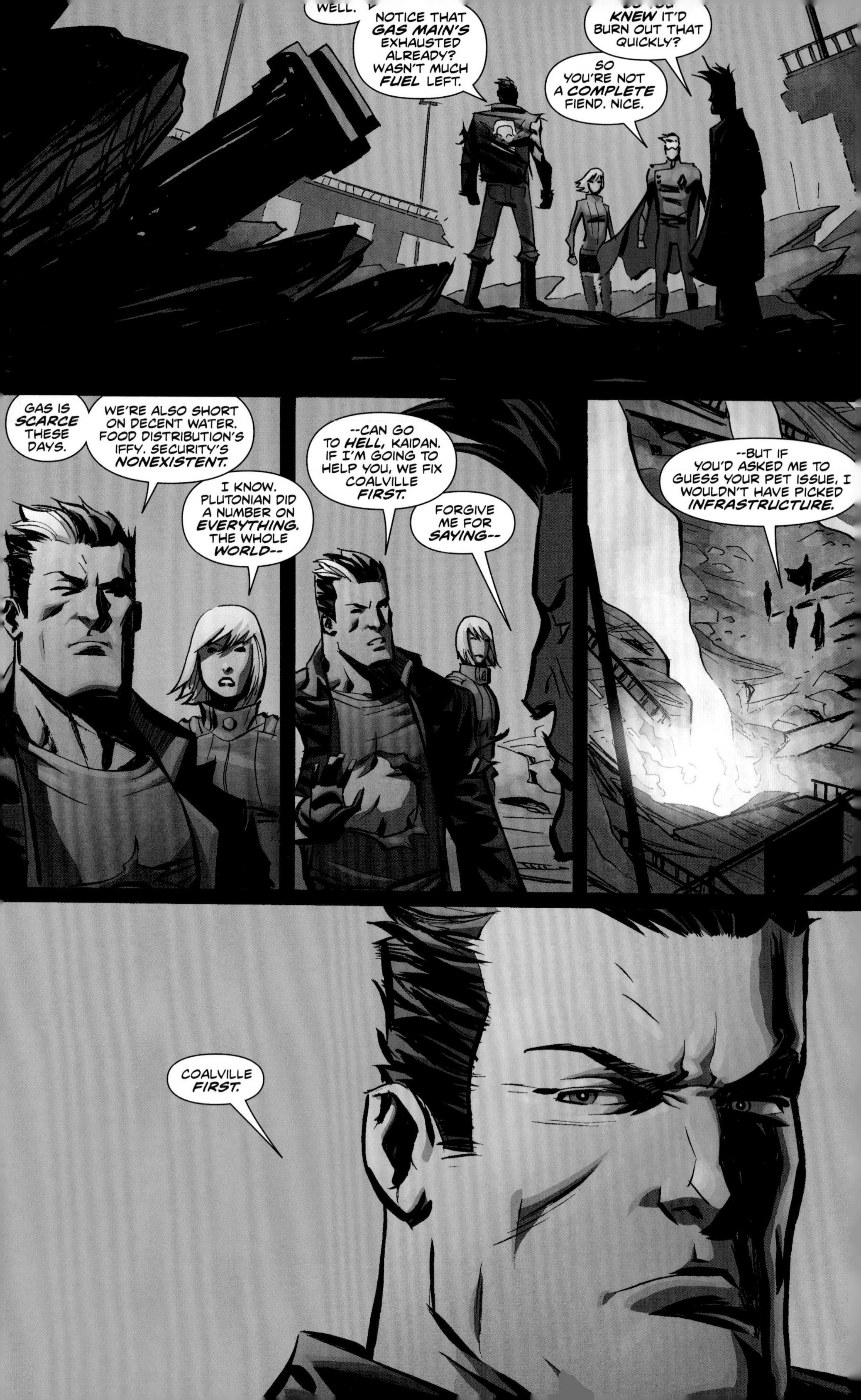
WELL.
NOTICE THAT GAS MAIN'S EXHAUSTED ALREADY? WASN'T MUCH FUEL LEFT.
KNEW IT'D BURN OUT THAT QUICKLY?
SO YOU'RE NOT A COMPLETE FIEND. NICE.
GAS IS SCARCE THESE DAYS.
WE'RE ALSO SHORT ON DECENT WATER. FOOD DISTRIBUTION'S IFFY. SECURITY'S NONEXISTENT.
I KNOW. PLUTONIAN DID A NUMBER ON EVERYTHING. THE WHOLE WORLD--
--CAN GO TO HELL, KAIDAN. IF I'M GOING TO HELP YOU, WE FIX COALVILLE FIRST.
FORGIVE ME FOR SAYING--
--BUT IF YOU'D ASKED ME TO GUESS YOUR PET ISSUE, I WOULDN'T HAVE PICKED INFRASTRUCTURE.
COALVILLE FIRST.

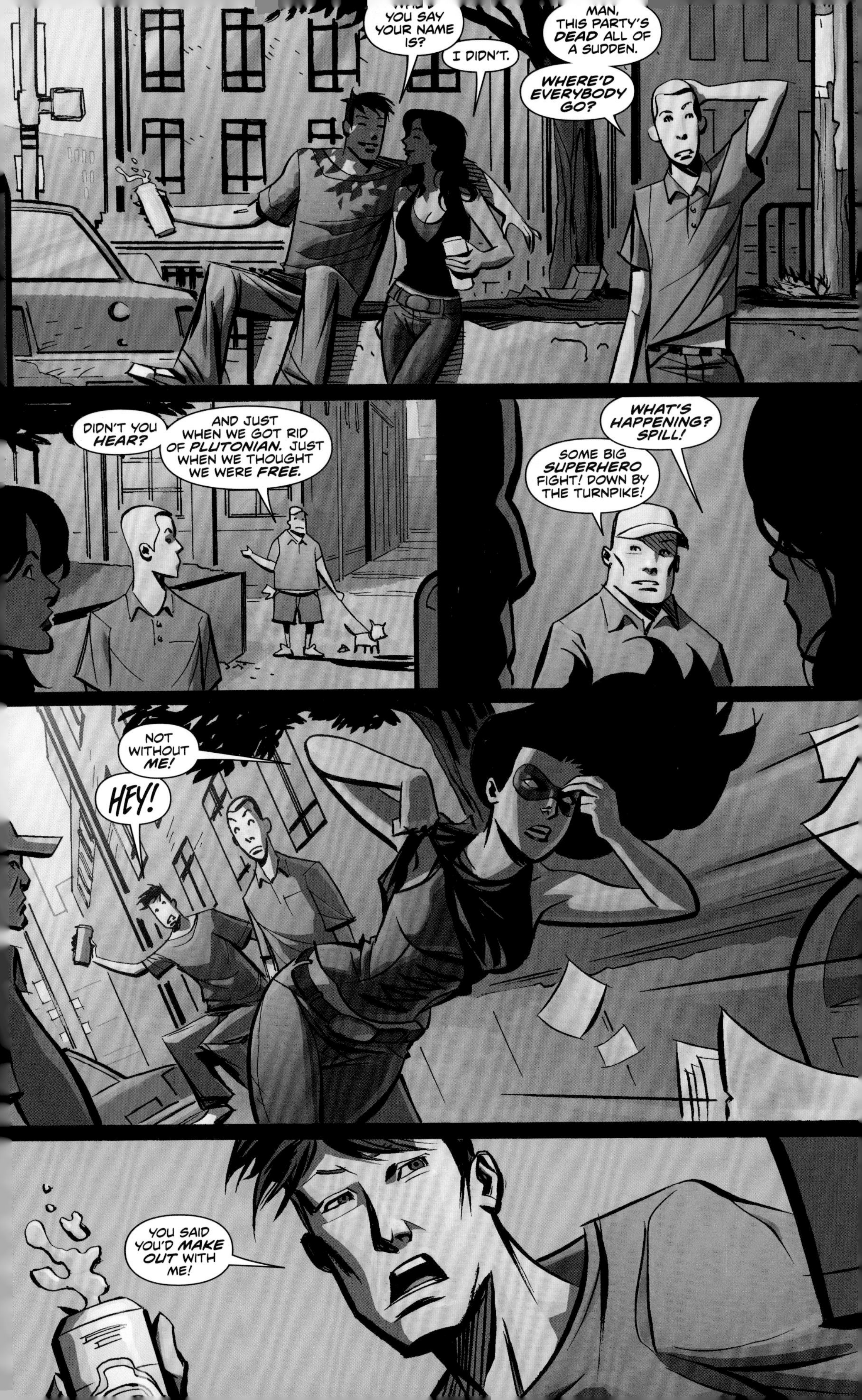

YOU SAY YOUR NAME IS?
I DIDN'T.
MAN, THIS PARTY'S DEAD ALL OF A SUDDEN.
WHERE'D EVERYBODY GO?
DIDN'T YOU HEAR?
AND JUST WHEN WE GOT RID OF PLUTONIAN. JUST WHEN WE THOUGHT WE WERE FREE.
WHAT'S HAPPENING? SPILL!
SOME BIG SUPERHERO FIGHT! DOWN BY THE TURNPIKE!
NOT WITHOUT ME!
HEY!
YOU SAID YOU'D MAKE OUT WITH ME!

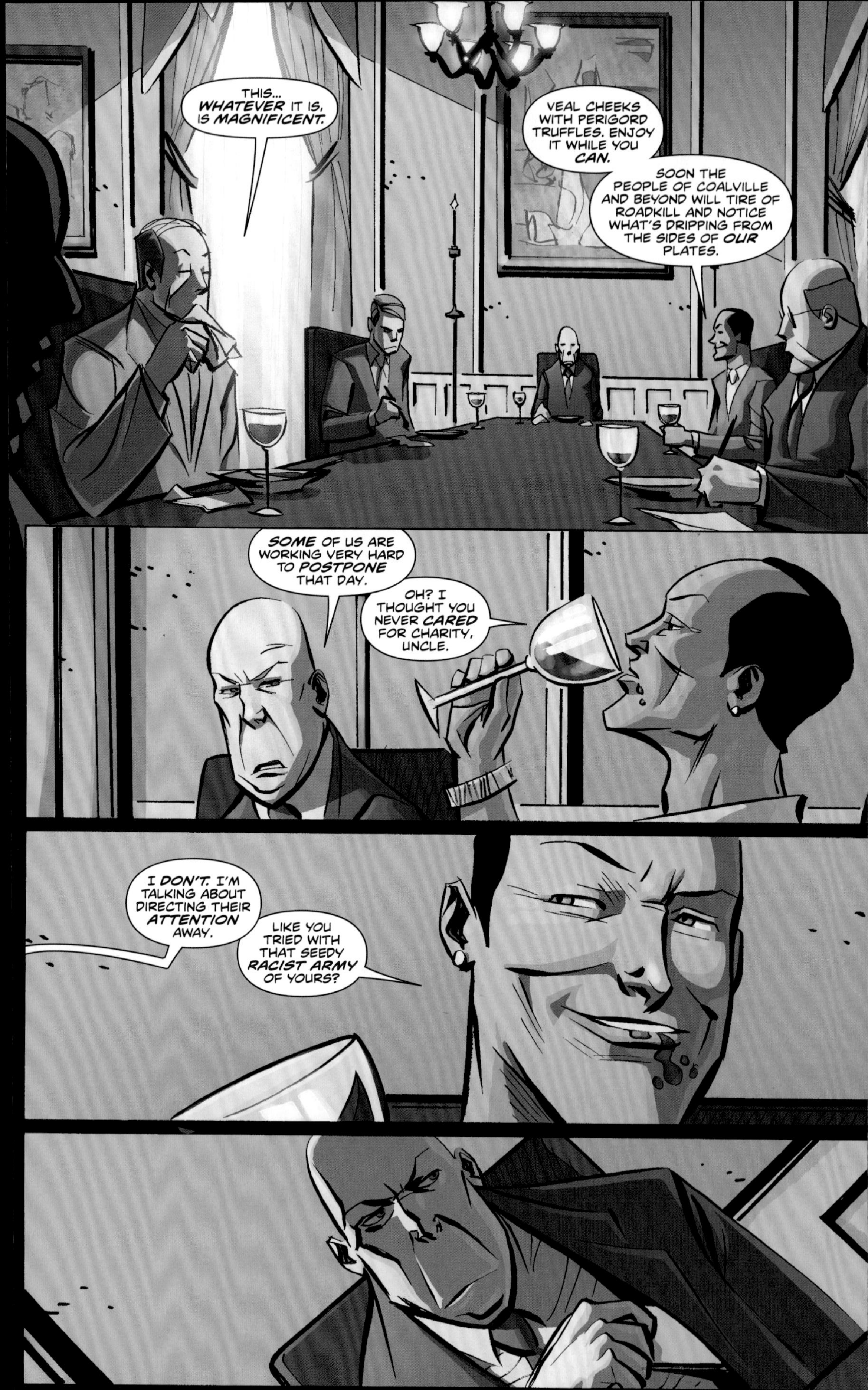
THIS... WHATEVER IT IS, IS MAGNIFICENT.
VEAL CHEEKS WITH PERIGORD TRUFFLES. ENJOY IT WHILE YOU CAN.
SOON THE PEOPLE OF COALVILLE AND BEYOND WILL TIRE OF ROADKILL AND NOTICE WHAT'S DRIPPING FROM THE SIDES OF OUR PLATES.
SOME OF US ARE WORKING VERY HARD TO POSTPONE THAT DAY.
OH? I THOUGHT YOU NEVER CARED FOR CHARITY, UNCLE.
I DON'T. I'M TALKING ABOUT DIRECTING THEIR ATTENTION AWAY.
LIKE YOU TRIED WITH THAT SEEDY RACIST ARMY OF YOURS?

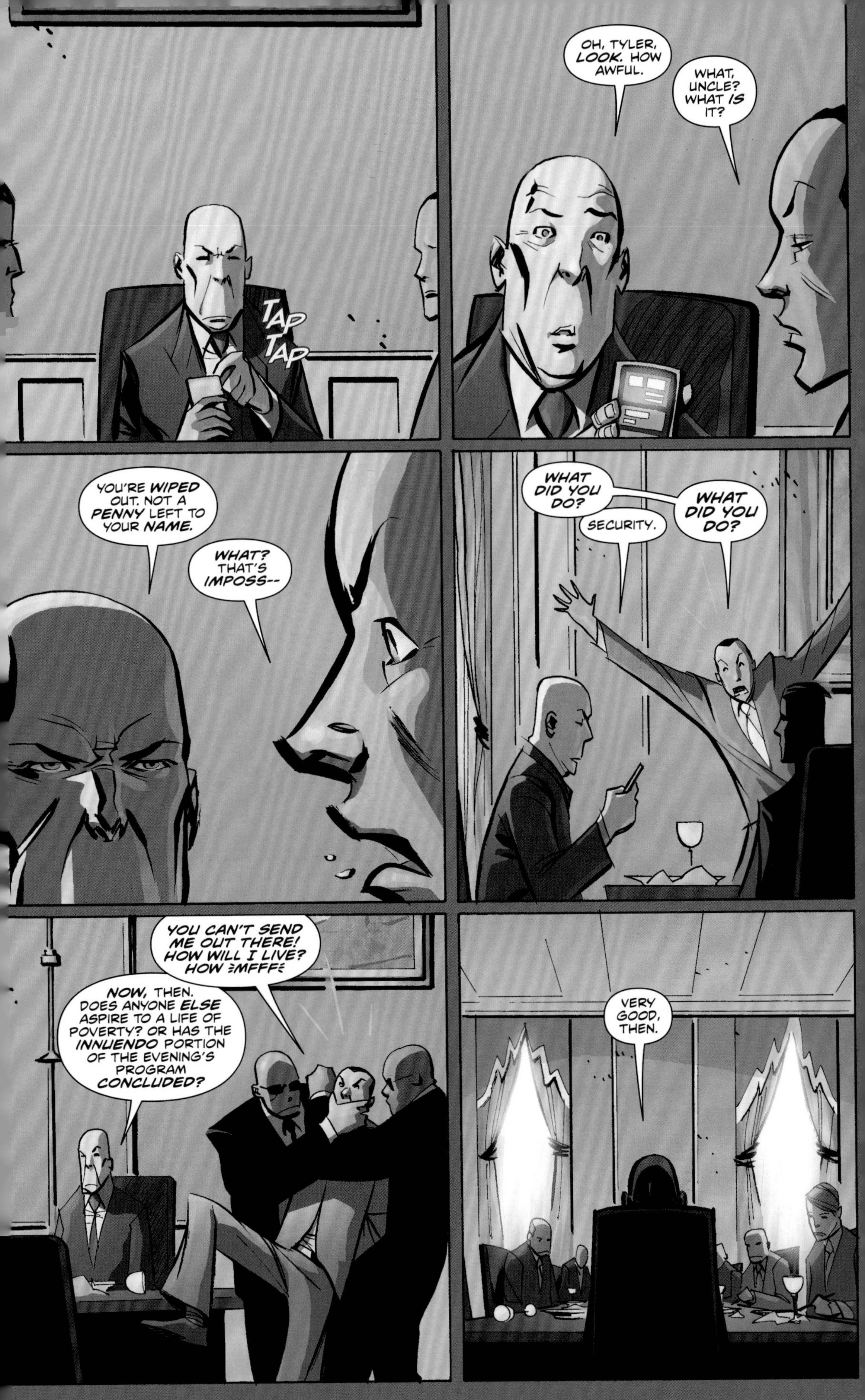
TAP TAP
OH, TYLER, LOOK. HOW AWFUL.
WHAT, UNCLE? WHAT IS IT?
YOU'RE WIPED OUT. NOT A PENNY LEFT TO YOUR NAME.
WHAT? THAT'S IMPOSS--
WHAT DID YOU DO?
SECURITY.
WHAT DID YOU DO?
YOU CAN'T SEND ME OUT THERE! HOW WILL I LIVE? HOW MFFF
NOW, THEN. DOES ANYONE ELSE ASPIRE TO A LIFE OF POVERTY? OR HAS THE INNUENDO PORTION OF THE EVENING'S PROGRAM CONCLUDED?
VERY GOOD, THEN.

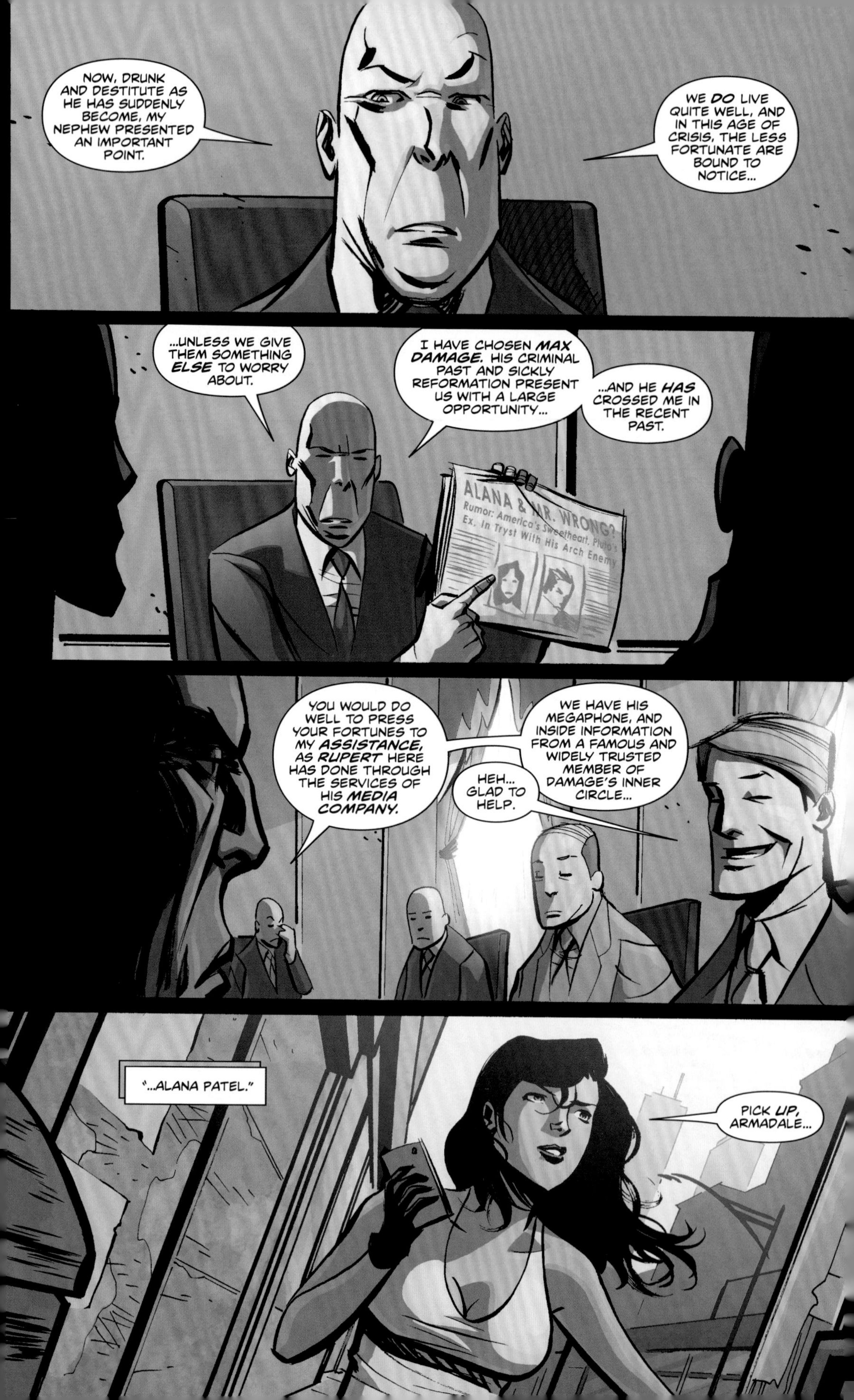
NOW, DRUNK AND DESTITUTE AS HE HAS SUDDENLY BECOME, MY NEPHEW PRESENTED AN IMPORTANT POINT.
WE DO LIVE QUITE WELL, AND IN THIS AGE OF CRISIS, THE LESS FORTUNATE ARE BOUND TO NOTICE...
...UNLESS WE GIVE THEM SOMETHING ELSE TO WORRY ABOUT.
I HAVE CHOSEN MAX DAMAGE. HIS CRIMINAL PAST AND SICKLY REFORMATION PRESENT US WITH A LARGE OPPORTUNITY...
...AND HE HAS CROSSED ME IN THE RECENT PAST.
ALANA & MR. WRONG?
Rumor: America's Sweetheart, Pluto's Ex, In Tryst With His Arch Enemy
YOU WOULD DO WELL TO PRESS YOUR FORTUNES TO MY ASSISTANCE, AS RUPERT HERE HAS DONE THROUGH THE SERVICES OF HIS MEDIA COMPANY.
WE HAVE HIS MEGAPHONE, AND INSIDE INFORMATION FROM A FAMOUS AND WIDELY TRUSTED MEMBER OF DAMAGE'S INNER CIRCLE...
HEH... GLAD TO HELP.
"...ALANA PATEL."
PICK UP, ARMADALE...

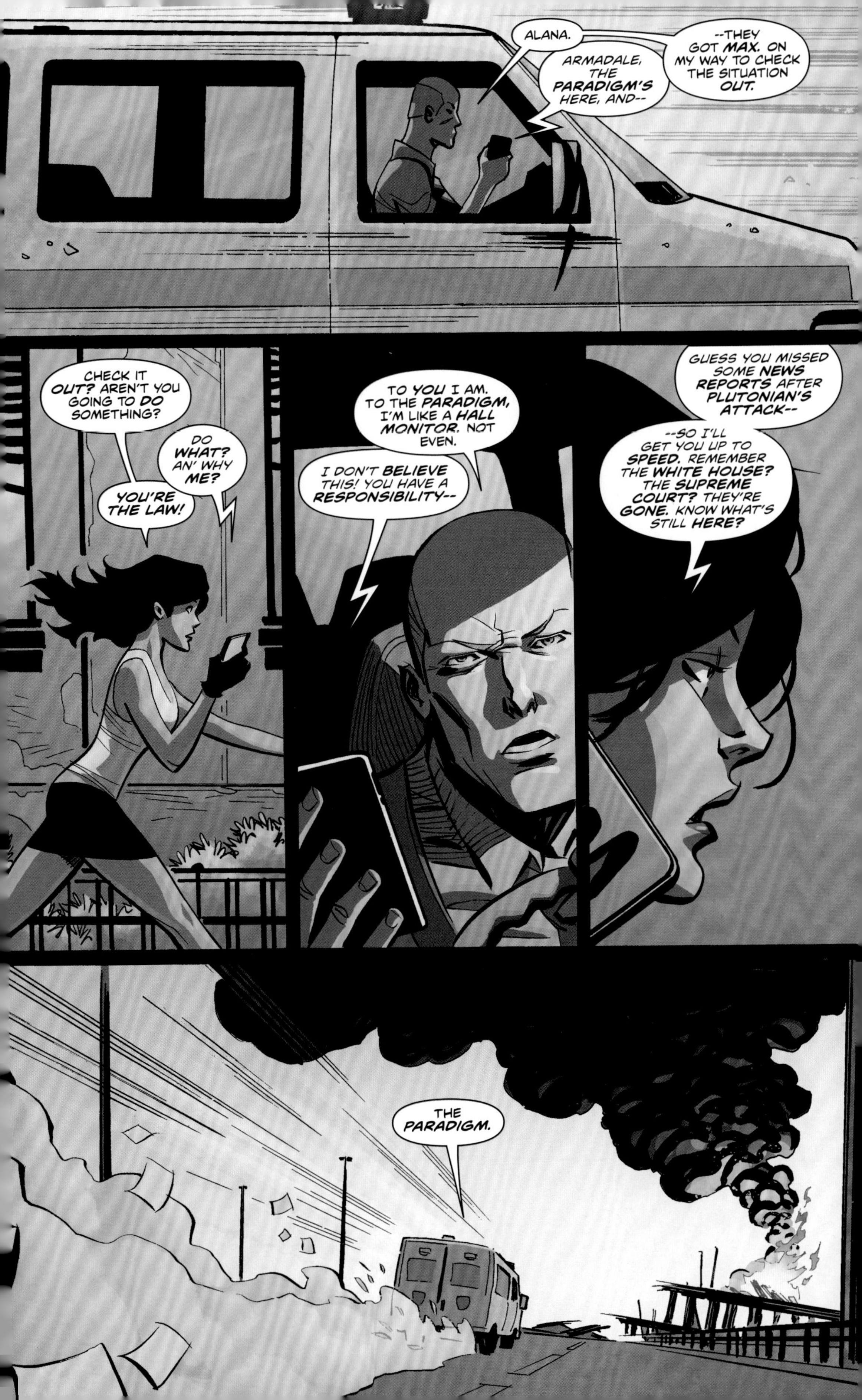
ALANA.
ARMADALE, THE PARADIGM'S HERE, AND--
--THEY GOT MAX. ON MY WAY TO CHECK THE SITUATION OUT.
CHECK IT OUT? AREN'T YOU GOING TO DO SOMETHING?
DO WHAT? AN' WHY ME?
YOU'RE THE LAW!
TO YOU I AM. TO THE PARADIGM, I'M LIKE A HALL MONITOR. NOT EVEN.
I DON'T BELIEVE THIS! YOU HAVE A RESPONSIBILITY--
GUESS YOU MISSED SOME NEWS REPORTS AFTER PLUTONIAN'S ATTACK--
--SO I'LL GET YOU UP TO SPEED. REMEMBER THE WHITE HOUSE? THE SUPREME COURT? THEY'RE GONE. KNOW WHAT'S STILL HERE?
THE PARADIGM.

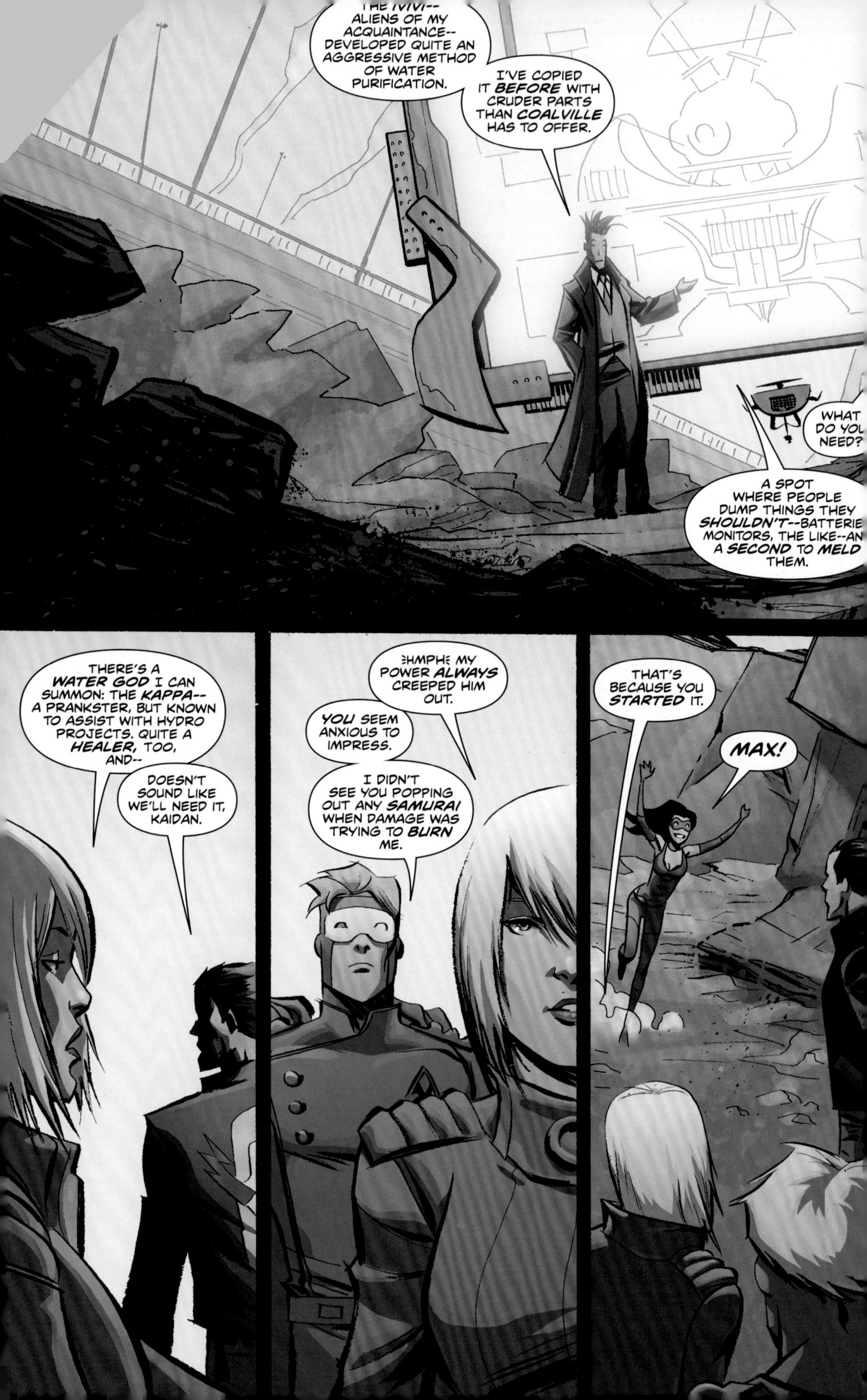

THE IVIVI-- ALIENS OF MY ACQUAINTANCE-- DEVELOPED QUITE AN AGGRESSIVE METHOD OF WATER PURIFICATION.
I'VE COPIED IT BEFORE WITH CRUDER PARTS THAN COALVILLE HAS TO OFFER.
WHAT DO YO NEED?
A SPOT WHERE PEOPLE DUMP THINGS THEY SHOULDN'T--BATTERIE MONITORS, THE LIKE--AN A SECOND TO MELD THEM.
THERE'S A WATER GOD I CAN SUMMON: THE KAPPA-- A PRANKSTER, BUT KNOWN TO ASSIST WITH HYDRO PROJECTS. QUITE A HEALER, TOO, AND--
DOESN'T SOUND LIKE WE'LL NEED IT, KAIDAN.
HMPH MY POWER ALWAYS CREEPED HIM OUT.
YOU SEEM ANXIOUS TO IMPRESS.
I DIDN'T SEE YOU POPPING OUT ANY SAMURAI WHEN DAMAGE WAS TRYING TO BURN ME.
THAT'S BECAUSE YOU STARTED IT.
MAX!

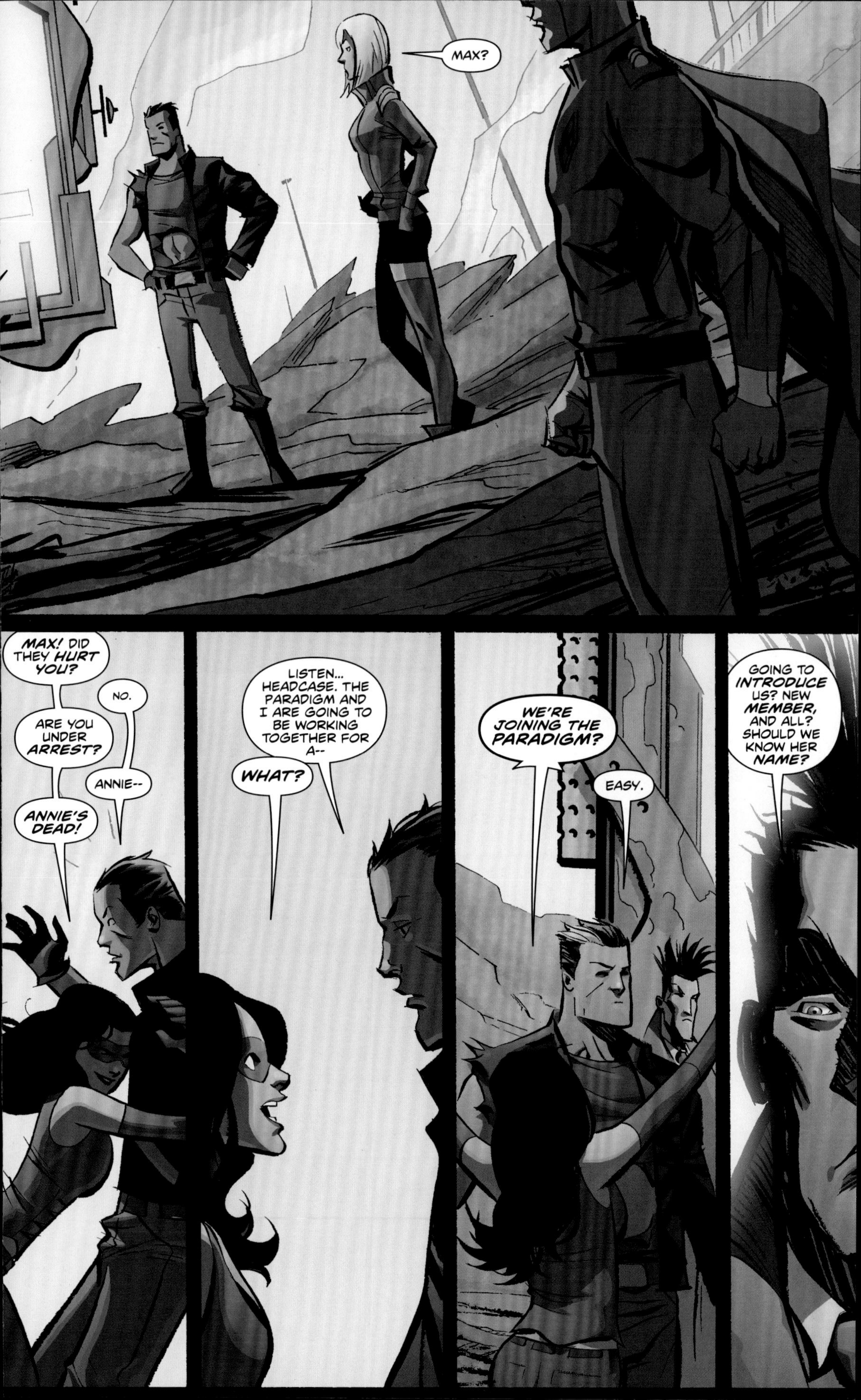
MAX?
MAX! DID THEY HURT YOU?
NO.
ARE YOU UNDER ARREST?
ANNIE--
ANNIE'S DEAD!
LISTEN... HEADCASE. THE PARADIGM AND I ARE GOING TO BE WORKING TOGETHER FOR A--
WHAT?
WE'RE JOINING THE PARADIGM?
EASY.
GOING TO INTRODUCE US? NEW MEMBER, AND ALL? SHOULD WE KNOW HER NAME?

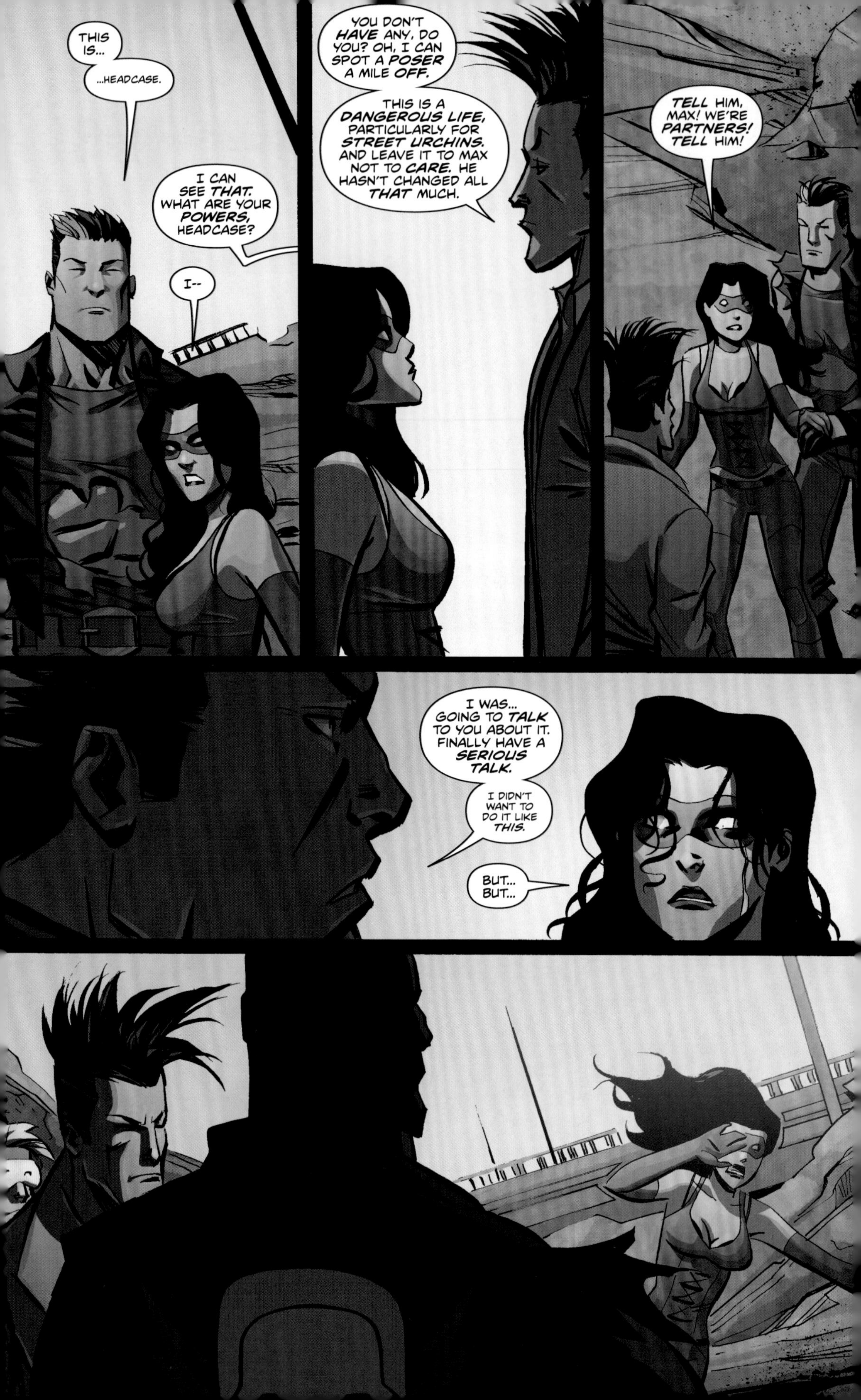
THIS IS...
...HEADCASE.
I CAN SEE THAT. WHAT ARE YOUR POWERS, HEADCASE?
I--
YOU DON'T HAVE ANY, DO YOU? OH, I CAN SPOT A POSER A MILE OFF.
THIS IS A DANGEROUS LIFE, PARTICULARLY FOR STREET URCHINS. AND LEAVE IT TO MAX NOT TO CARE. HE HASN'T CHANGED ALL THAT MUCH.
TELL HIM, MAX! WE'RE PARTNERS! TELL HIM!
I WAS... GOING TO TALK TO YOU ABOUT IT. FINALLY HAVE A SERIOUS TALK.
I DIDN'T WANT TO DO IT LIKE THIS.
BUT... BUT...

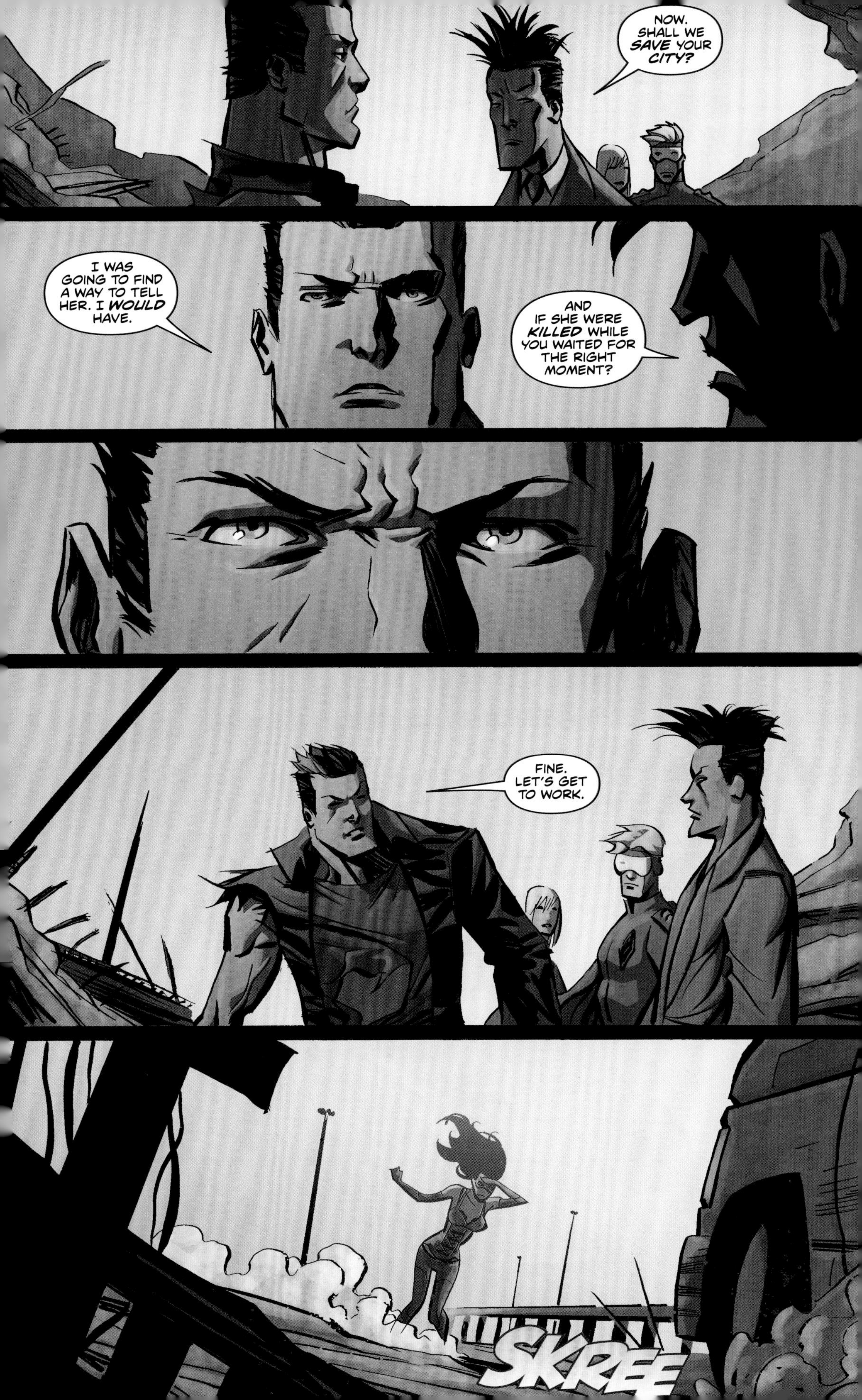
NOW. SHALL WE SAVE YOUR CITY?
I WAS GOING TO FIND A WAY TO TELL HER. I WOULD HAVE.
AND IF SHE WERE KILLED WHILE YOU WAITED FOR THE RIGHT MOMENT?
FINE. LET'S GET TO WORK.
SKREE

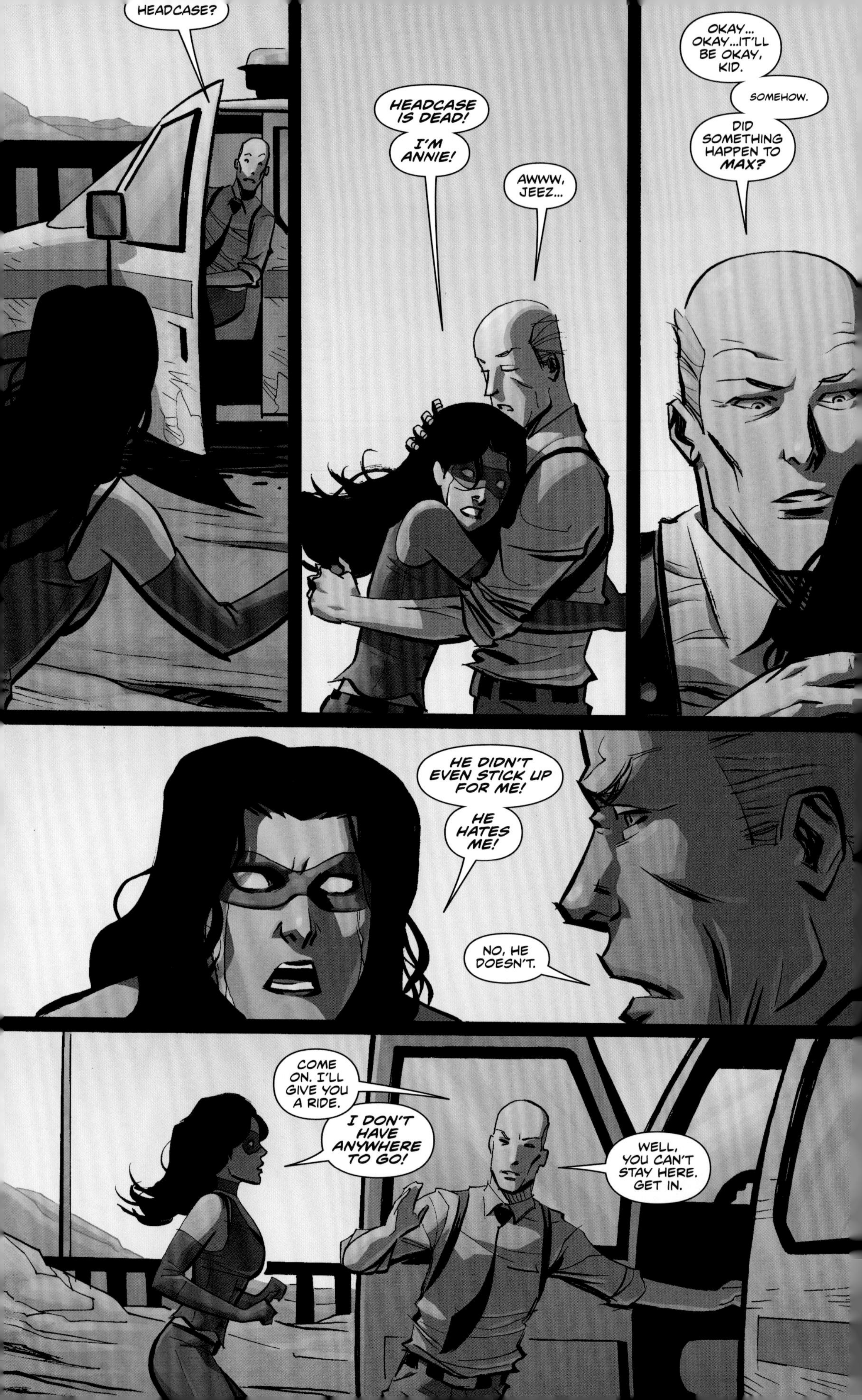
HEADCASE?
HEADCASE IS DEAD!
I'M ANNIE!
AWWW, JEEZ...
OKAY... OKAY...IT'LL BE OKAY, KID.
SOMEHOW.
DID SOMETHING HAPPEN TO MAX?
HE DIDN'T EVEN STICK UP FOR ME!
HE HATES ME!
NO, HE DOESN'T.
COME ON. I'LL GIVE YOU A RIDE.
I DON'T HAVE ANYWHERE TO GO!
WELL, YOU CAN'T STAY HERE. GET IN.

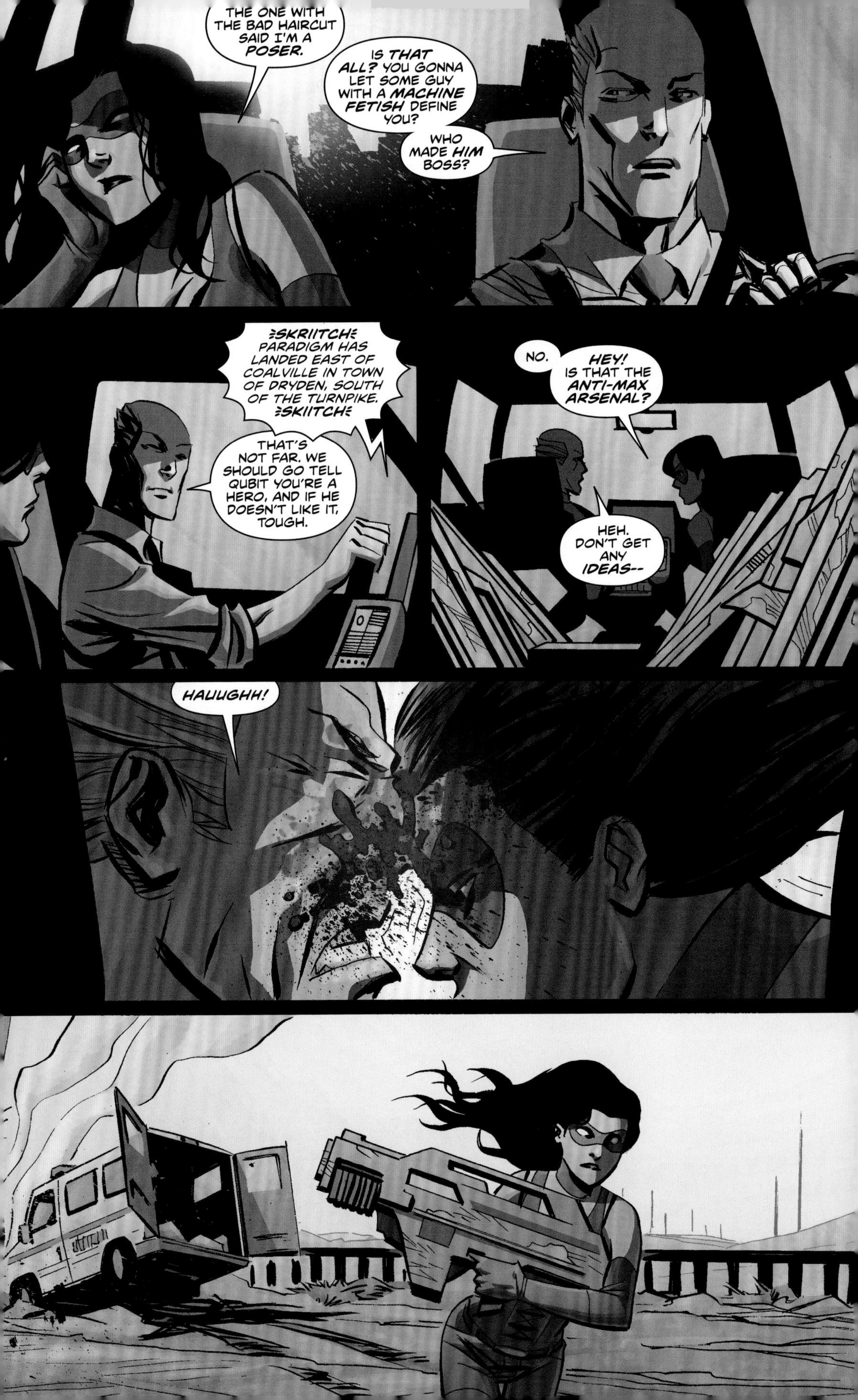
THE ONE WITH THE BAD HAIRCUT SAID I'M A POSER.
IS THAT ALL? YOU GONNA LET SOME GUY WITH A MACHINE FETISH DEFINE YOU?
WHO MADE HIM BOSS?
SKRIITCH PARADIGM HAS LANDED EAST OF COALVILLE IN TOWN OF DRYDEN, SOUTH OF THE TURNPIKE. SKIITCH
THAT'S NOT FAR. WE SHOULD GO TELL QUBIT YOU'RE A HERO, AND IF HE DOESN'T LIKE IT, TOUGH.
NO.
HEY! IS THAT THE ANTI-MAX ARSENAL?
HEH. DON'T GET ANY IDEAS--
HAUUGHH!

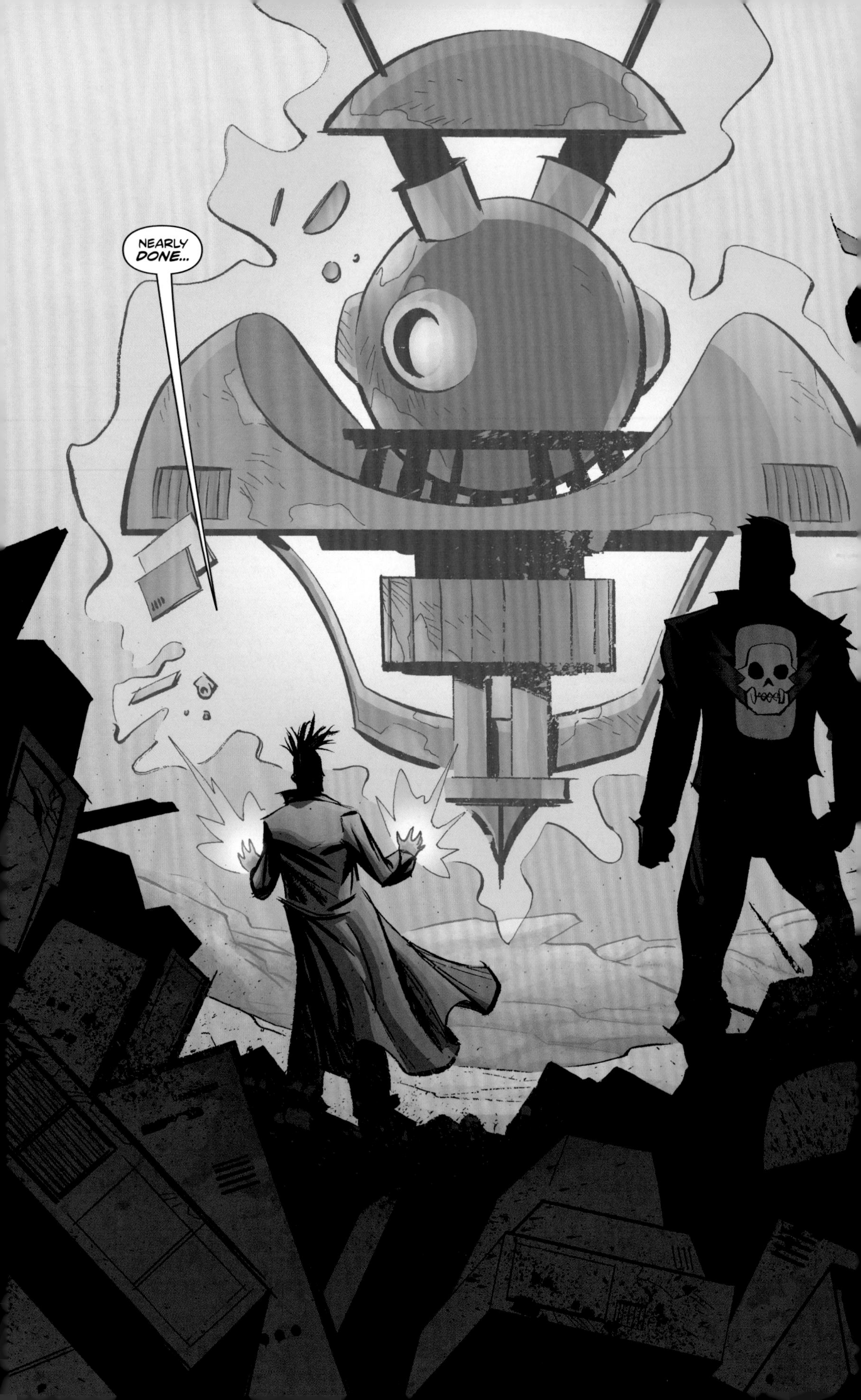
NEARLY DONE...

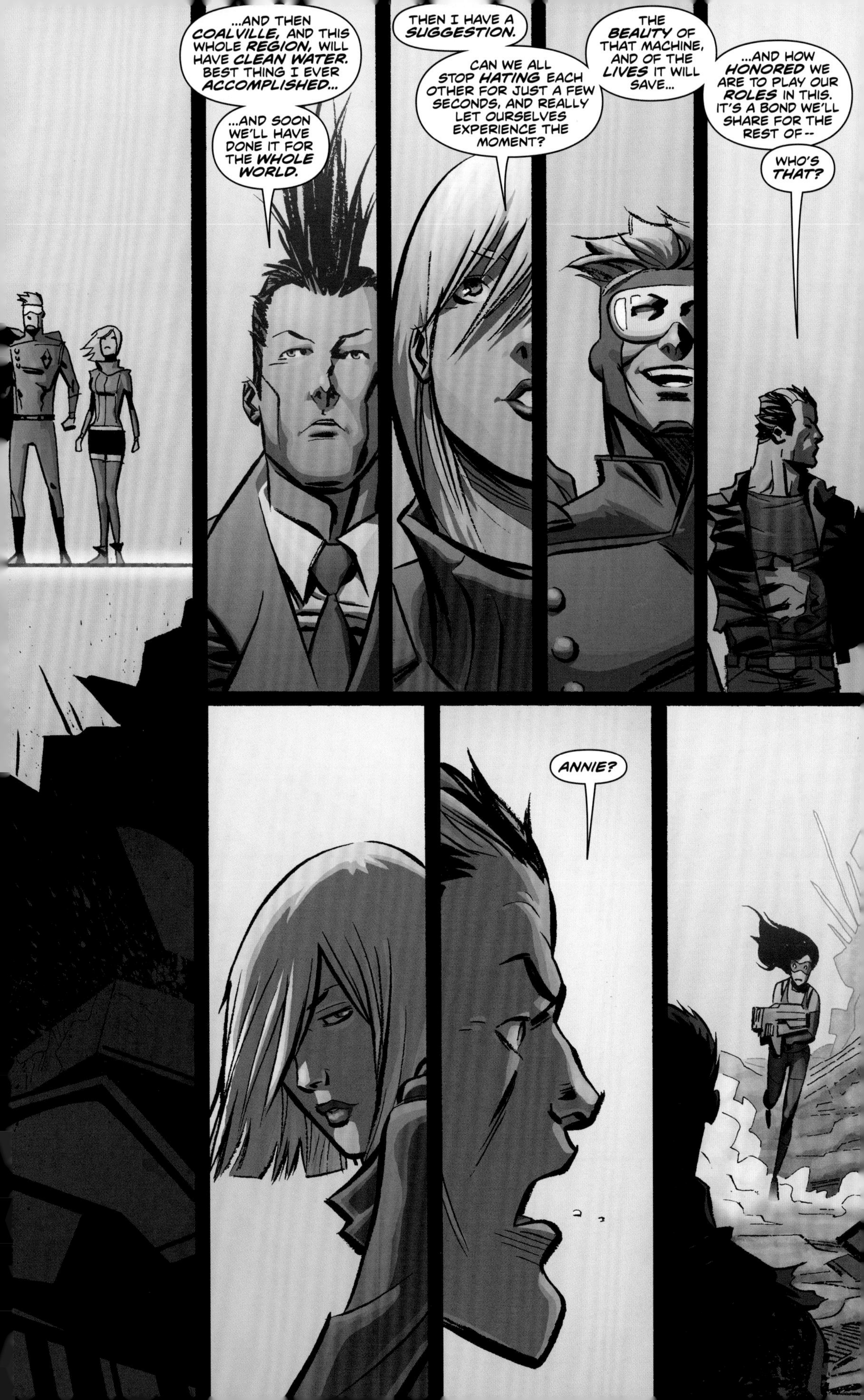
...AND THEN COALVILLE, AND THIS WHOLE REGION, WILL HAVE CLEAN WATER. BEST THING I EVER ACCOMPLISHED...
...AND SOON WE'LL HAVE DONE IT FOR THE WHOLE WORLD.
THEN I HAVE A SUGGESTION.
CAN WE ALL STOP HATING EACH OTHER FOR JUST A FEW SECONDS, AND REALLY LET OURSELVES EXPERIENCE THE MOMENT?
THE BEAUTY OF THAT MACHINE, AND OF THE LIVES IT WILL SAVE...
...AND HOW HONORED WE ARE TO PLAY OUR ROLES IN THIS. IT'S A BOND WE'LL SHARE FOR THE REST OF --
WHO'S THAT?
ANNIE?

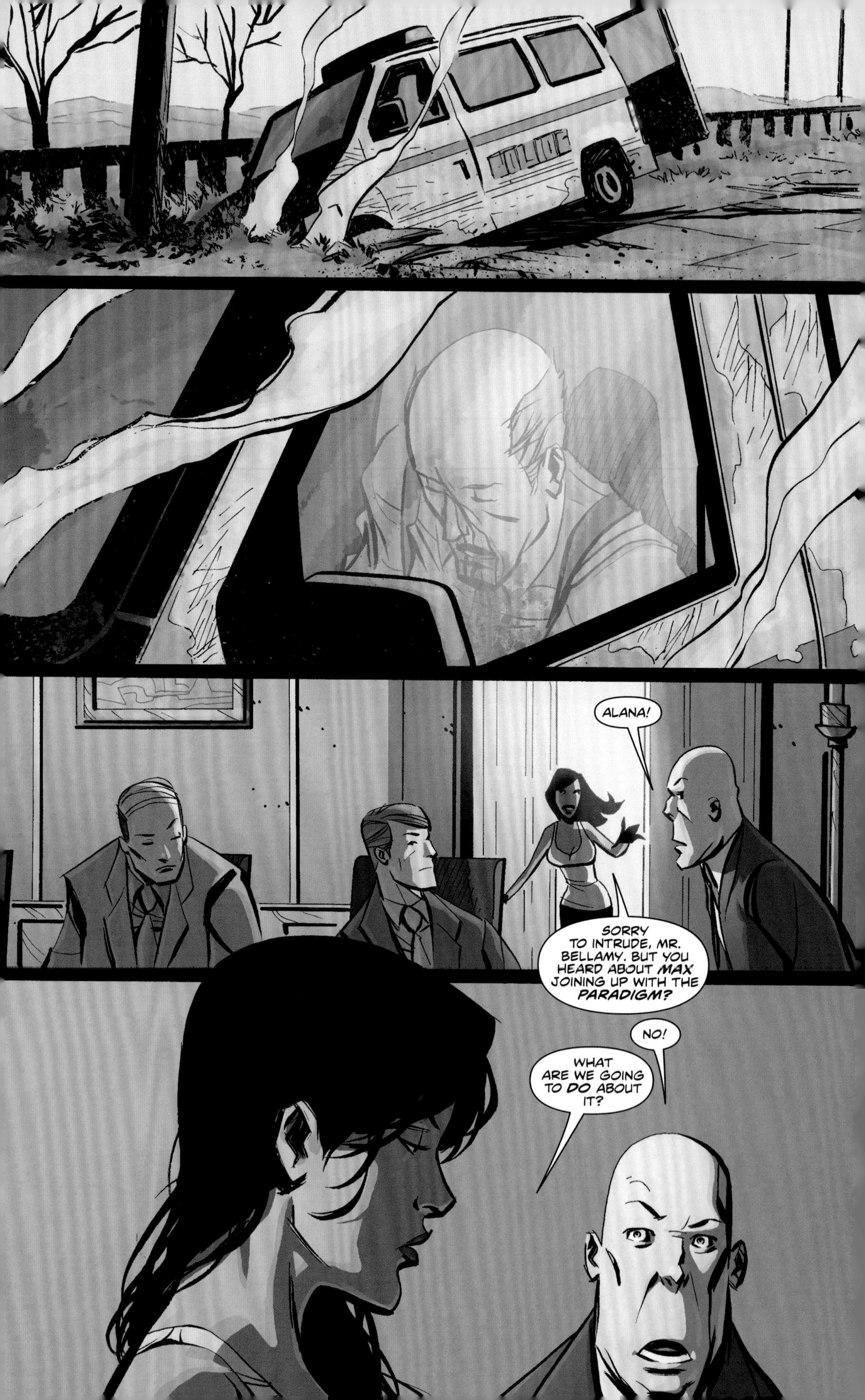
ALANA!
SORRY TO INTRUDE, MR. BELLAMY. BUT YOU HEARD ABOUT MAX JOINING UP WITH THE PARADIGM?
NO!
WHAT ARE WE GOING TO DO ABOUT IT?

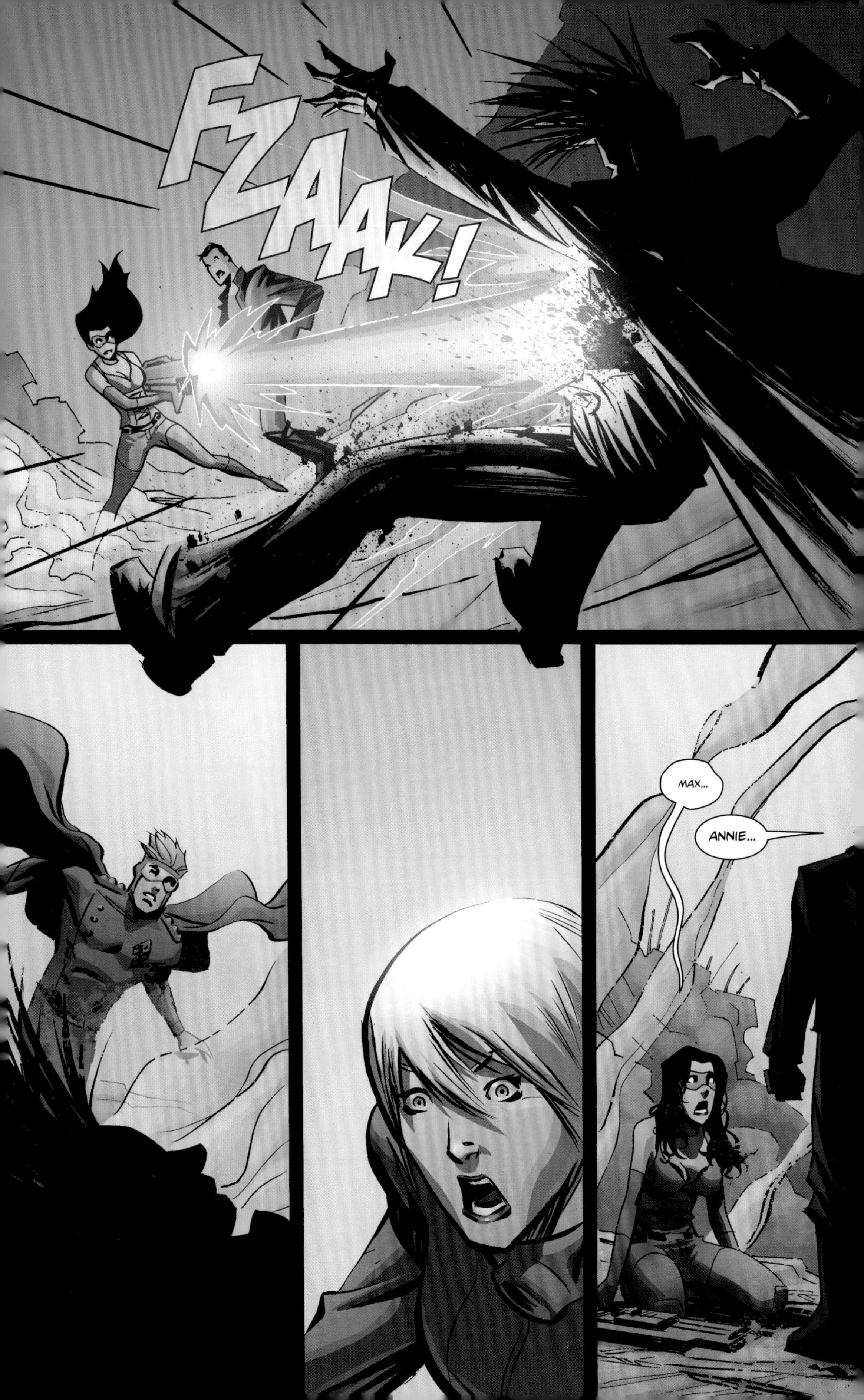
FZAAK!
MAX...
ANNIE...

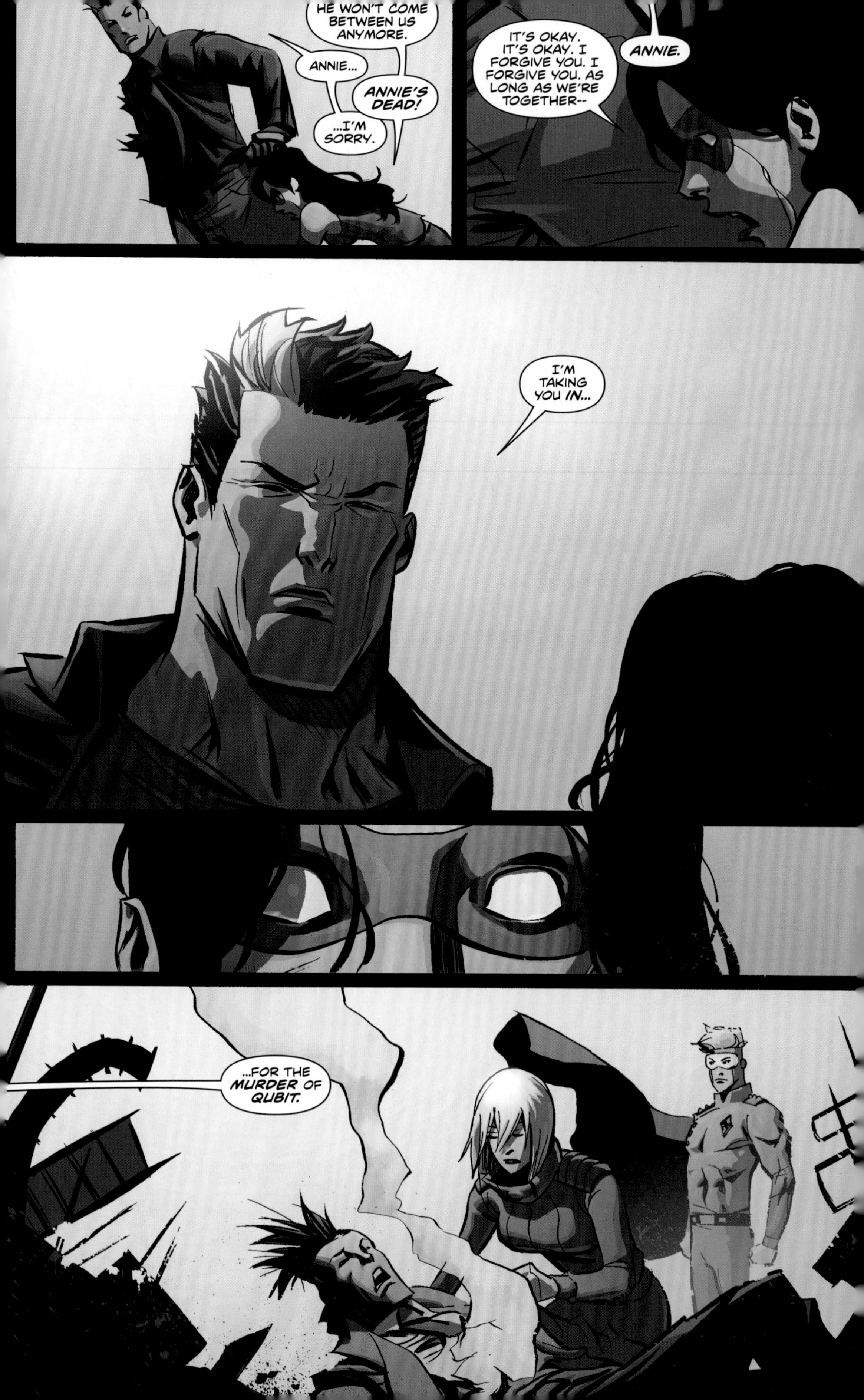

HE WON'T COME BETWEEN US ANYMORE.
ANNIE...
ANNIE'S DEAD!
...I'M SORRY.
IT'S OKAY. IT'S OKAY. I FORGIVE YOU. I FORGIVE YOU. AS LONG AS WE'RE TOGETHER--
ANNIE.
I'M TAKING YOU IN...
...FOR THE MURDER OF QUBIT.

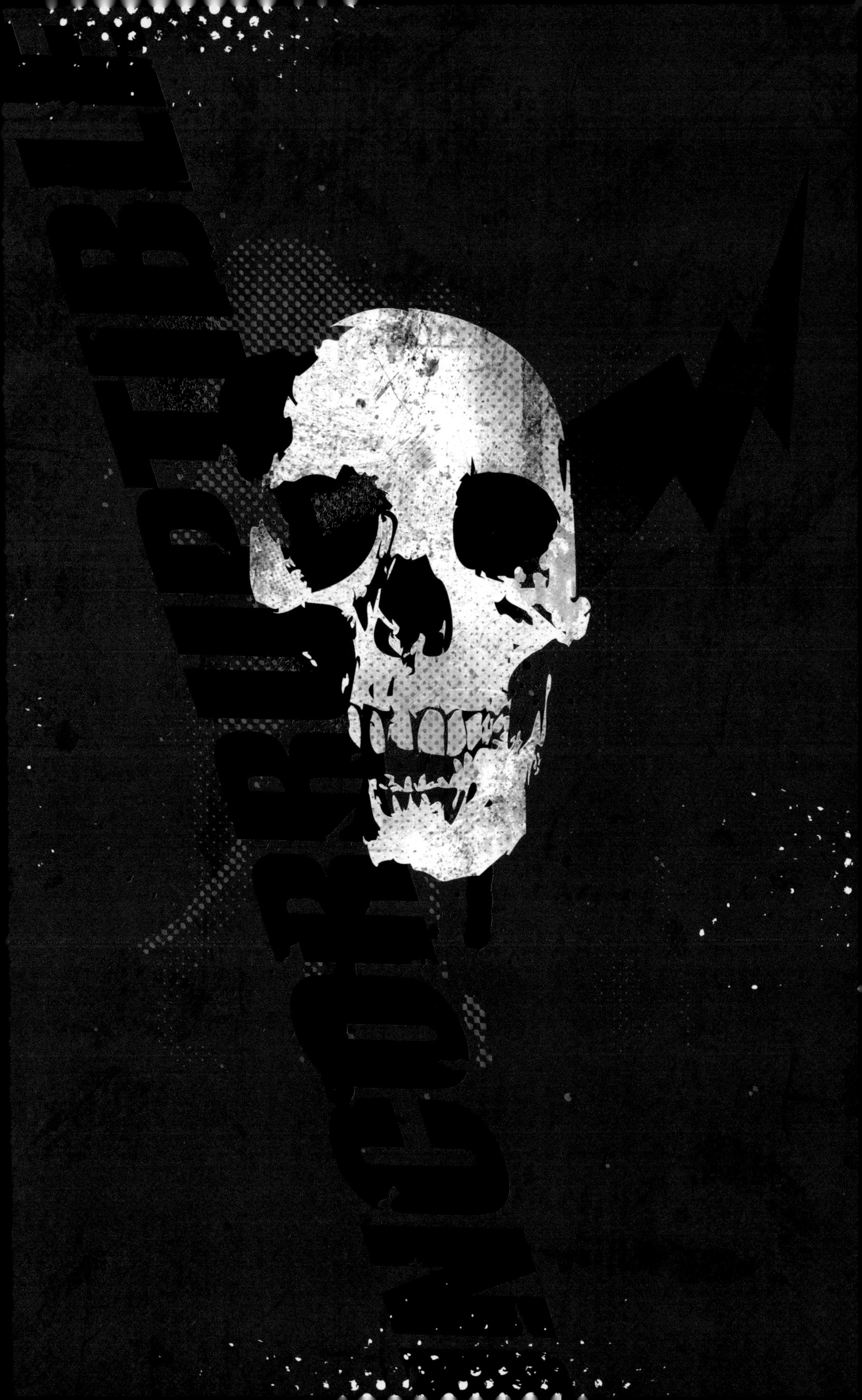

# CHAPTER 16

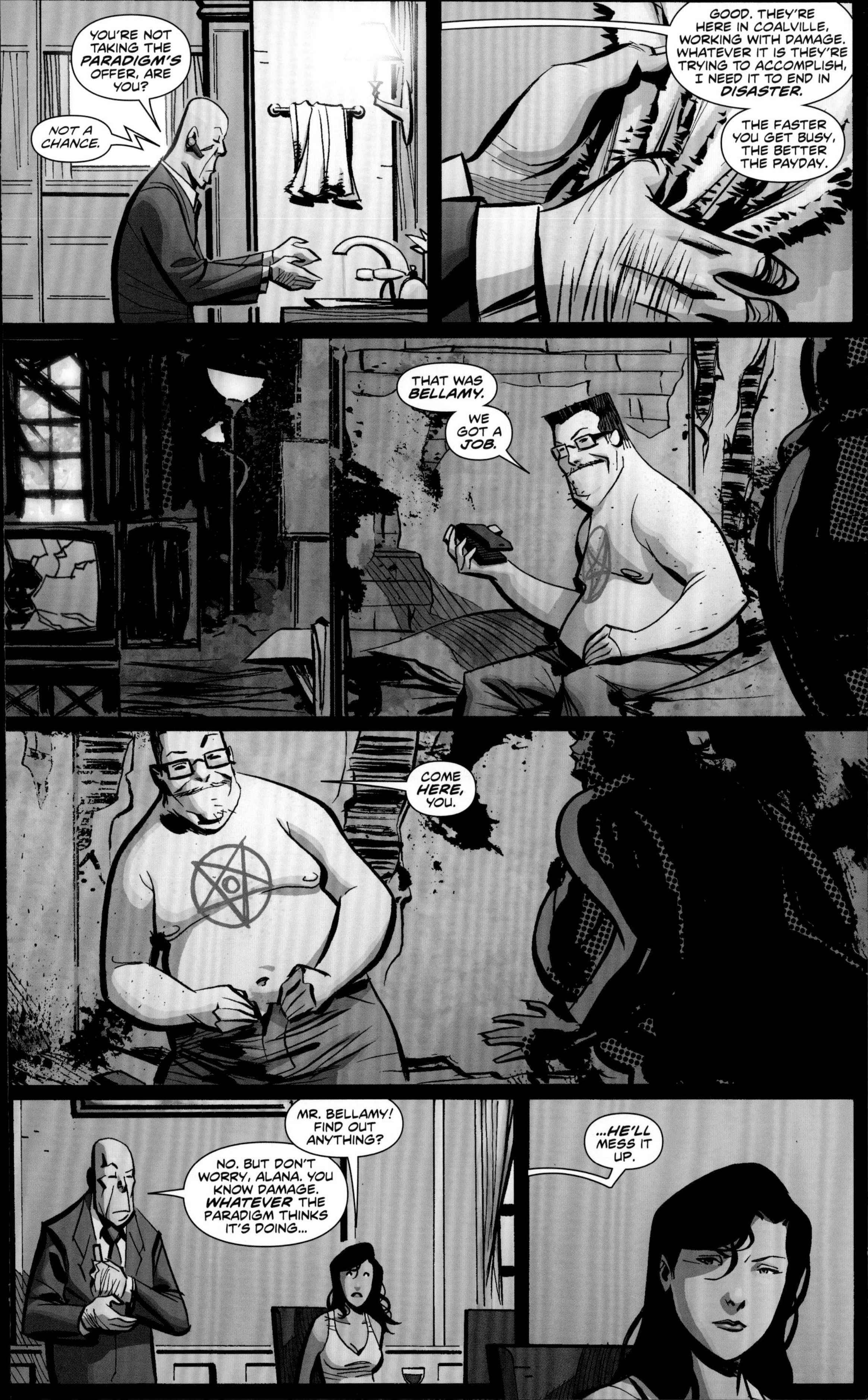
YOU'RE NOT TAKING THE PARADIGM'S OFFER, ARE YOU?
NOT A CHANCE.
GOOD. THEY'RE HERE IN COALVILLE, WORKING WITH DAMAGE. WHATEVER IT IS THEY'RE TRYING TO ACCOMPLISH, I NEED IT TO END IN DISASTER.
THE FASTER YOU GET BUSY, THE BETTER THE PAYDAY.
THAT WAS BELLAMY.
WE GOT A JOB.
COME HERE, YOU.
MR. BELLAMY! FIND OUT ANYTHING?
NO. BUT DON'T WORRY, ALANA. YOU KNOW DAMAGE. WHATEVER THE PARADIGM THINKS IT'S DOING...
...HE'LL MESS IT UP.

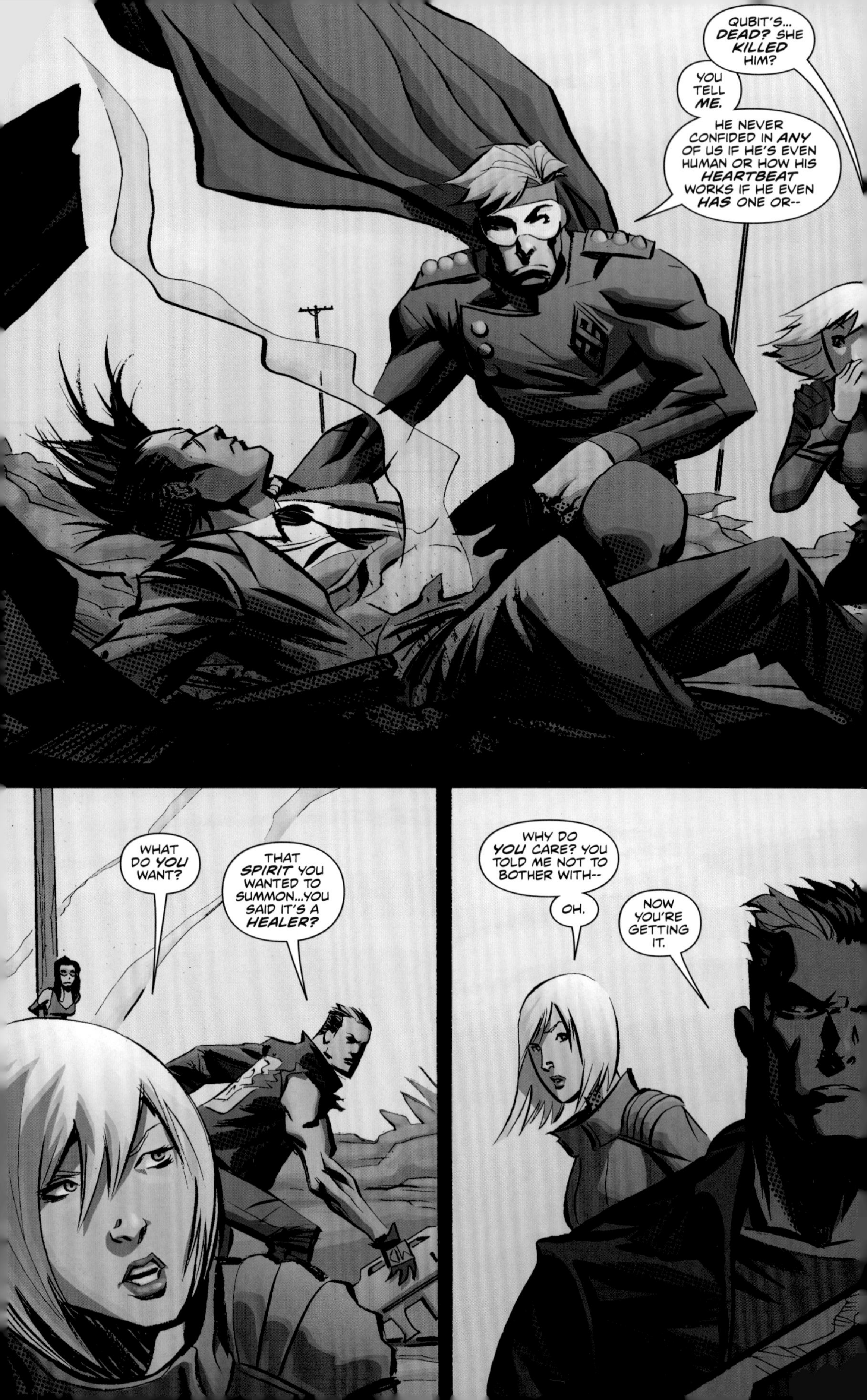
QUBIT'S... DEAD? SHE KILLED HIM?
YOU TELL ME.
HE NEVER CONFIDED IN ANY OF US IF HE'S EVEN HUMAN OR HOW HIS HEARTBEAT WORKS IF HE EVEN HAS ONE OR--
WHAT DO YOU WANT?
THAT SPIRIT YOU WANTED TO SUMMON...YOU SAID IT'S A HEALER?
WHY DO YOU CARE? YOU TOLD ME NOT TO BOTHER WITH--
OH.
NOW YOU'RE GETTING IT.

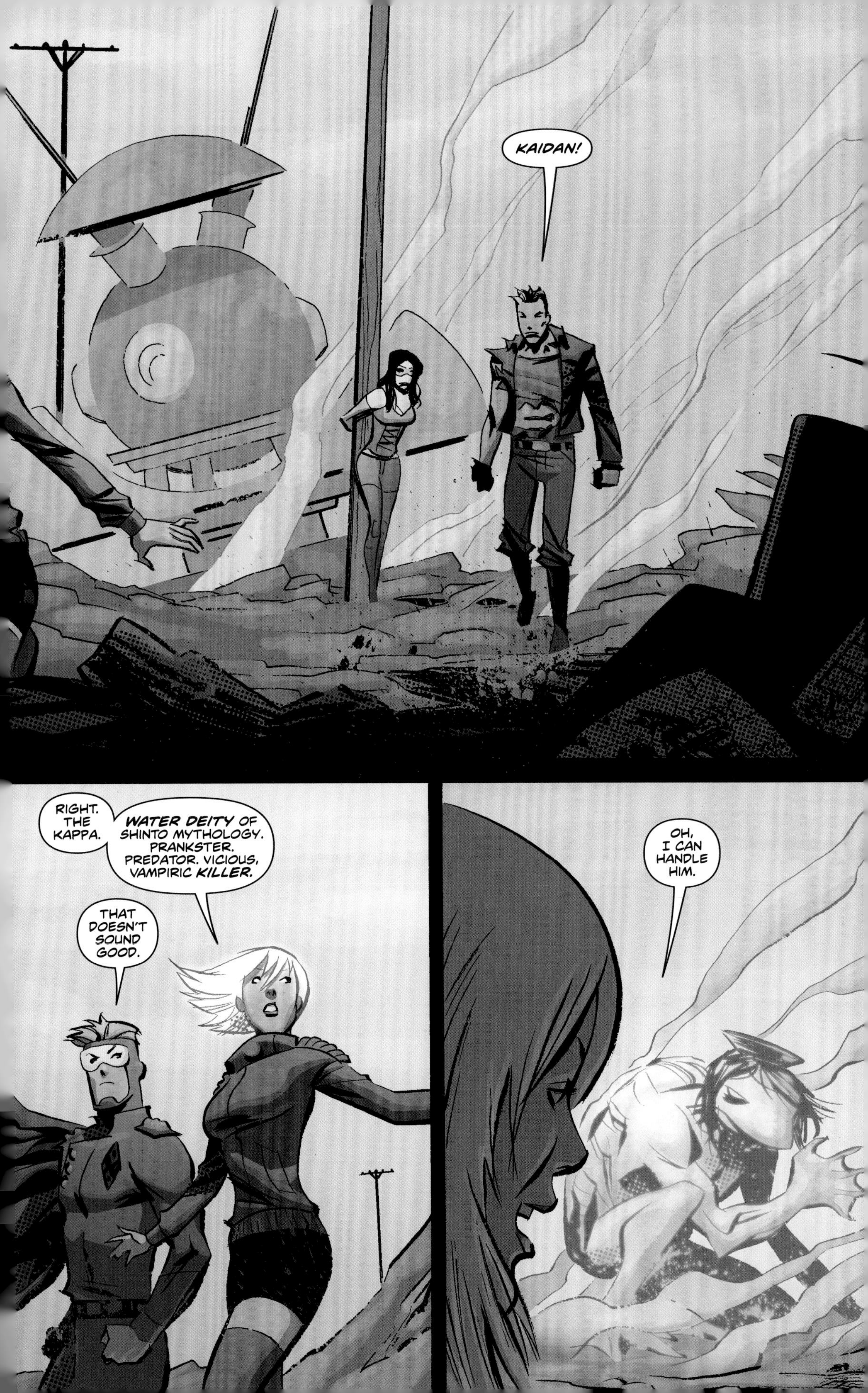
KAIDAN!
RIGHT. THE KAPPA.
WATER DEITY OF SHINTO MYTHOLOGY. PRANKSTER. PREDATOR. VICIOUS, VAMPIRIC KILLER.
THAT DOESN'T SOUND GOOD.
OH, I CAN HANDLE HIM.

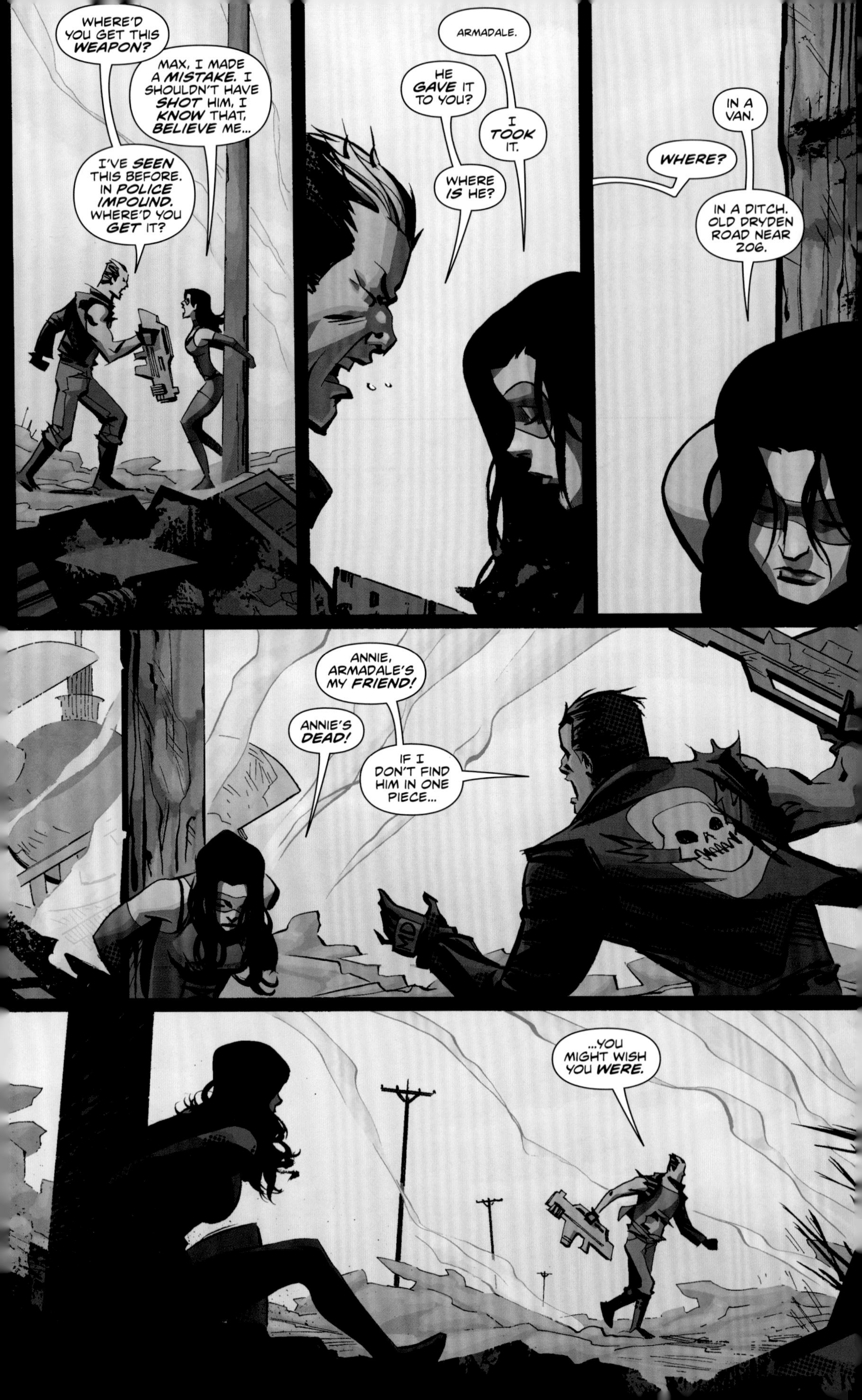
WHERE'D YOU GET THIS WEAPON?
MAX, I MADE A MISTAKE. I SHOULDN'T HAVE SHOT HIM, I KNOW THAT, BELIEVE ME...
I'VE SEEN THIS BEFORE. IN POLICE IMPOUND. WHERE'D YOU GET IT?
ARMADALE.
HE GAVE IT TO YOU?
I TOOK IT.
WHERE IS HE?
IN A VAN.
WHERE?
IN A DITCH. OLD DRYDEN ROAD NEAR 206.
ANNIE, ARMADALE'S MY FRIEND!
ANNIE'S DEAD!
IF I DON'T FIND HIM IN ONE PIECE...
...YOU MIGHT WISH YOU WERE.

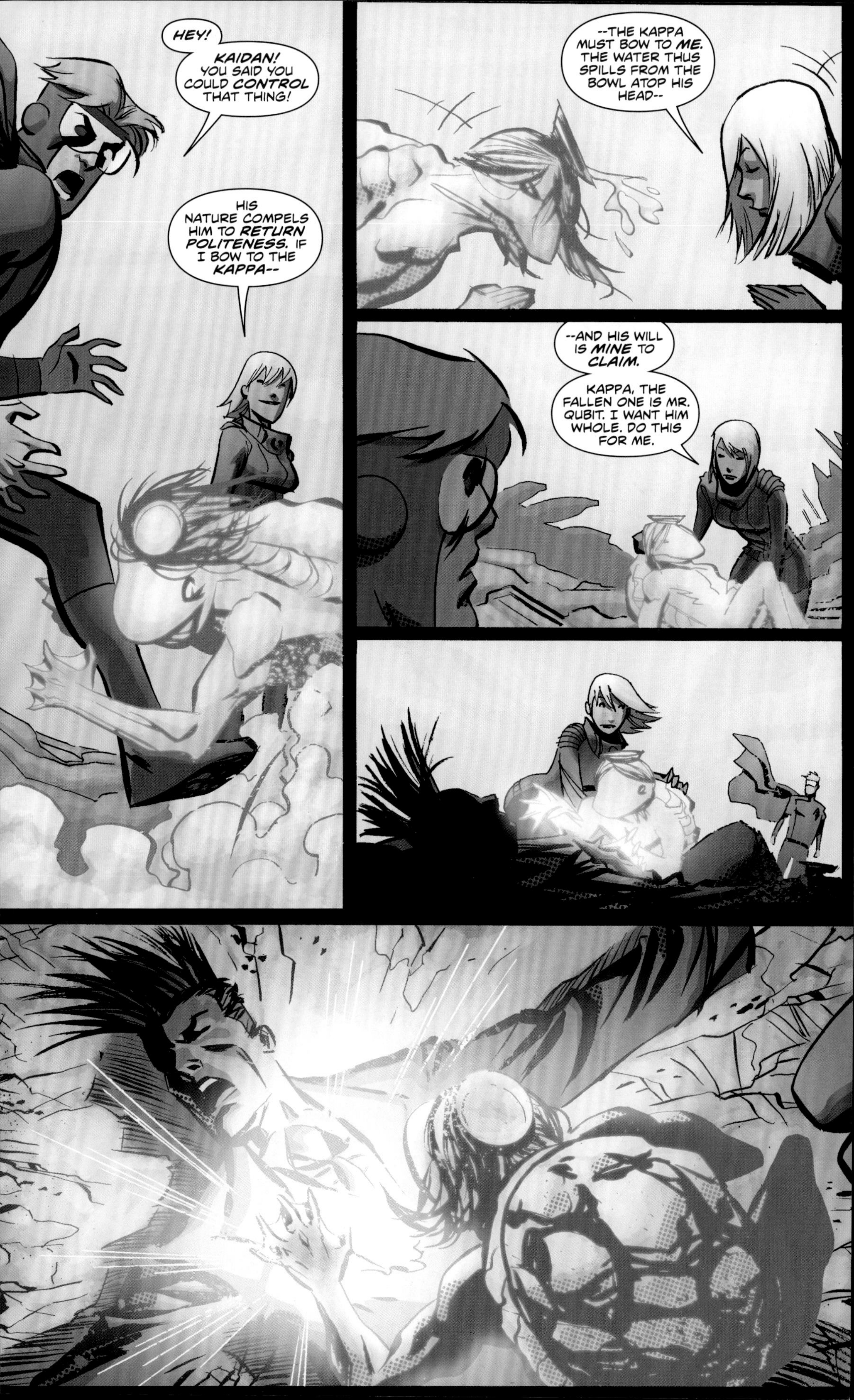
HEY!
KAIDAN! YOU SAID YOU COULD CONTROL THAT THING!
HIS NATURE COMPELS HIM TO RETURN POLITENESS. IF I BOW TO THE KAPPA--
--THE KAPPA MUST BOW TO ME. THE WATER THUS SPILLS FROM THE BOWL ATOP HIS HEAD--
--AND HIS WILL IS MINE TO CLAIM.
KAPPA, THE FALLEN ONE IS MR. QUBIT. I WANT HIM WHOLE. DO THIS FOR ME.

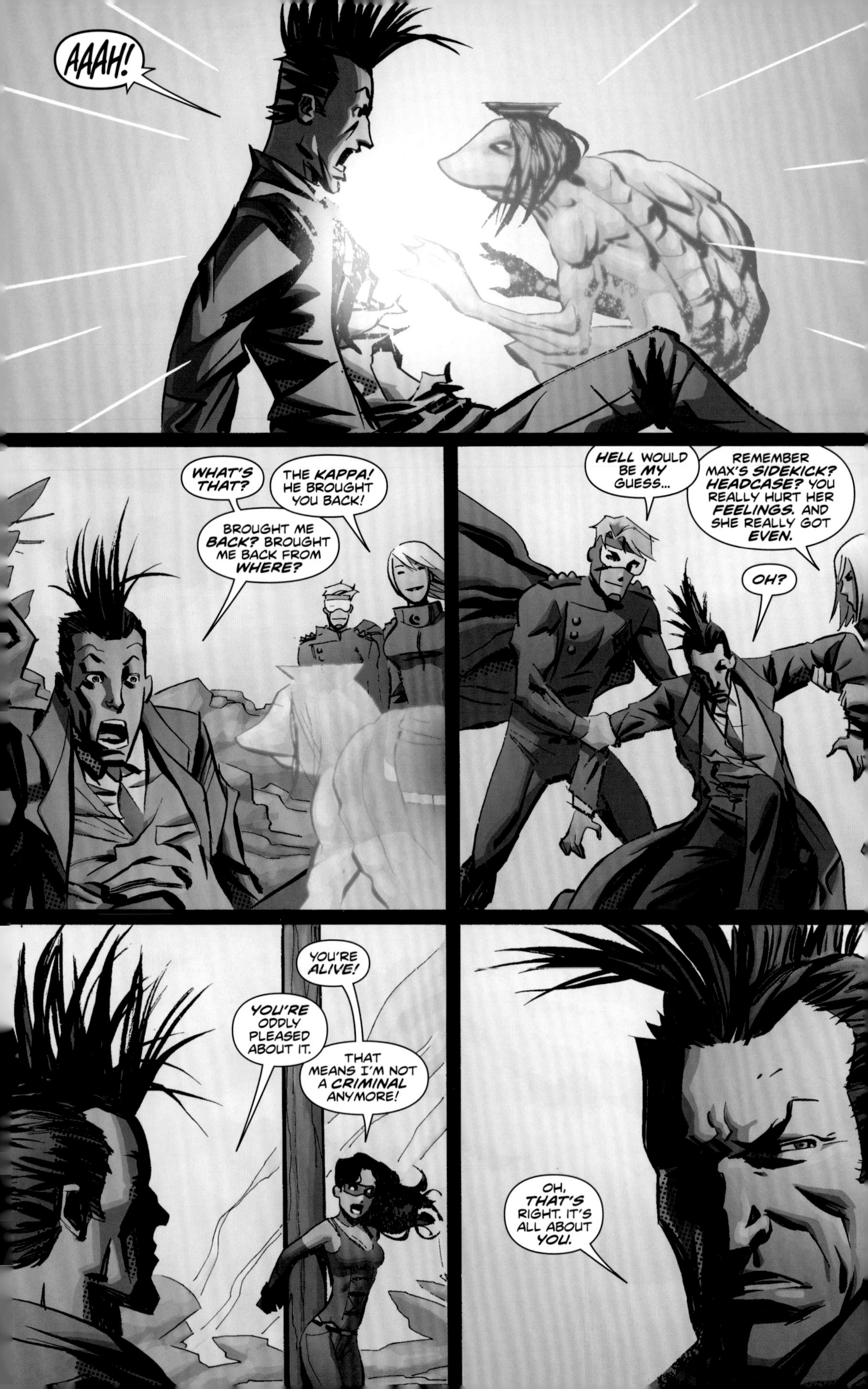
AAAH!
WHAT'S THAT?
THE KAPPA! HE BROUGHT YOU BACK!
BROUGHT ME BACK? BROUGHT ME BACK FROM WHERE?
HELL WOULD BE MY GUESS...
REMEMBER MAX'S SIDEKICK? HEADCASE? YOU REALLY HURT HER FEELINGS. AND SHE REALLY GOT EVEN.
OH?
YOU'RE ALIVE!
YOU'RE ODDLY PLEASED ABOUT IT.
THAT MEANS I'M NOT A CRIMINAL ANYMORE!
OH, THAT'S RIGHT. IT'S ALL ABOUT YOU.

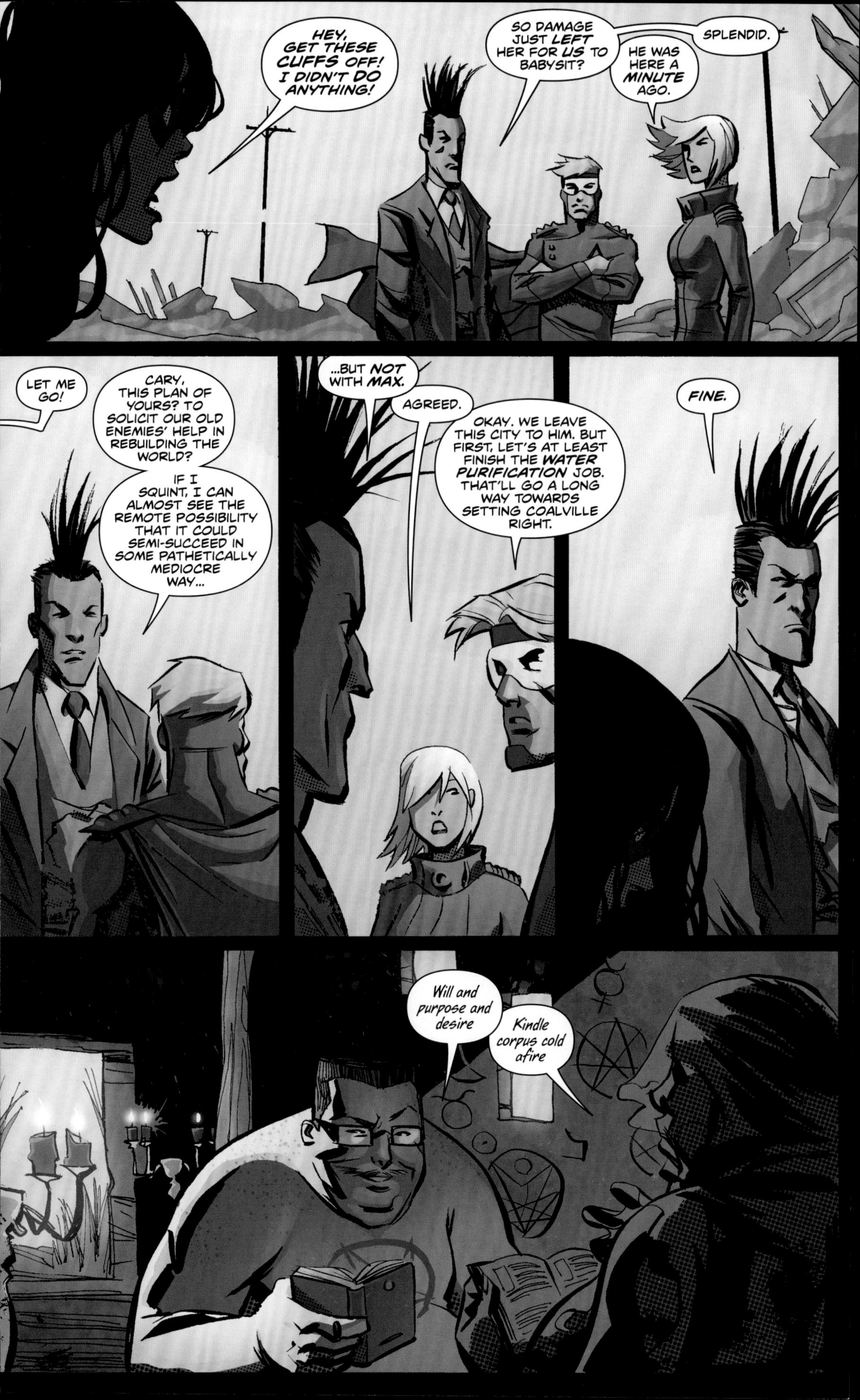
HEY, GET THESE CUFFS OFF! I DIDN'T DO ANYTHING!
SO DAMAGE JUST LEFT HER FOR US TO BABYSIT?
SPLENDID.
HE WAS HERE A MINUTE AGO.
LET ME GO!
CARY, THIS PLAN OF YOURS? TO SOLICIT OUR OLD ENEMIES' HELP IN REBUILDING THE WORLD?
IF I SQUINT, I CAN ALMOST SEE THE REMOTE POSSIBILITY THAT IT COULD SEMI-SUCCEED IN SOME PATHETICALLY MEDIOCRE WAY...
...BUT NOT WITH MAX.
AGREED.
OKAY. WE LEAVE THIS CITY TO HIM. BUT FIRST, LET'S AT LEAST FINISH THE WATER PURIFICATION JOB. THAT'LL GO A LONG WAY TOWARDS SETTING COALVILLE RIGHT.
FINE.
Will and purpose and desire
Kindle corpus cold afire

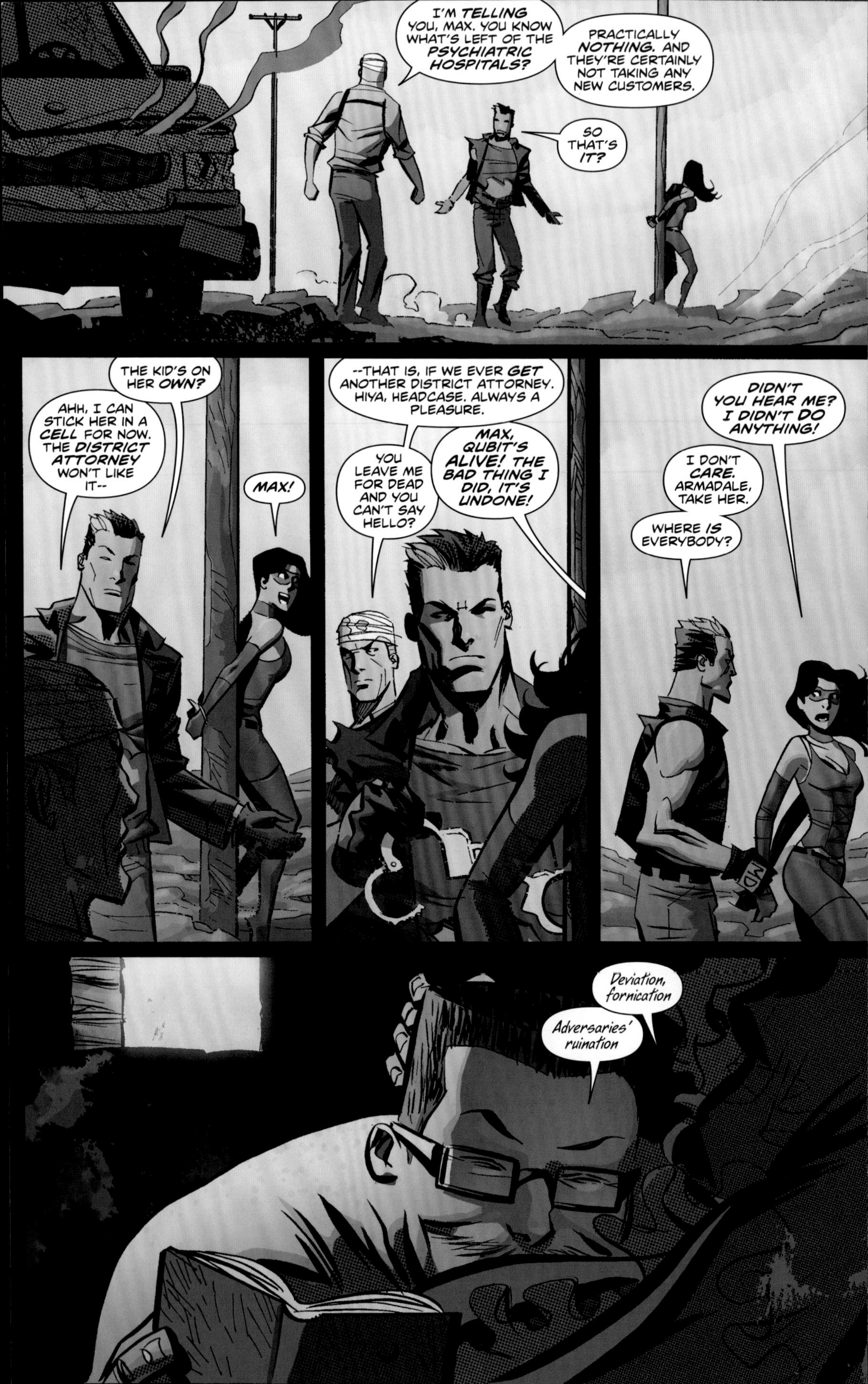
I'M TELLING YOU, MAX. YOU KNOW WHAT'S LEFT OF THE PSYCHIATRIC HOSPITALS?
PRACTICALLY NOTHING. AND THEY'RE CERTAINLY NOT TAKING ANY NEW CUSTOMERS.
SO THAT'S IT?
THE KID'S ON HER OWN?
AHH, I CAN STICK HER IN A CELL FOR NOW. THE DISTRICT ATTORNEY WON'T LIKE IT--
MAX!
--THAT IS, IF WE EVER GET ANOTHER DISTRICT ATTORNEY. HIYA, HEADCASE. ALWAYS A PLEASURE.
YOU LEAVE ME FOR DEAD AND YOU CAN'T SAY HELLO?
MAX, QUBIT'S ALIVE! THE BAD THING I DID, IT'S UNDONE!
DIDN'T YOU HEAR ME? I DIDN'T DO ANYTHING!
I DON'T CARE. ARMADALE, TAKE HER.
WHERE IS EVERYBODY?
MD
Deviation, fornication
Adversaries' ruination

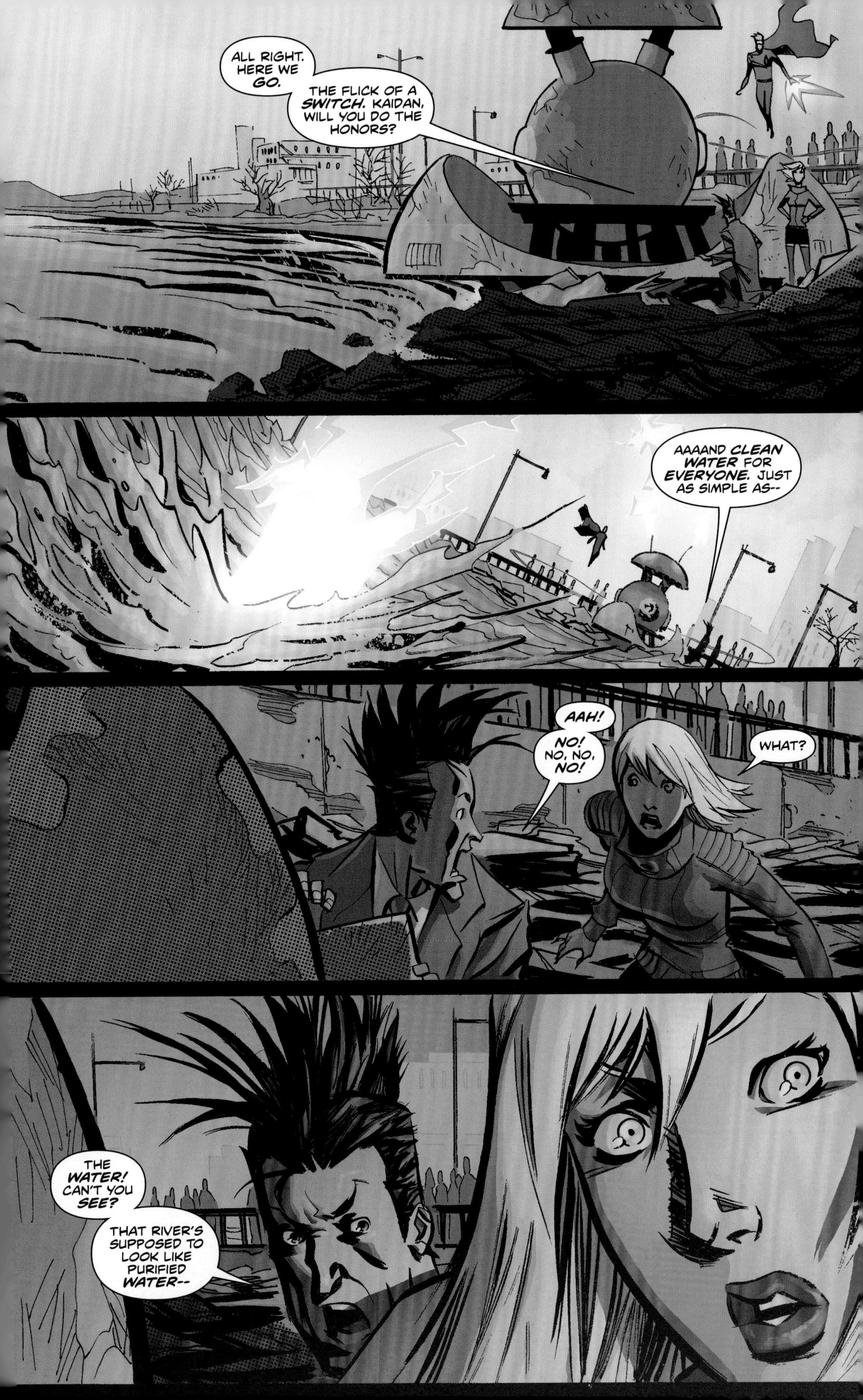
ALL RIGHT. HERE WE GO.
THE FLICK OF A SWITCH. KAIDAN, WILL YOU DO THE HONORS?
AAAAND CLEAN WATER FOR EVERYONE. JUST AS SIMPLE AS--
AAH!
NO! NO, NO, NO!
WHAT?
THE WATER! CAN'T YOU SEE?
THAT RIVER'S SUPPOSED TO LOOK LIKE PURIFIED WATER--

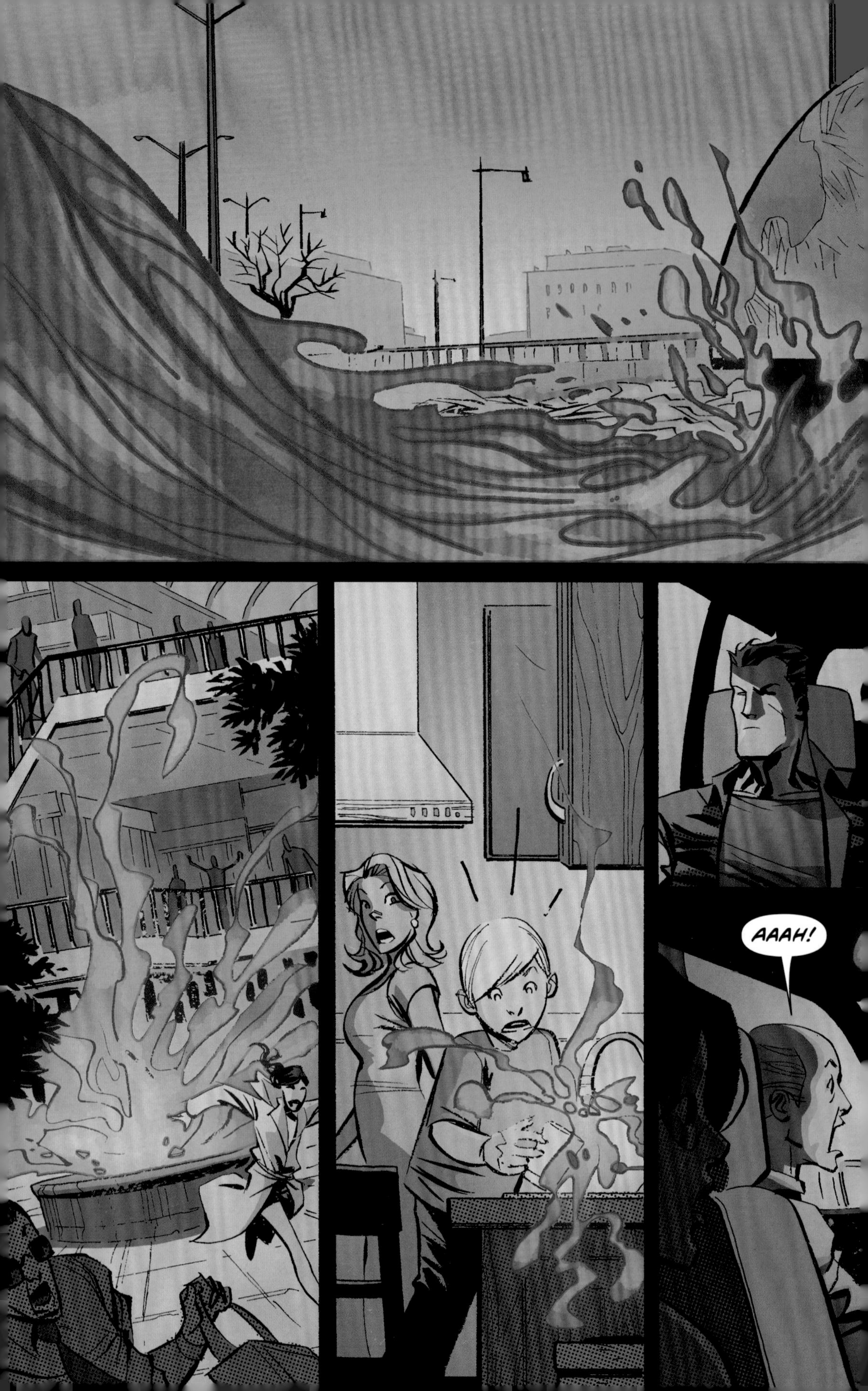
AAAH!

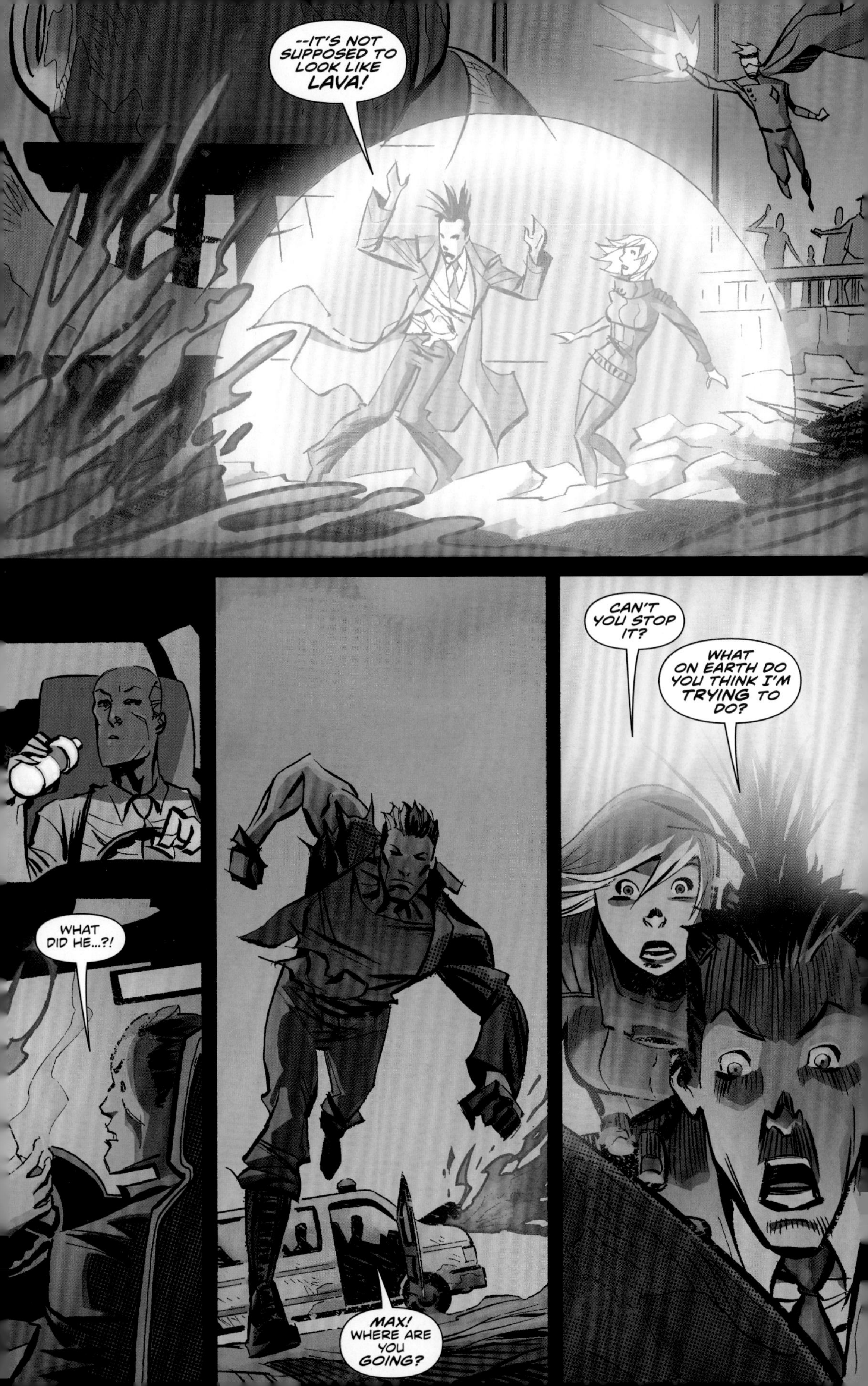
--IT'S NOT SUPPOSED TO LOOK LIKE LAVA!
WHAT DID HE...?!
MAX! WHERE ARE YOU GOING?
CAN'T YOU STOP IT?
WHAT ON EARTH DO YOU THINK I'M TRYING TO DO?

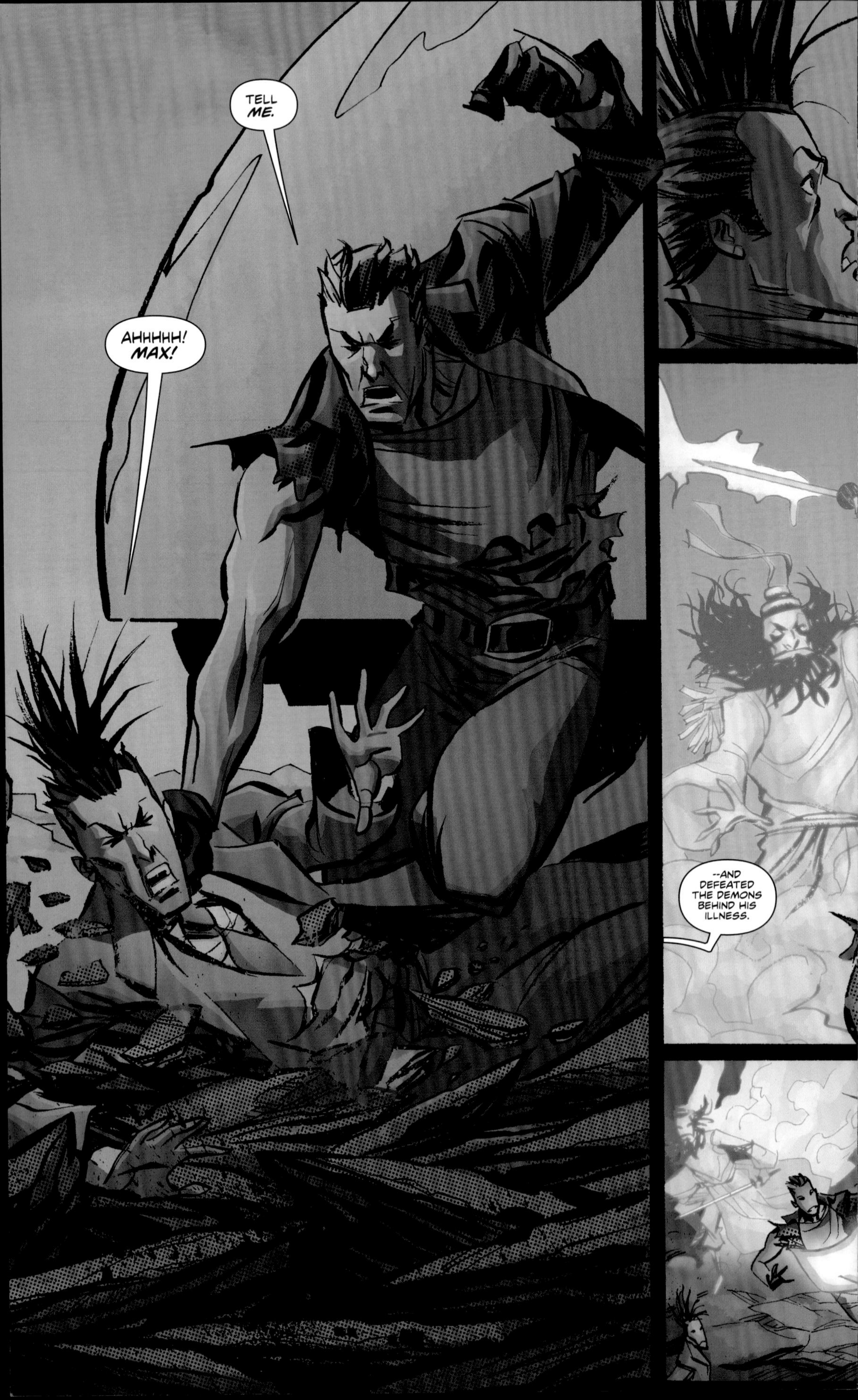
TELL ME.
AHHHHH! MAX!
--AND DEFEATED THE DEMONS BEHIND HIS ILLNESS.

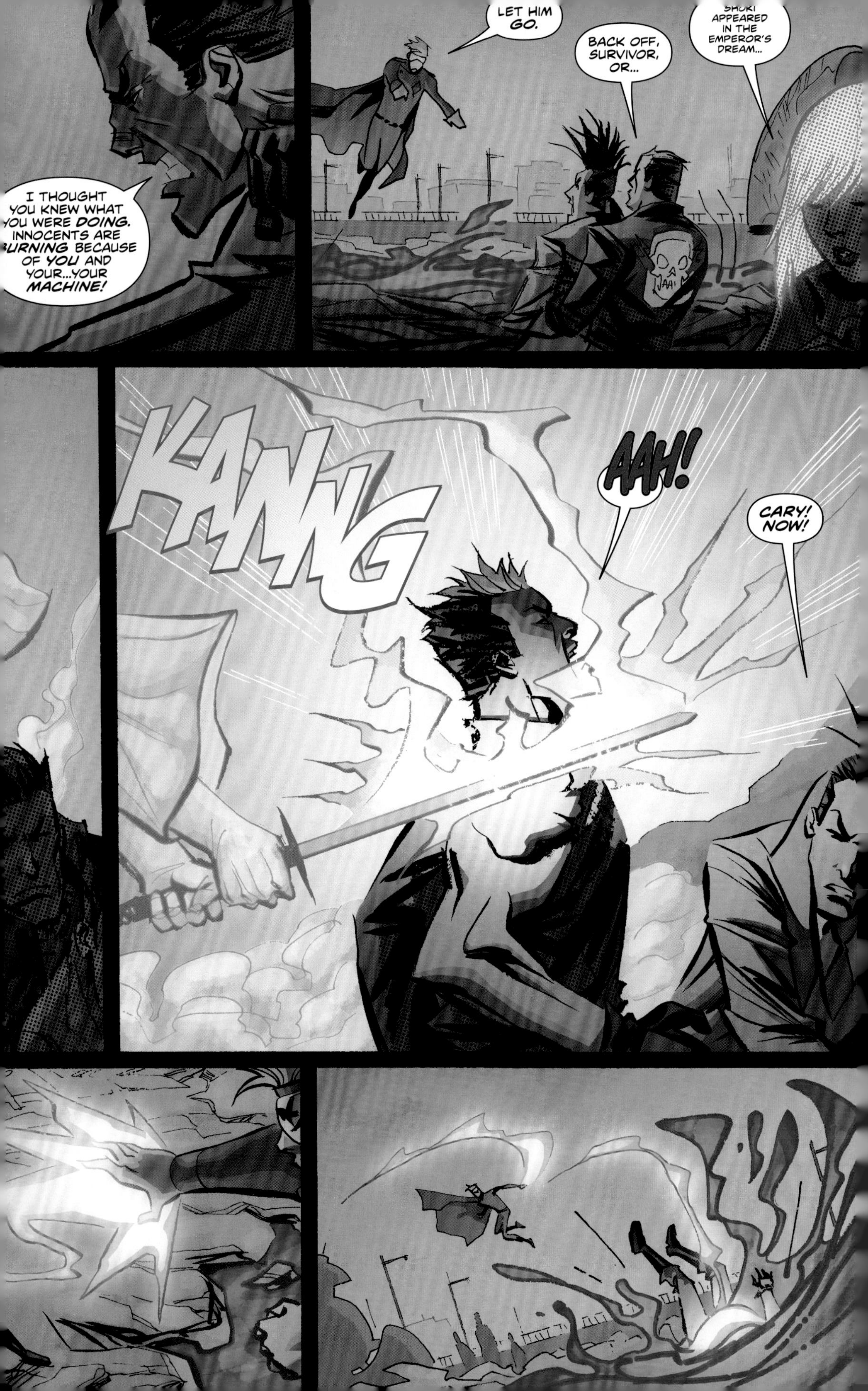
I THOUGHT YOU KNEW WHAT YOU WERE DOING. INNOCENTS ARE URNING BECAUSE OF YOU AND YOUR...YOUR MACHINE!
LET HIM GO.
BACK OFF, SURVIVOR, OR...
APPEARED IN THE EMPEROR'S DREAM...
KANNG
AAH!
CARY! NOW!

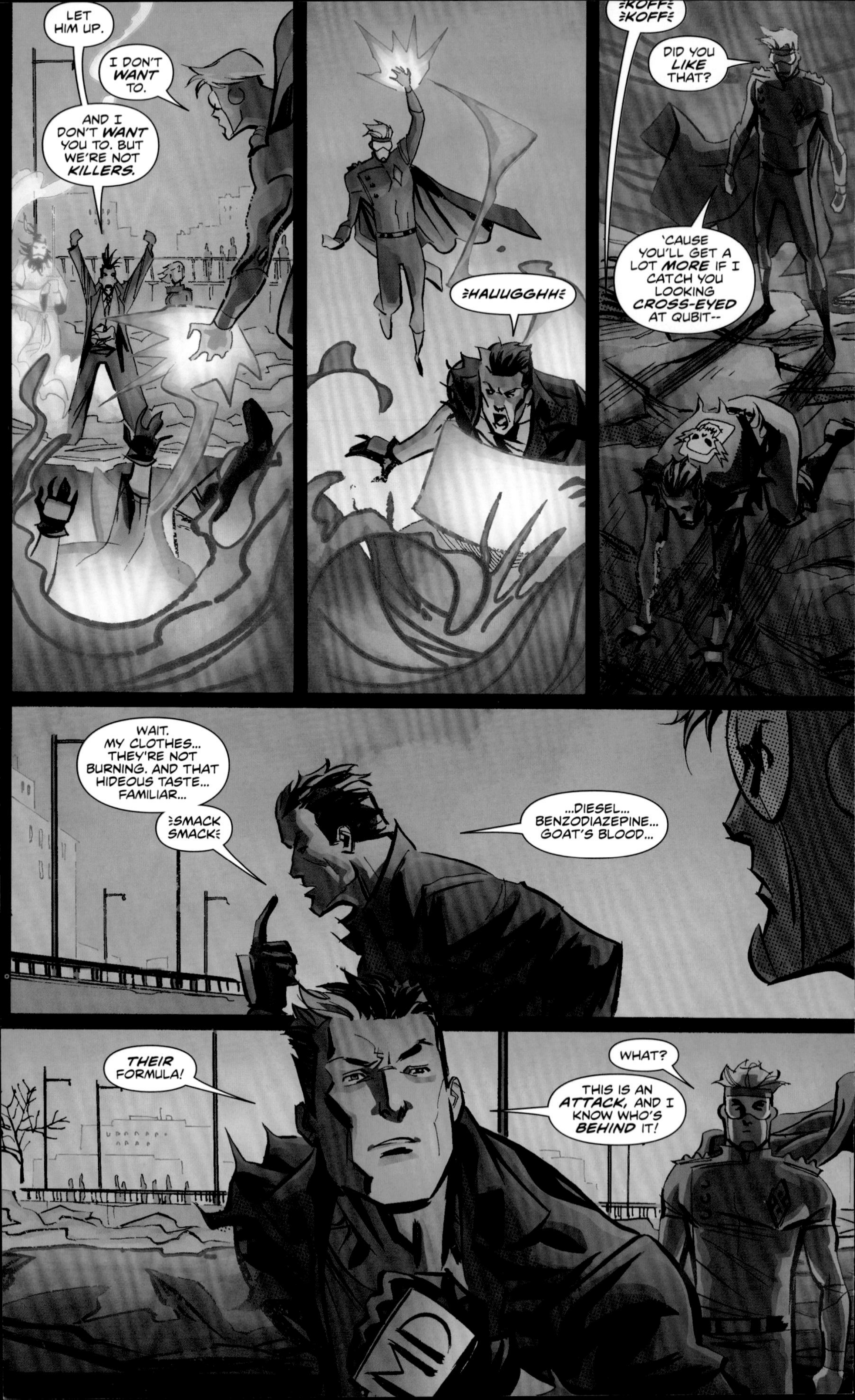
LET HIM UP.
I DON'T WANT TO.
AND I DON'T WANT YOU TO. BUT WE'RE NOT KILLERS.
HAUUGGHH
KOFF KOFF
DID YOU LIKE THAT?
'CAUSE YOU'LL GET A LOT MORE IF I CATCH YOU LOOKING CROSS-EYED AT QUBIT--
WAIT. MY CLOTHES... THEY'RE NOT BURNING. AND THAT HIDEOUS TASTE... FAMILIAR...
SMACK SMACK
...DIESEL... BENZODIAZEPINE... GOAT'S BLOOD...
THEIR FORMULA!
WHAT?
THIS IS AN ATTACK, AND I KNOW WHO'S BEHIND IT!

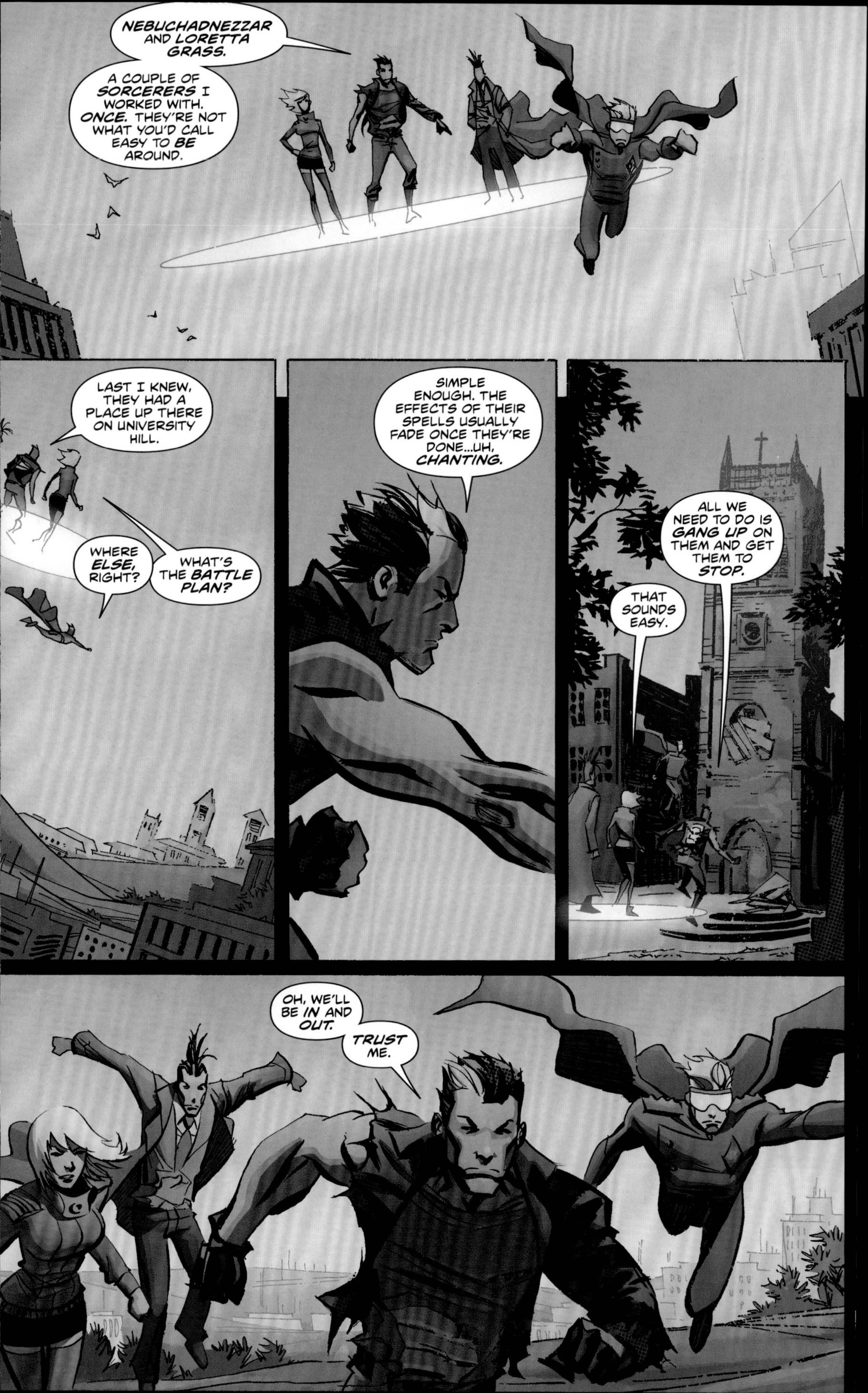
NEBUCHADNEZZAR AND LORETTA GRASS.
A COUPLE OF SORCERERS I WORKED WITH. ONCE. THEY'RE NOT WHAT YOU'D CALL EASY TO BE AROUND.
LAST I KNEW, THEY HAD A PLACE UP THERE ON UNIVERSITY HILL.
WHERE ELSE, RIGHT?
WHAT'S THE BATTLE PLAN?
SIMPLE ENOUGH. THE EFFECTS OF THEIR SPELLS USUALLY FADE ONCE THEY'RE DONE...UH, CHANTING.
ALL WE NEED TO DO IS GANG UP ON THEM AND GET THEM TO STOP.
THAT SOUNDS EASY.
OH, WE'LL BE IN AND OUT.
TRUST ME.

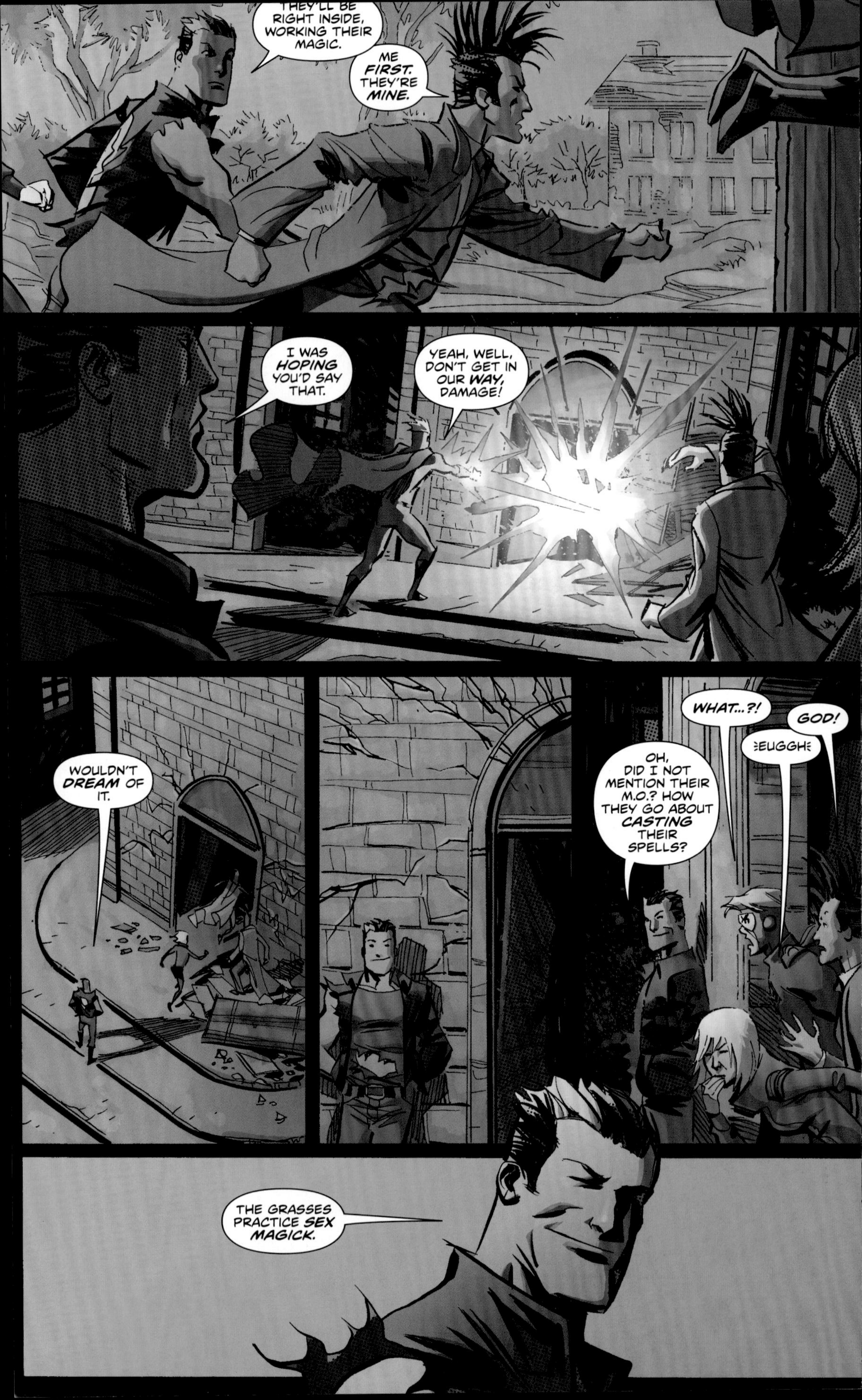
THEY'LL BE RIGHT INSIDE, WORKING THEIR MAGIC.
ME FIRST. THEY'RE MINE.
I WAS HOPING YOU'D SAY THAT.
YEAH, WELL, DON'T GET IN OUR WAY, DAMAGE!
WOULDN'T DREAM OF IT.
OH, DID I NOT MENTION THEIR M.O.? HOW THEY GO ABOUT CASTING THEIR SPELLS?
WHAT...?!
GOD!
EUGGH
THE GRASSES PRACTICE SEX MAGICK.

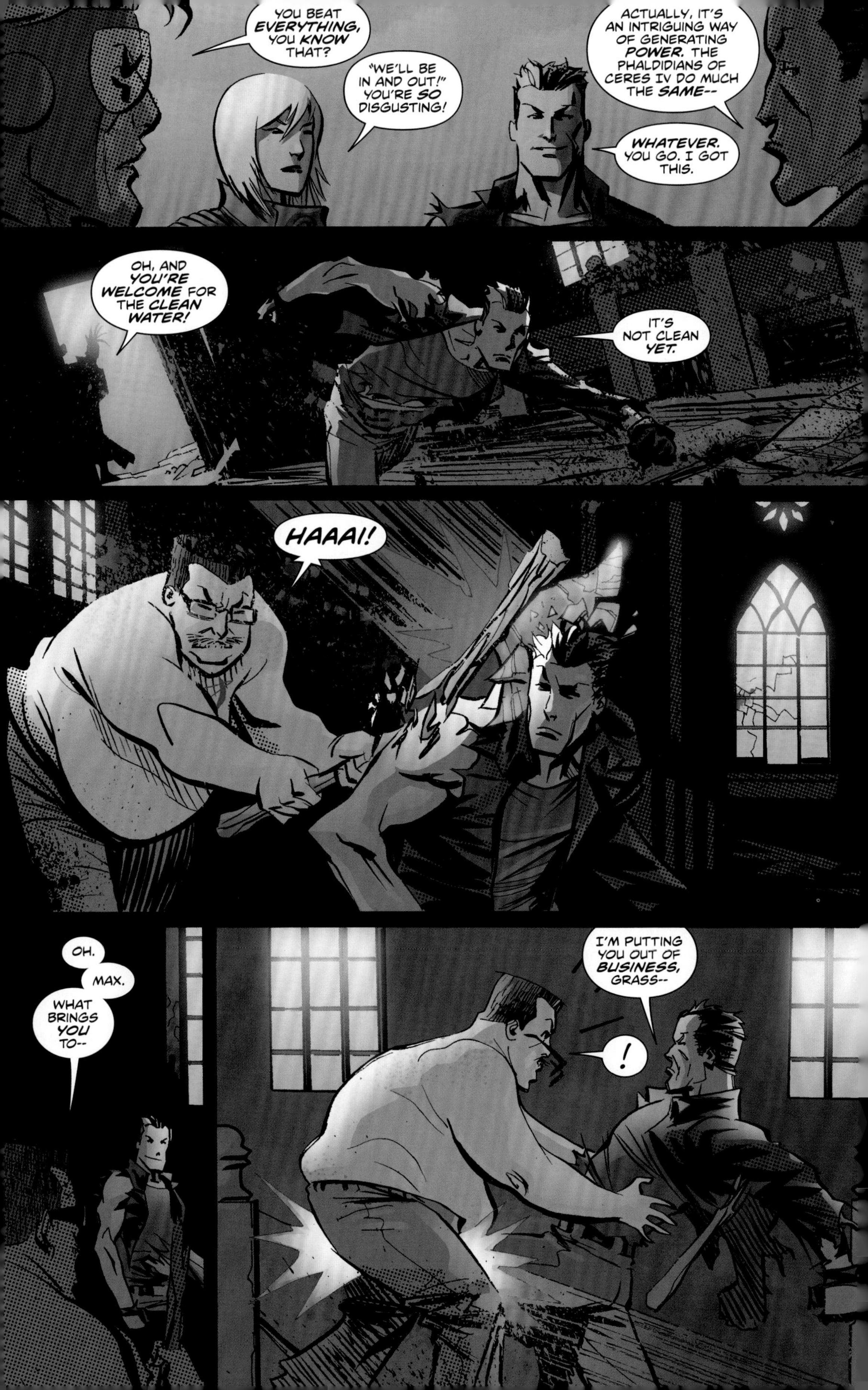
YOU BEAT EVERYTHING, YOU KNOW THAT?
"WE'LL BE IN AND OUT!" YOU'RE SO DISGUSTING!
ACTUALLY, IT'S AN INTRIGUING WAY OF GENERATING POWER. THE PHALDIDIANS OF CERES IV DO MUCH THE SAME--
WHATEVER. YOU GO. I GOT THIS.
OH, AND YOU'RE WELCOME FOR THE CLEAN WATER!
IT'S NOT CLEAN YET.
HAAAI!
OH.
MAX.
WHAT BRINGS YOU TO--
I'M PUTTING YOU OUT OF BUSINESS, GRASS--
!

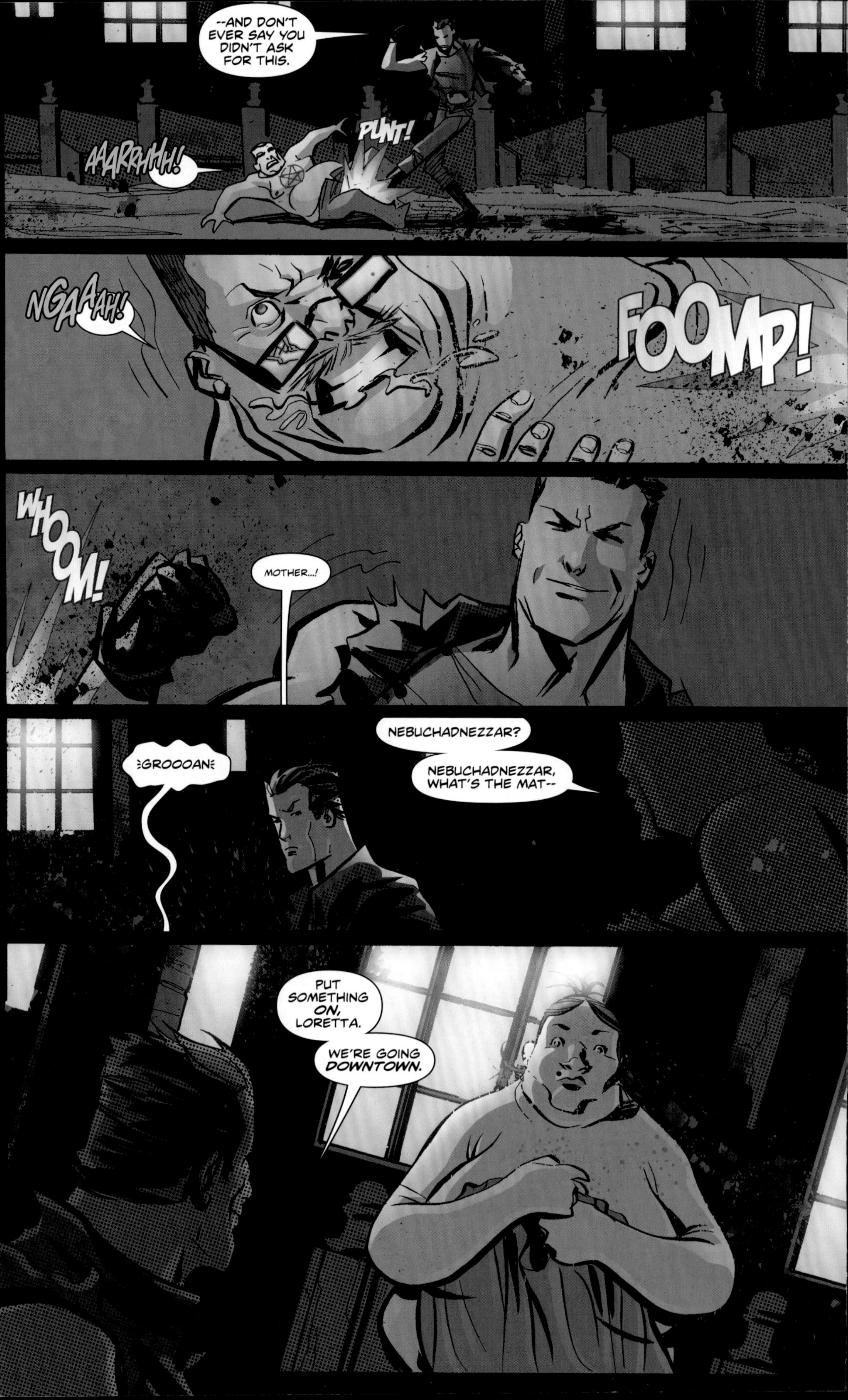
--AND DON'T EVER SAY YOU DIDN'T ASK FOR THIS.
PUNT!
AAARRHHH!
NGAAAAH!
FOOMP!
WHOOM!
MOTHER...!
GROOOAN
NEBUCHADNEZZAR?
NEBUCHADNEZZAR, WHAT'S THE MAT--
PUT SOMETHING ON, LORETTA.
WE'RE GOING DOWNTOWN.

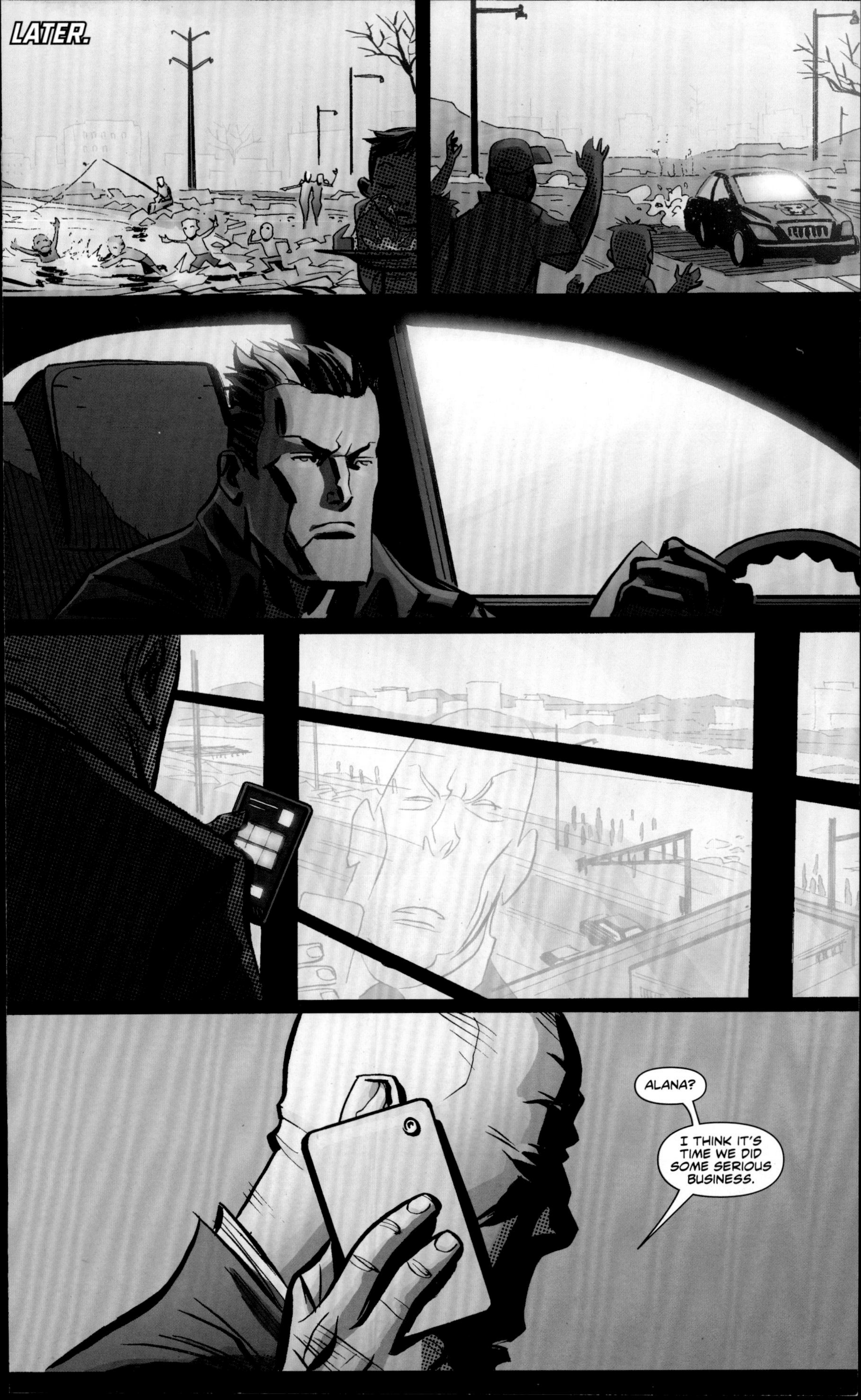
LATER.
ALANA?
I THINK IT'S TIME WE DID SOME SERIOUS BUSINESS.

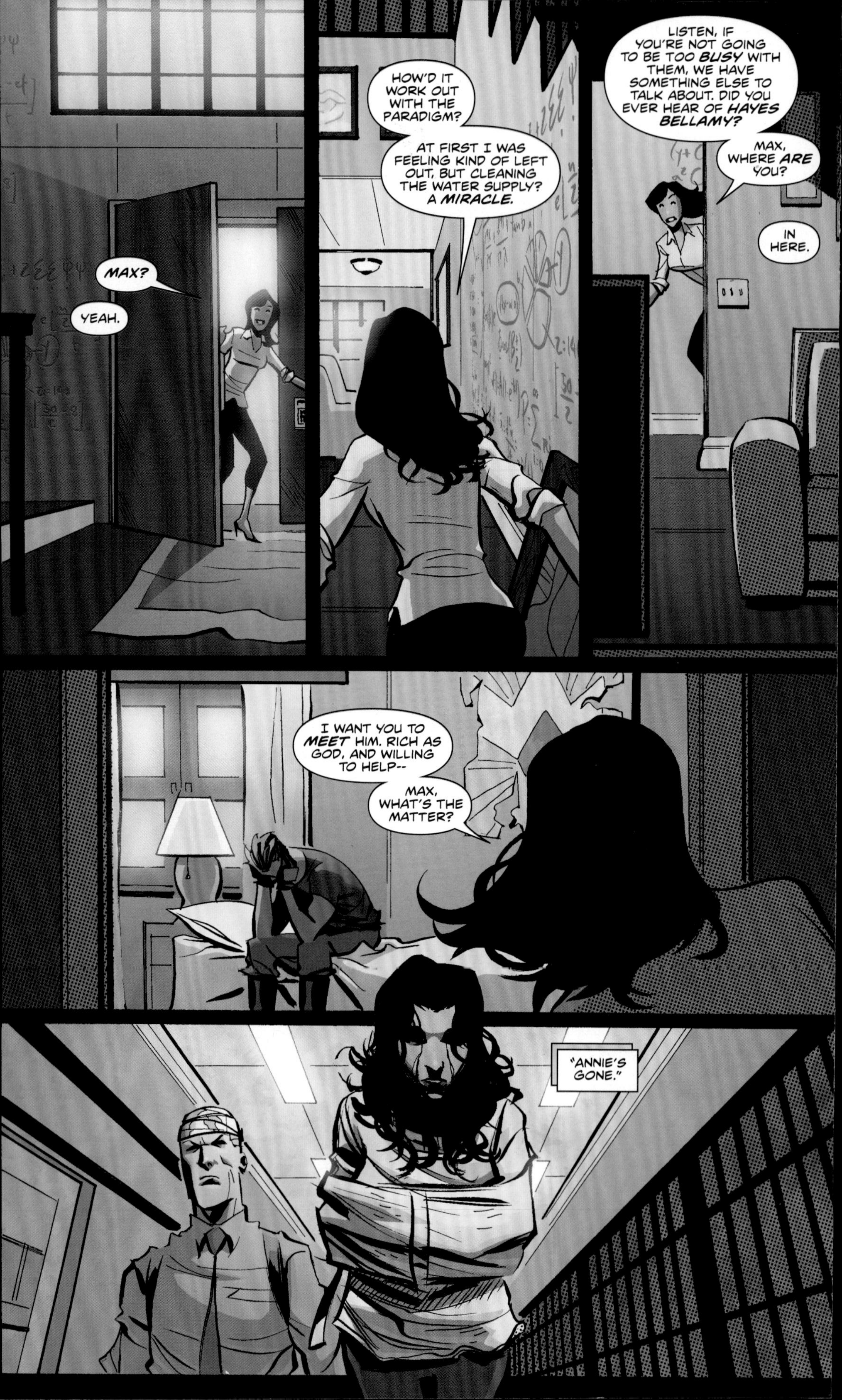
MAX?
YEAH.
HOW'D IT WORK OUT WITH THE PARADIGM?
AT FIRST I WAS FEELING KIND OF LEFT OUT, BUT CLEANING THE WATER SUPPLY? A MIRACLE.
LISTEN, IF YOU'RE NOT GOING TO BE TOO BUSY WITH THEM, WE HAVE SOMETHING ELSE TO TALK ABOUT. DID YOU EVER HEAR OF HAYES BELLAMY?
MAX, WHERE ARE YOU?
IN HERE.
I WANT YOU TO MEET HIM. RICH AS GOD, AND WILLING TO HELP--
MAX, WHAT'S THE MATTER?
"ANNIE'S GONE."

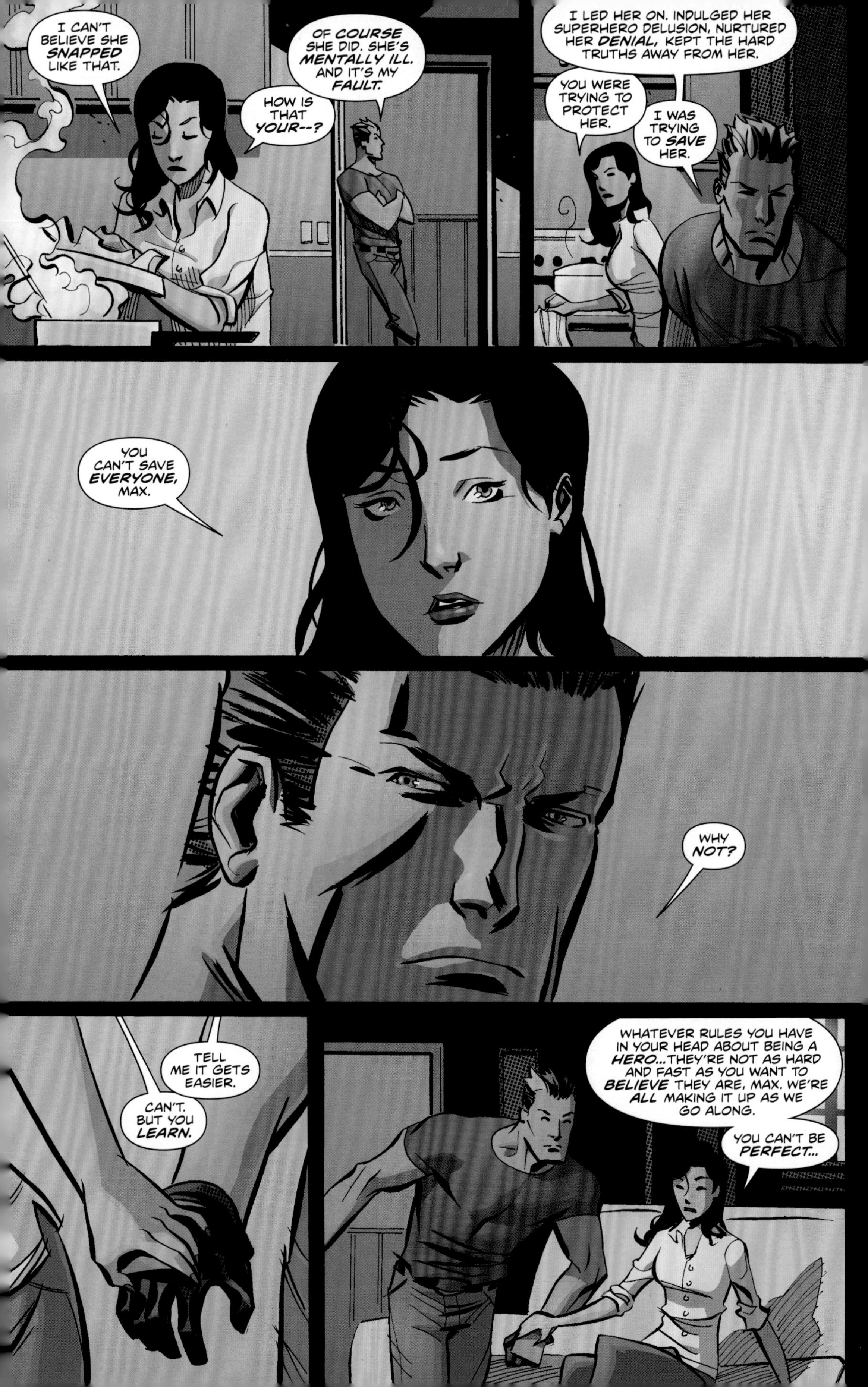
I CAN'T BELIEVE SHE SNAPPED LIKE THAT.
OF COURSE SHE DID. SHE'S MENTALLY ILL. AND IT'S MY FAULT.
HOW IS THAT YOUR--?
I LED HER ON. INDULGED HER SUPERHERO DELUSION, NURTURED HER DENIAL, KEPT THE HARD TRUTHS AWAY FROM HER.
YOU WERE TRYING TO PROTECT HER.
I WAS TRYING TO SAVE HER.
YOU CAN'T SAVE EVERYONE, MAX.
WHY NOT?
TELL ME IT GETS EASIER.
CAN'T. BUT YOU LEARN.
WHATEVER RULES YOU HAVE IN YOUR HEAD ABOUT BEING A HERO...THEY'RE NOT AS HARD AND FAST AS YOU WANT TO BELIEVE THEY ARE, MAX. WE'RE ALL MAKING IT UP AS WE GO ALONG.
YOU CAN'T BE PERFECT...

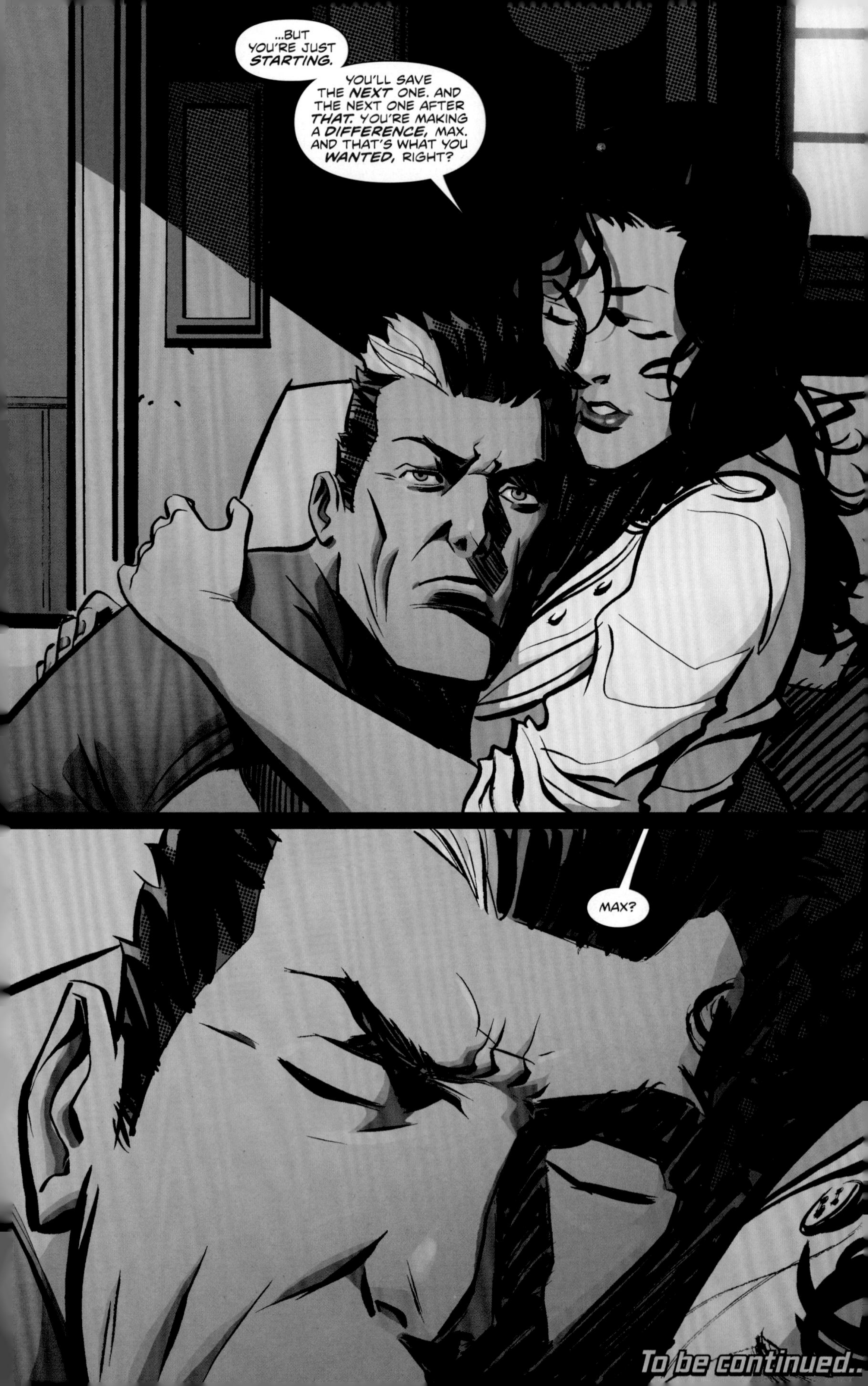
...BUT YOU'RE JUST STARTING.
YOU'LL SAVE THE NEXT ONE. AND THE NEXT ONE AFTER THAT. YOU'RE MAKING A DIFFERENCE, MAX. AND THAT'S WHAT YOU WANTED, RIGHT?
MAX?
To be continued...

# COVER GALLERY

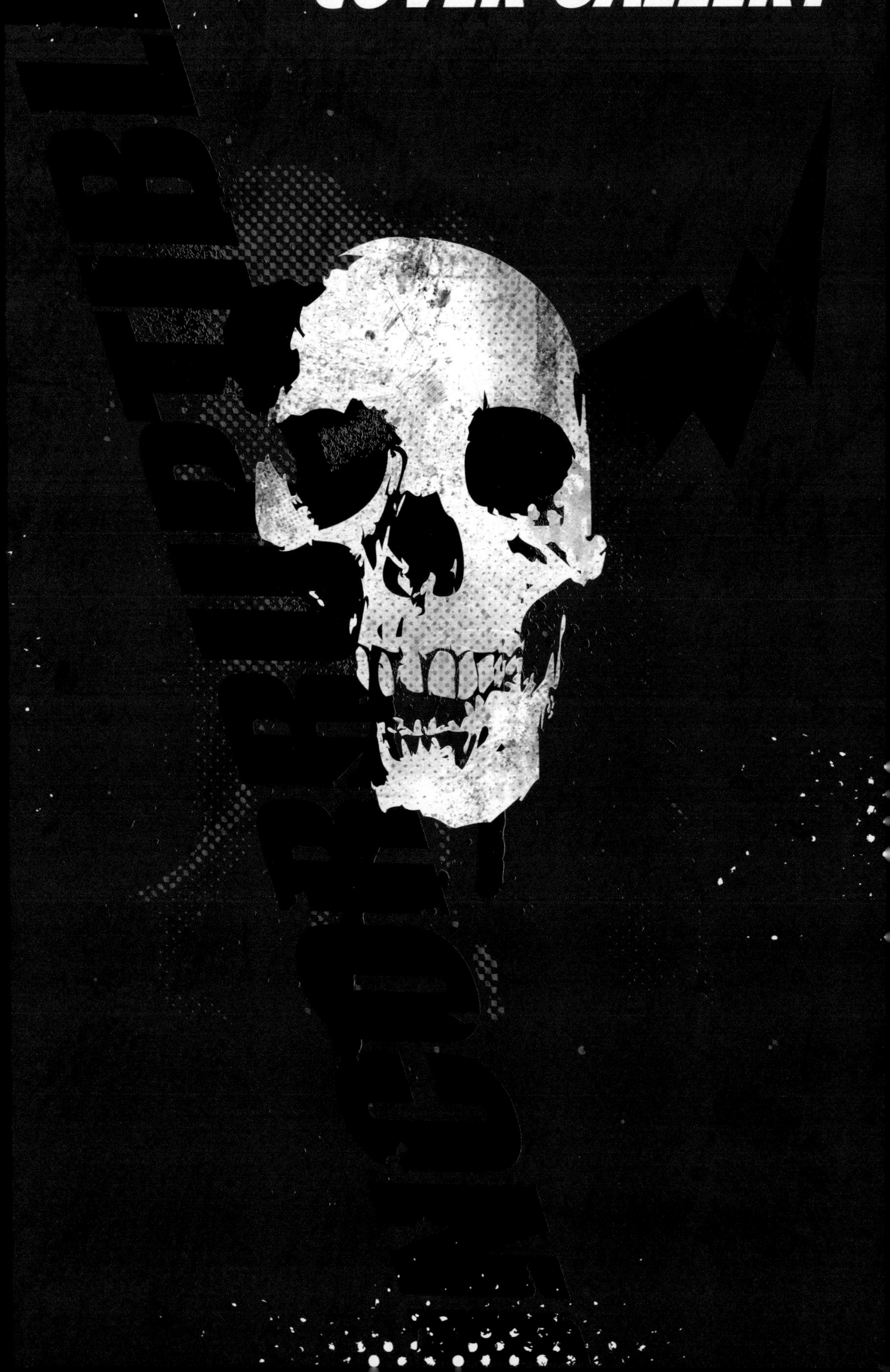

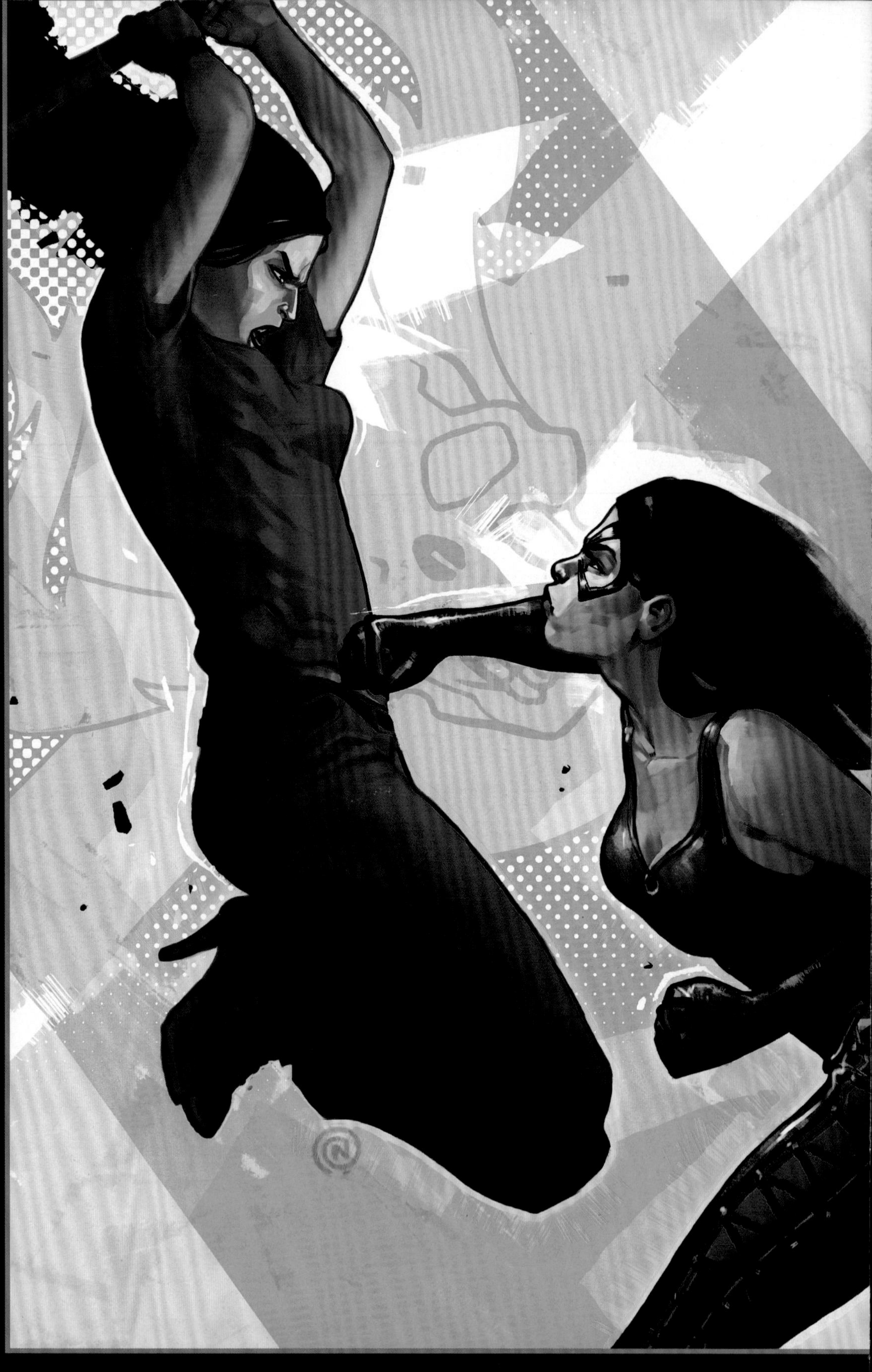

COVER 13A: CHRISTIAN NAUCK

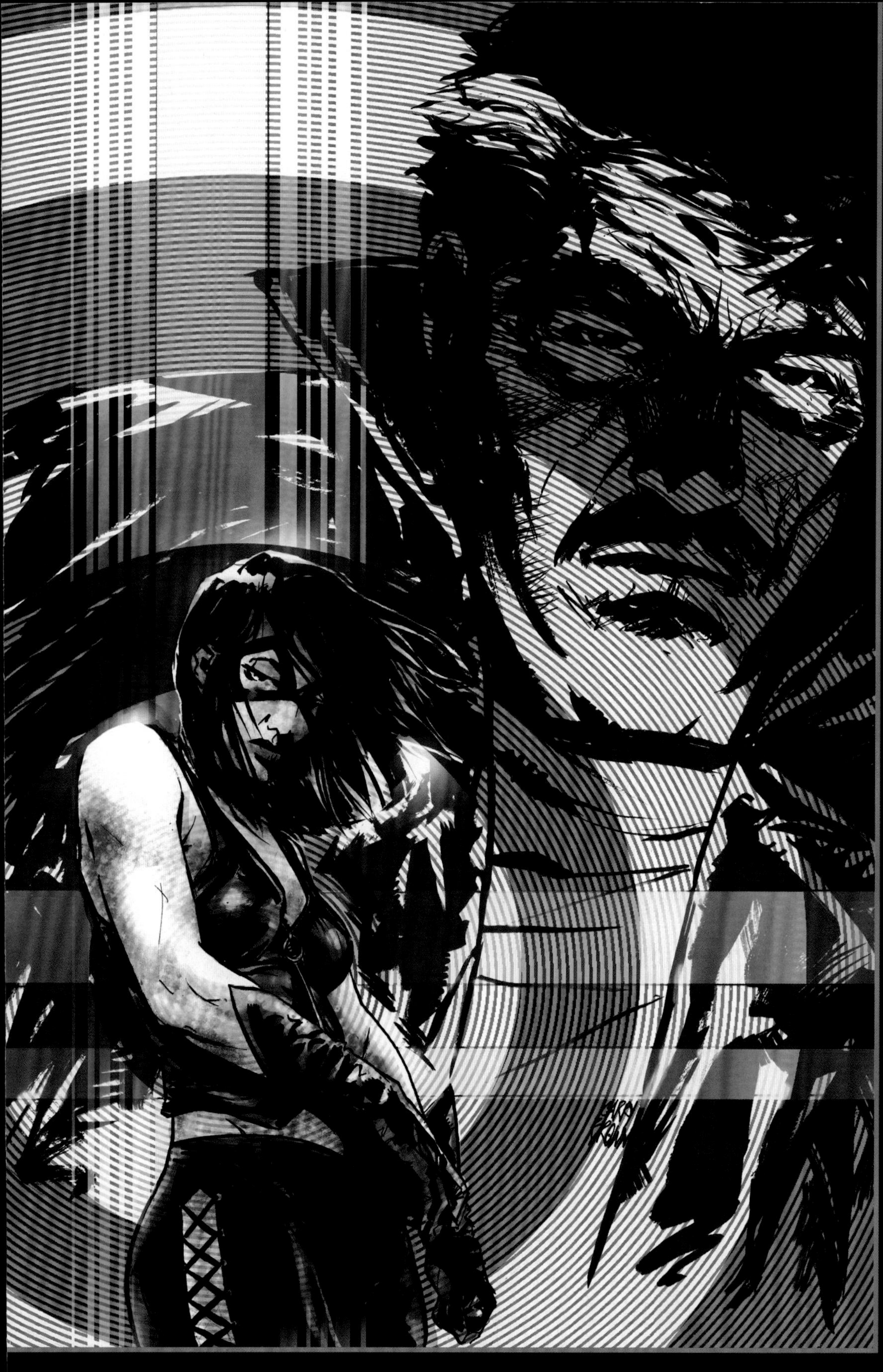

COVER 13B: GARRY BROWN

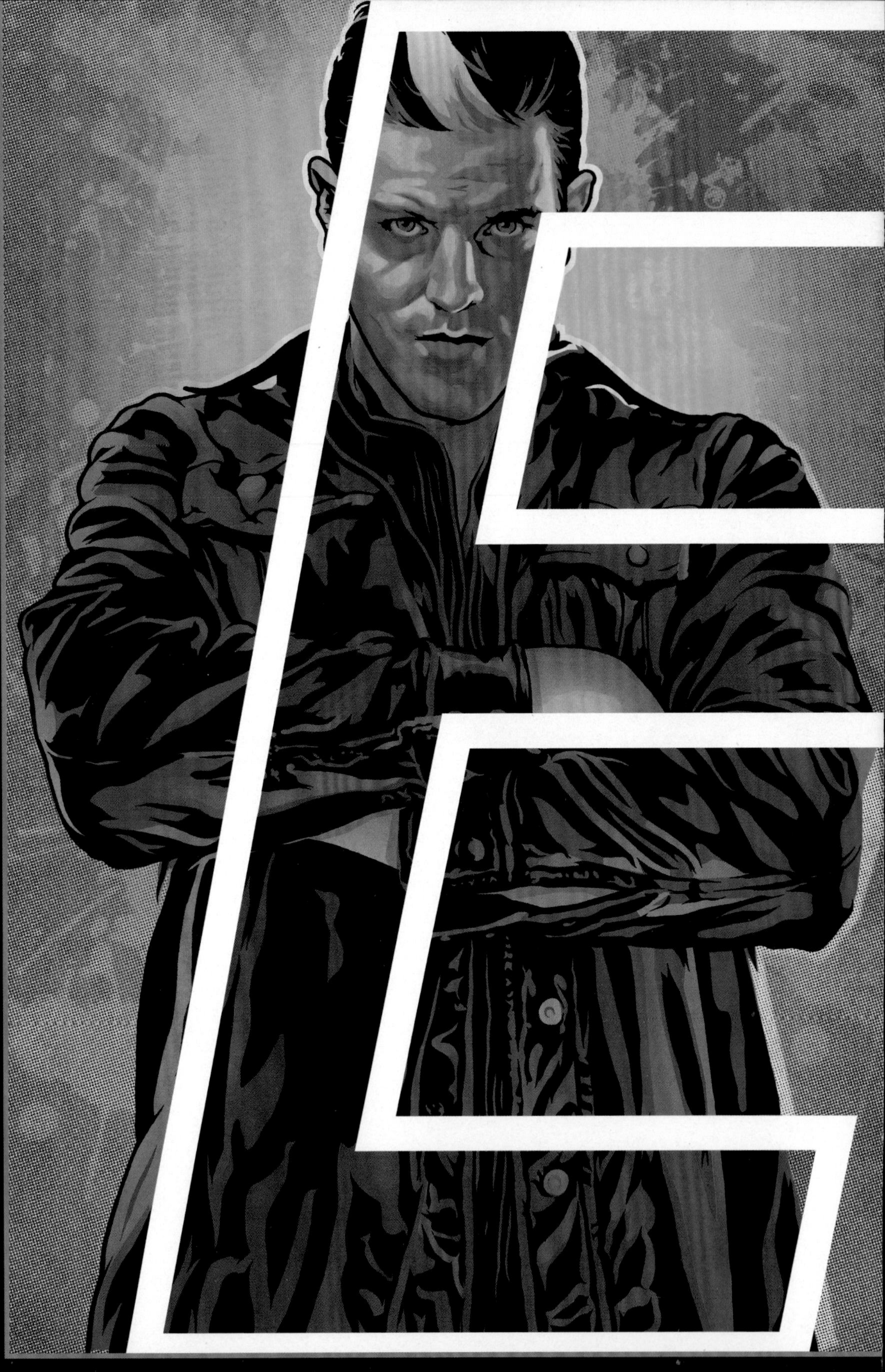

COVER 13C: JEFFREY SPOKES

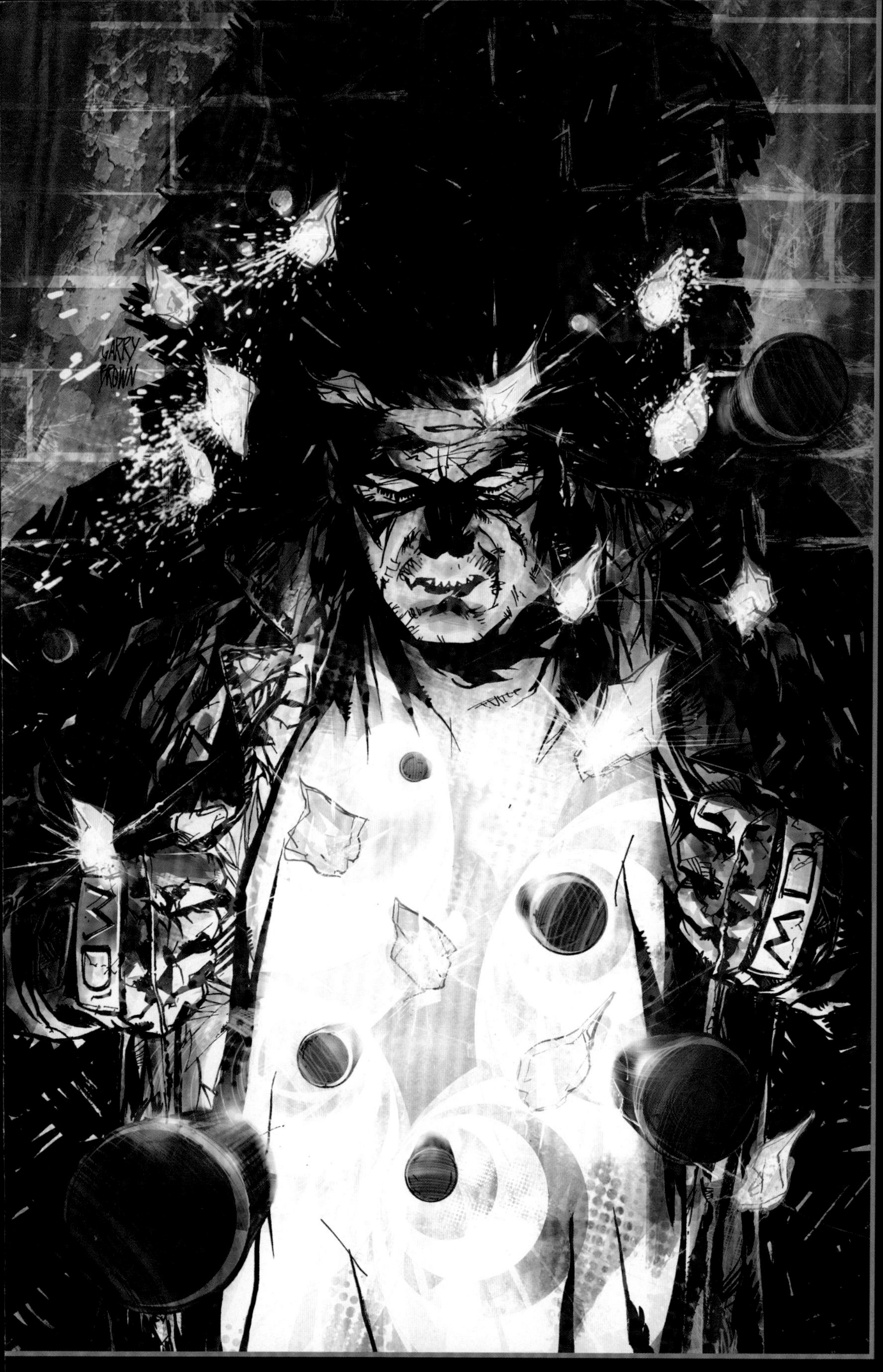
GARRY
BROWN

COVER 14A: GARRY BROWN

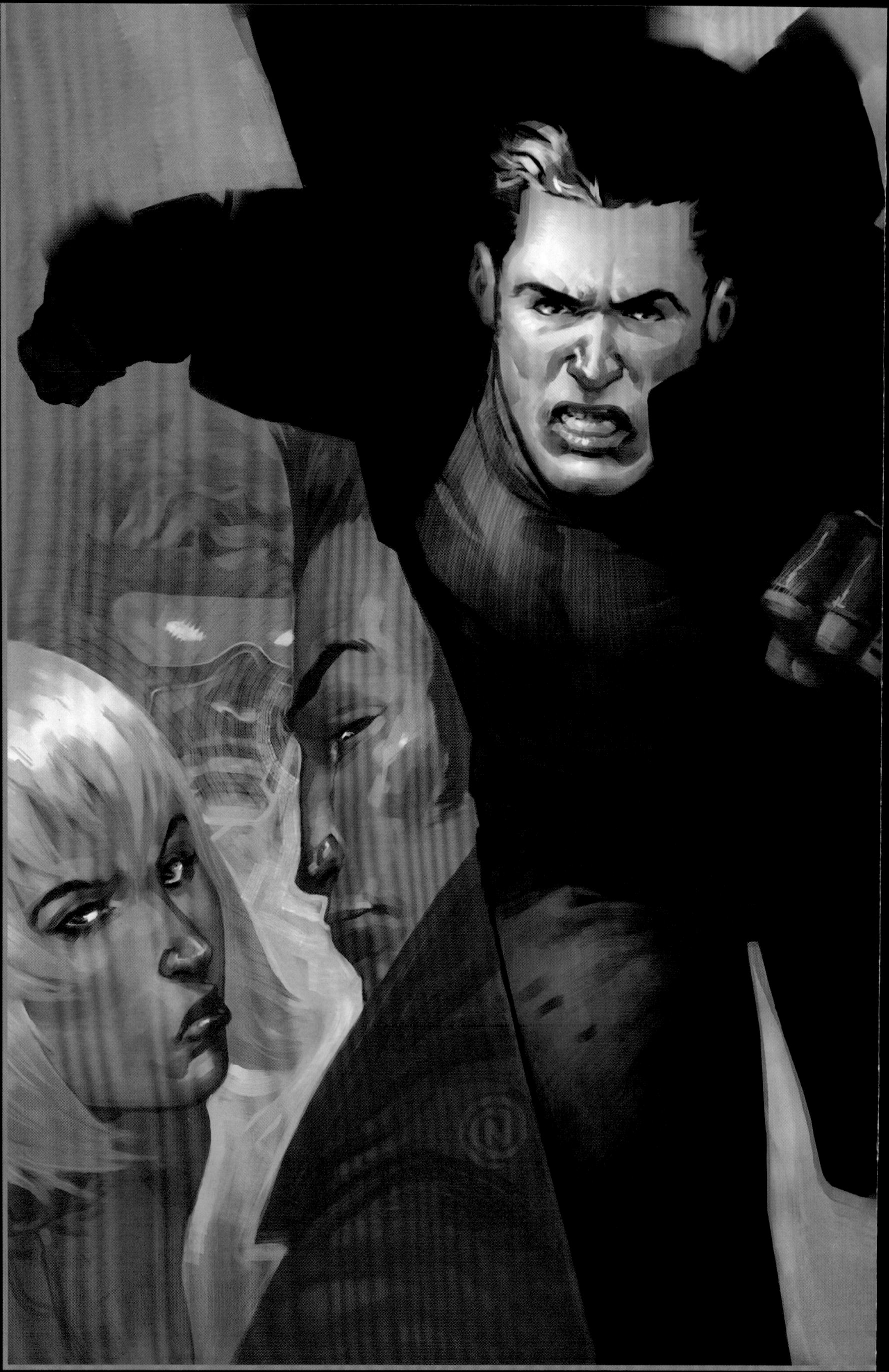

COVER 14B: CHRISTIAN NAUCK

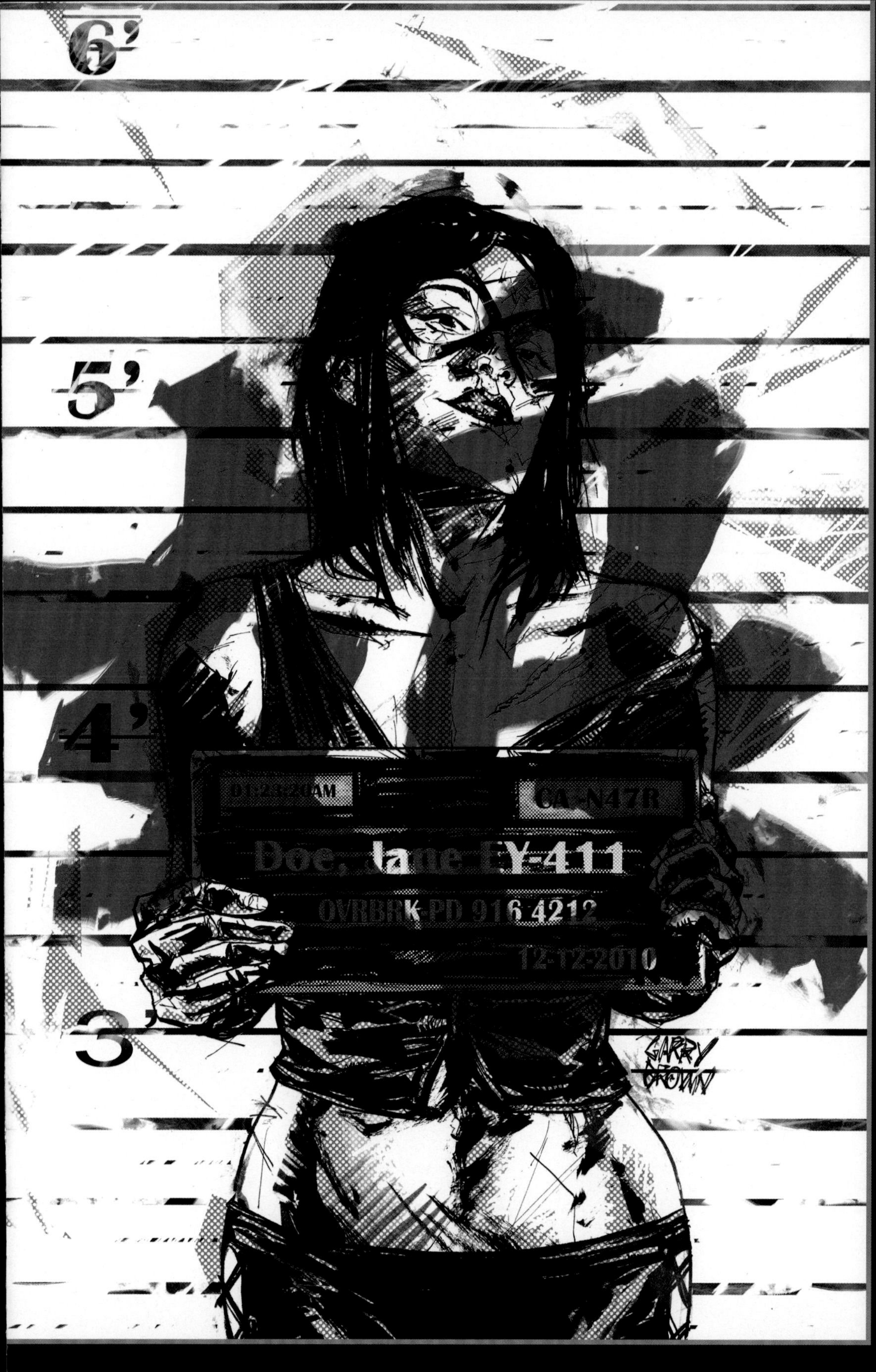
6'
5'
4'
3'
CA-N47R
Doe, Jane EY-411
OVRBRK-PD 916 4212
12-12-2010
GARRY BROWN

COVER 15A: GARRY BROWN

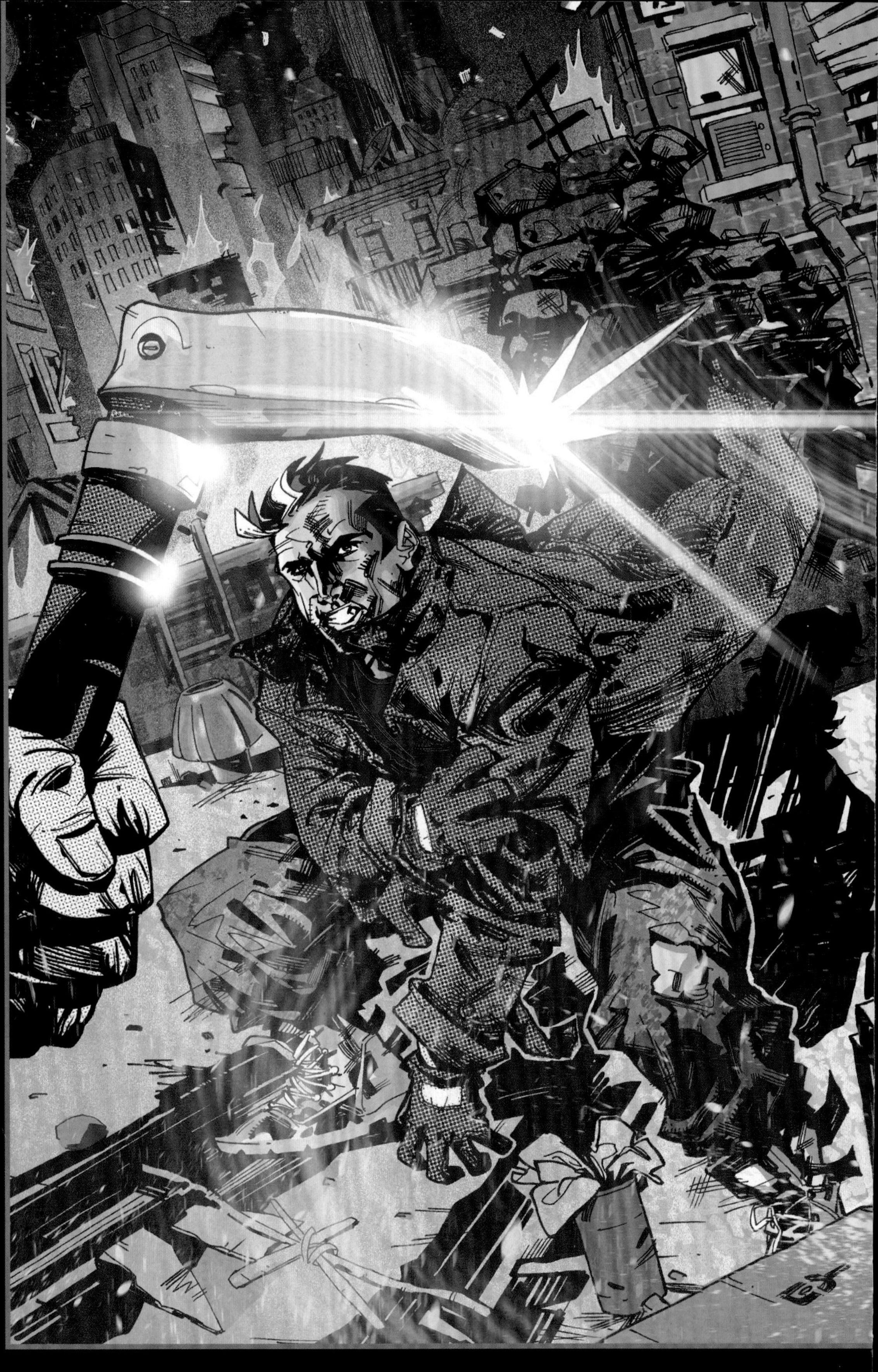

**COVER 15B: JOSE HOLDER**
**COLORIST: MITCH GERADS**

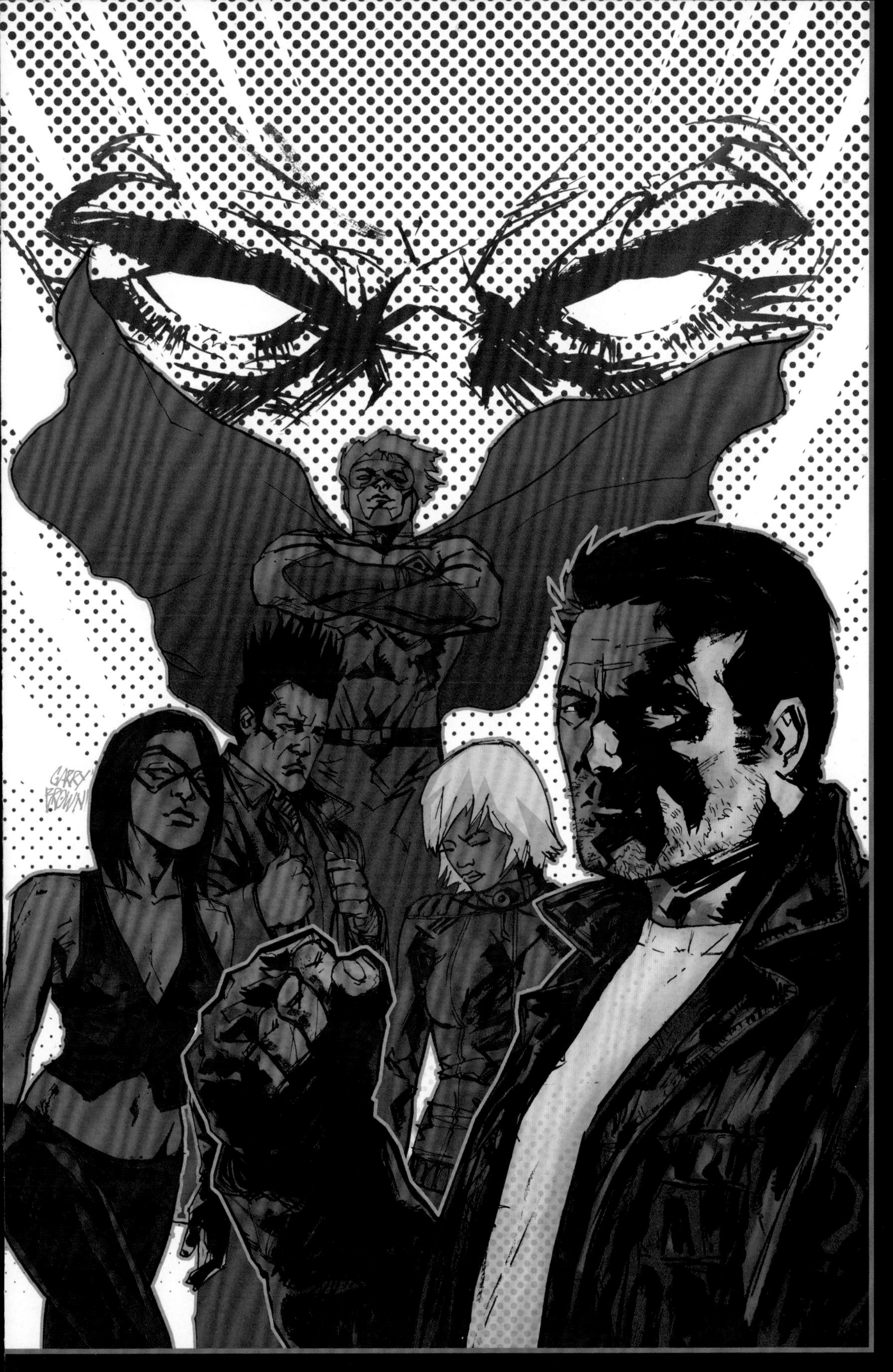
GARRY BROWN

COVER 16A: GARRY BROWN

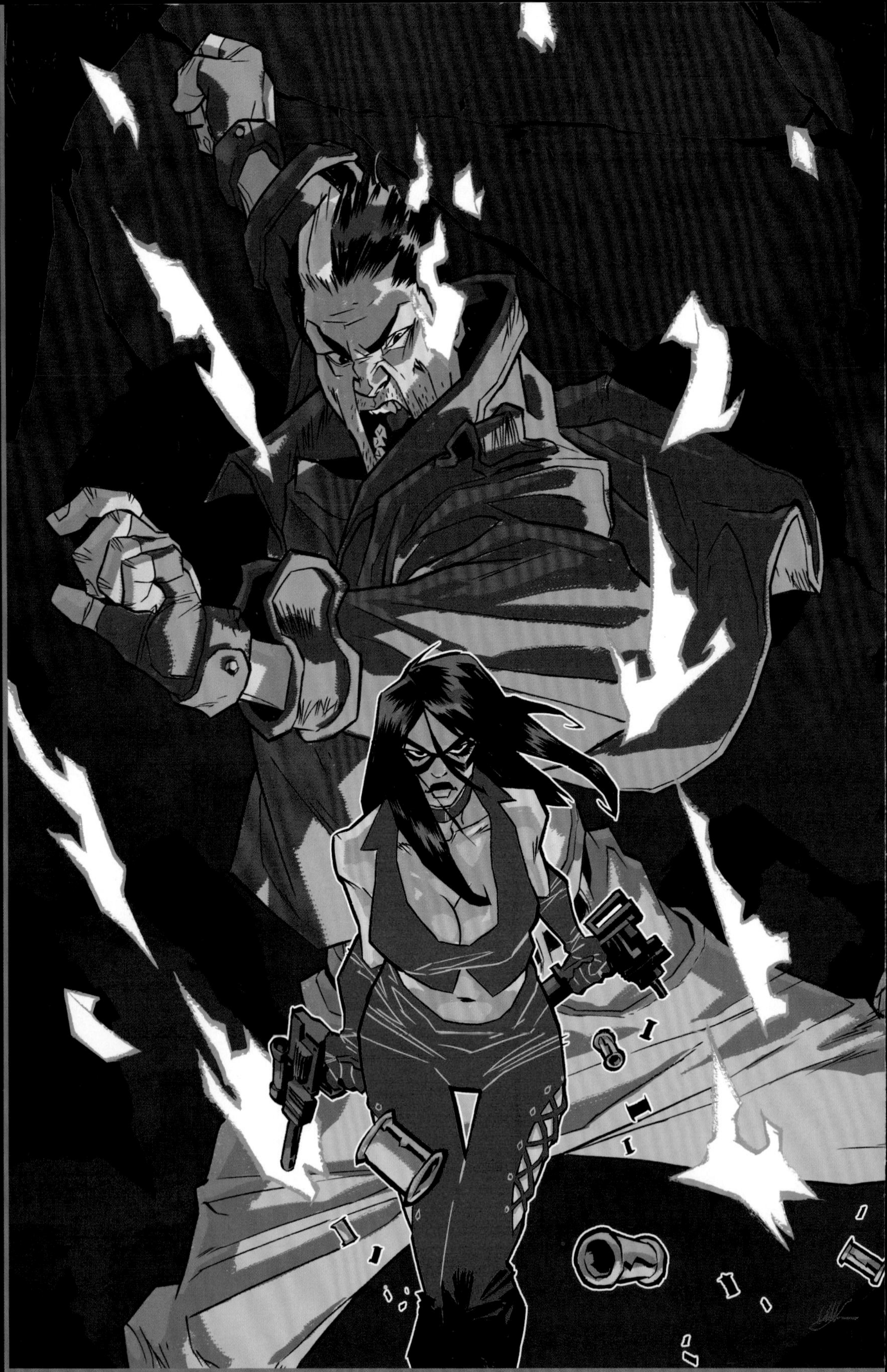

COVER 16B: MATTEO SCALERA

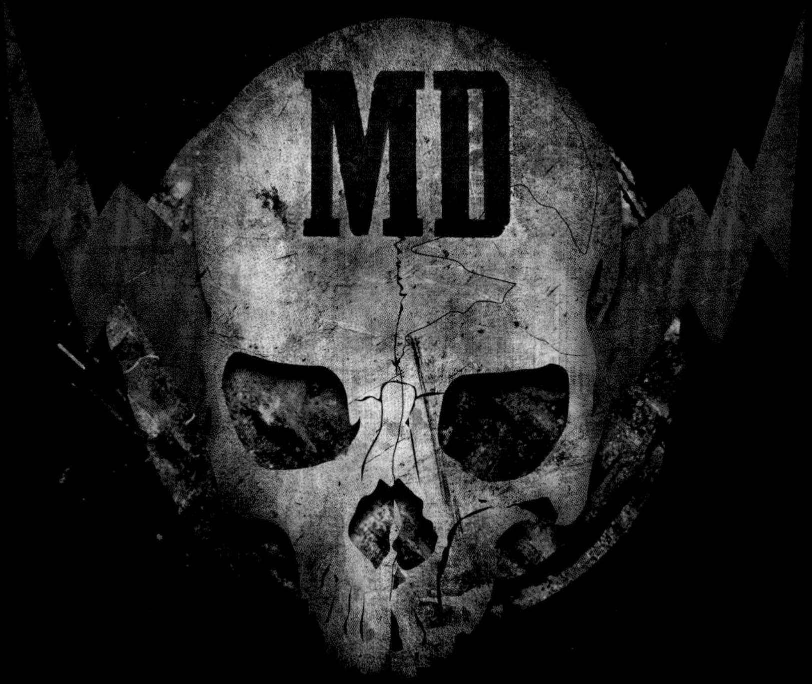
MD

# MARK WAID    PAUL AZACETA
# POTTER'S FIELD

INTRODUCTION BY **GREG RUCKA**

**FIRST TIME IN TRADE PAPERBACK!**

**A NEW VISION OF NOIR FROM LEGENDARY WRITER MARK WAID, AUTHOR OF THE MULTIPLE EISNER AWARD-WINNING KINGDOM COME, AND AMAZING SPIDER-MAN ARTIST PAUL AZACETA IN THEIR FIRST EVER COLLABORATION.**

ISBN: 978-1-60886-052-4 / DIAMOND CODE: APR110835

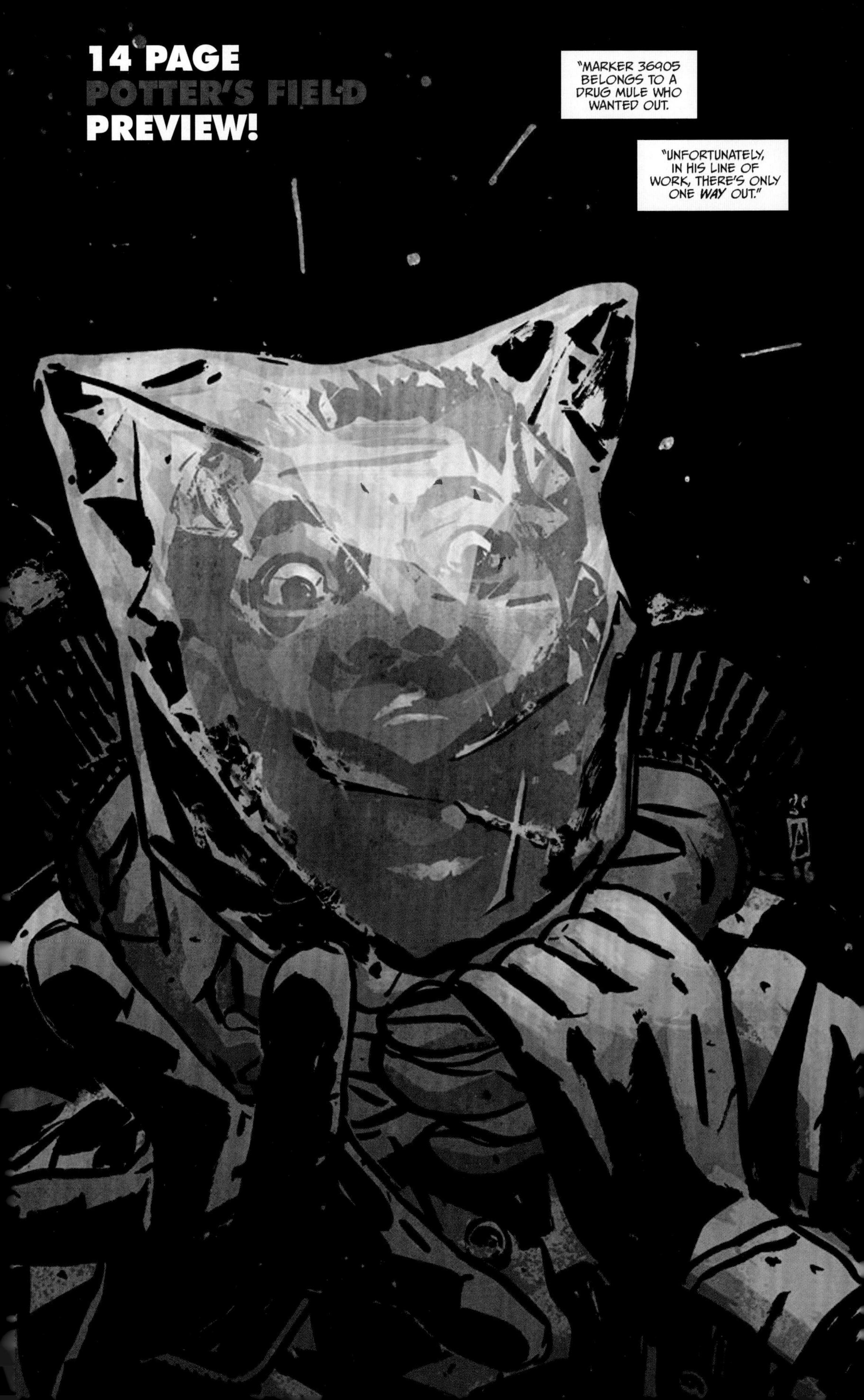
14 PAGE
POTTER'S FIELD
PREVIEW!
"MARKER 36905 BELONGS TO A DRUG MULE WHO WANTED OUT.
"UNFORTUNATELY, IN HIS LINE OF WORK, THERE'S ONLY ONE WAY OUT."

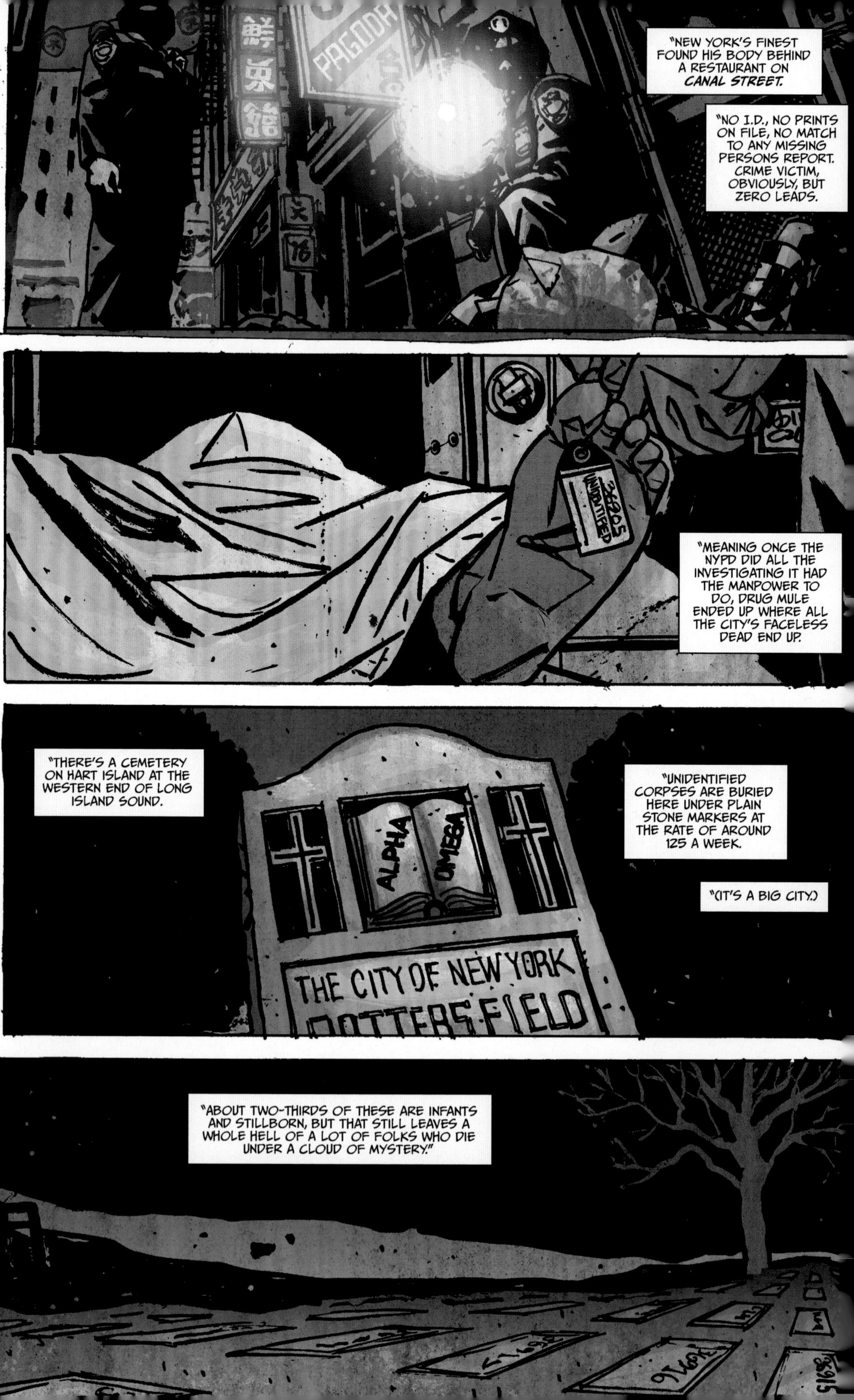
PAGODA
"NEW YORK'S FINEST FOUND HIS BODY BEHIND A RESTAURANT ON *CANAL STREET.*
"NO I.D., NO PRINTS ON FILE, NO MATCH TO ANY MISSING PERSONS REPORT. CRIME VICTIM, OBVIOUSLY, BUT ZERO LEADS.
UNIDENTIFIED
"MEANING ONCE THE NYPD DID ALL THE INVESTIGATING IT HAD THE MANPOWER TO DO, DRUG MULE ENDED UP WHERE ALL THE CITY'S FACELESS DEAD END UP.
"THERE'S A CEMETERY ON HART ISLAND AT THE WESTERN END OF LONG ISLAND SOUND.
ALPHA
OMEGA
THE CITY OF NEW YORK
"UNIDENTIFIED CORPSES ARE BURIED HERE UNDER PLAIN STONE MARKERS AT THE RATE OF AROUND 125 A WEEK.
"(IT'S A BIG CITY.)
"ABOUT TWO-THIRDS OF THESE ARE INFANTS AND STILLBORN, BUT THAT STILL LEAVES A WHOLE HELL OF A LOT OF FOLKS WHO DIE UNDER A CLOUD OF MYSTERY."

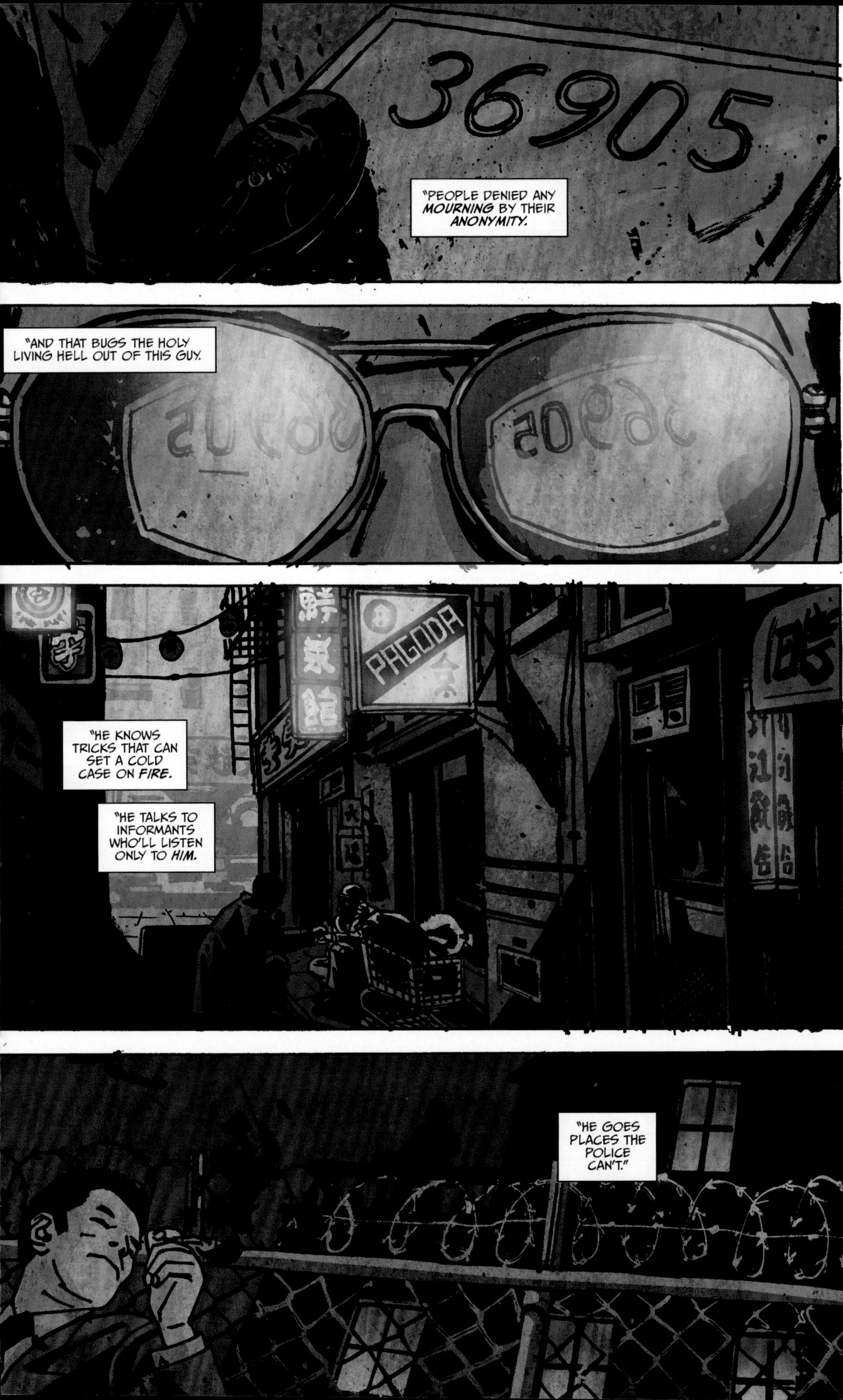
36905
"PEOPLE DENIED ANY *MOURNING* BY THEIR *ANONYMITY.*
"AND THAT BUGS THE HOLY LIVING HELL OUT OF THIS GUY.
PAGODA
"HE KNOWS TRICKS THAT CAN SET A COLD CASE ON *FIRE.*
"HE TALKS TO INFORMANTS WHO'LL LISTEN ONLY TO *HIM.*
"HE GOES PLACES THE POLICE CAN'T."

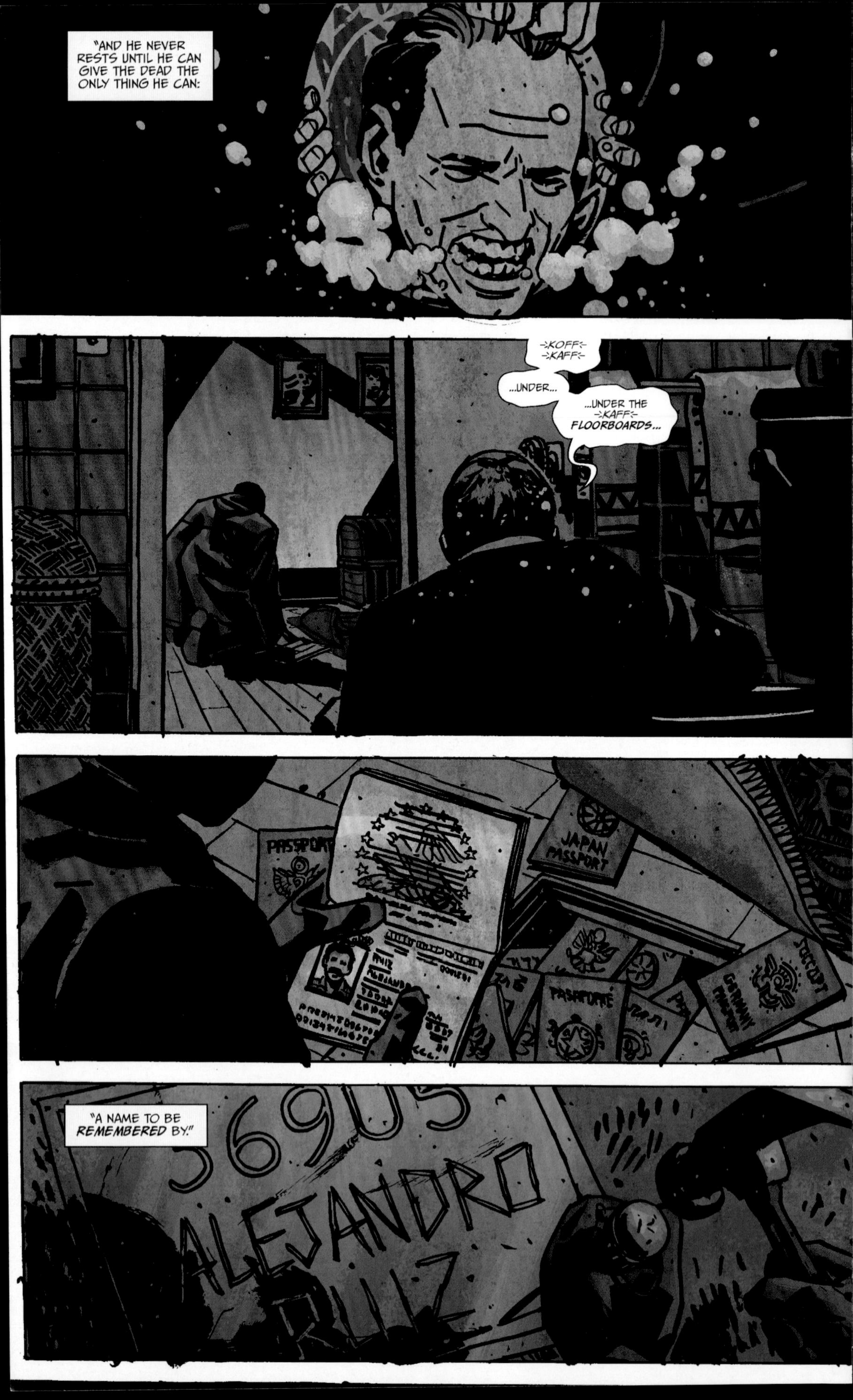
"AND HE NEVER RESTS UNTIL HE CAN GIVE THE DEAD THE ONLY THING HE CAN:
-KOFF- -KAFF-
...UNDER...
...UNDER THE -KAFF- FLOORBOARDS...
PASSPORT
JAPAN PASSPORT
PASAPORTE
GERMANY PASSPORT
"A NAME TO BE REMEMBERED BY."
569US
ALEJANDRO
RUIZ

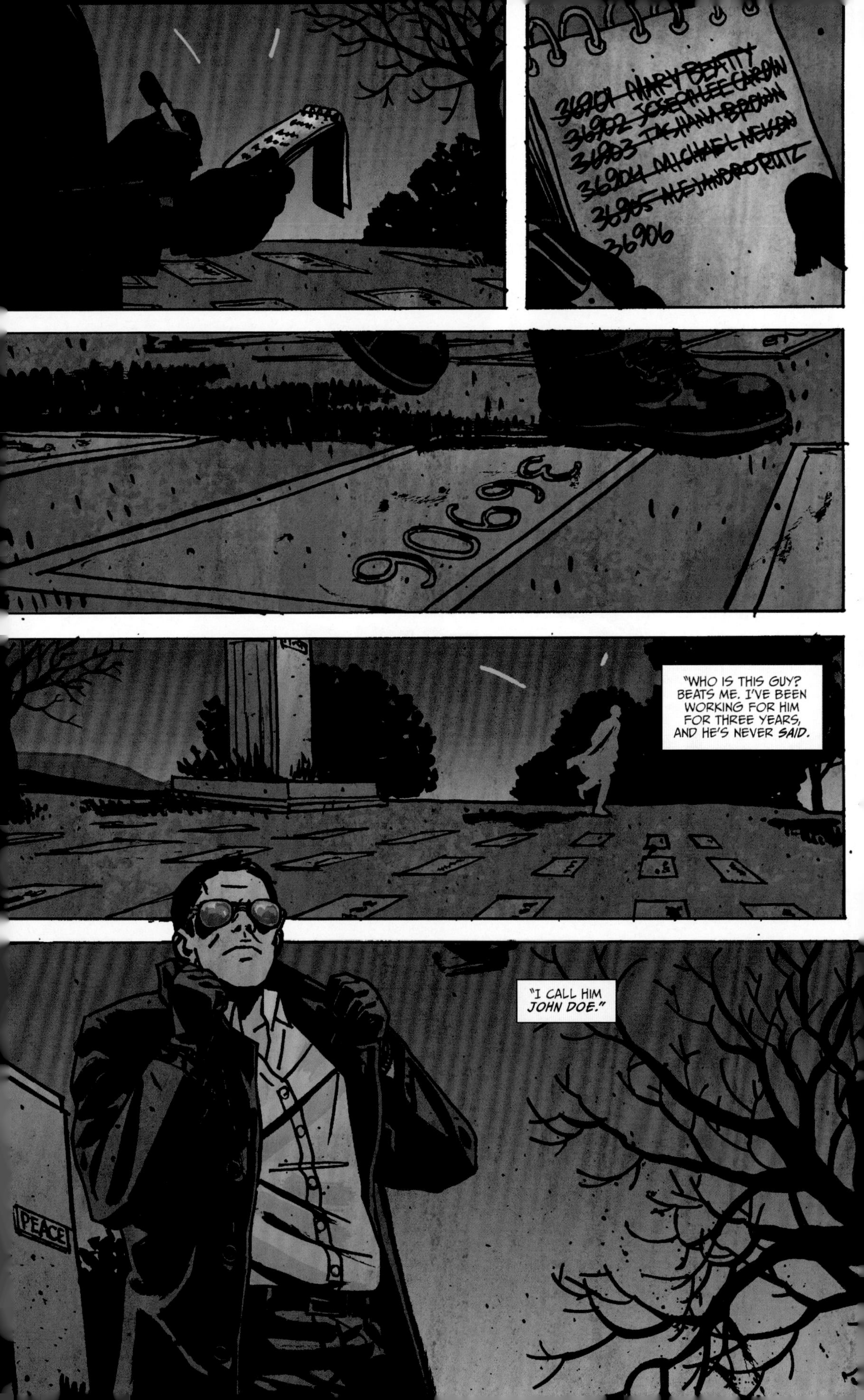
36901 MARY BEATTY
36902 JOSEPH LEE CARBIN
36903
36904 MICHAEL NELSON
36905 ALEJANDRO RUIZ
36906
36906
"WHO IS THIS GUY? BEATS ME. I'VE BEEN WORKING FOR HIM FOR THREE YEARS, AND HE'S NEVER *SAID*.
"I CALL HIM *JOHN DOE*."
PEACE

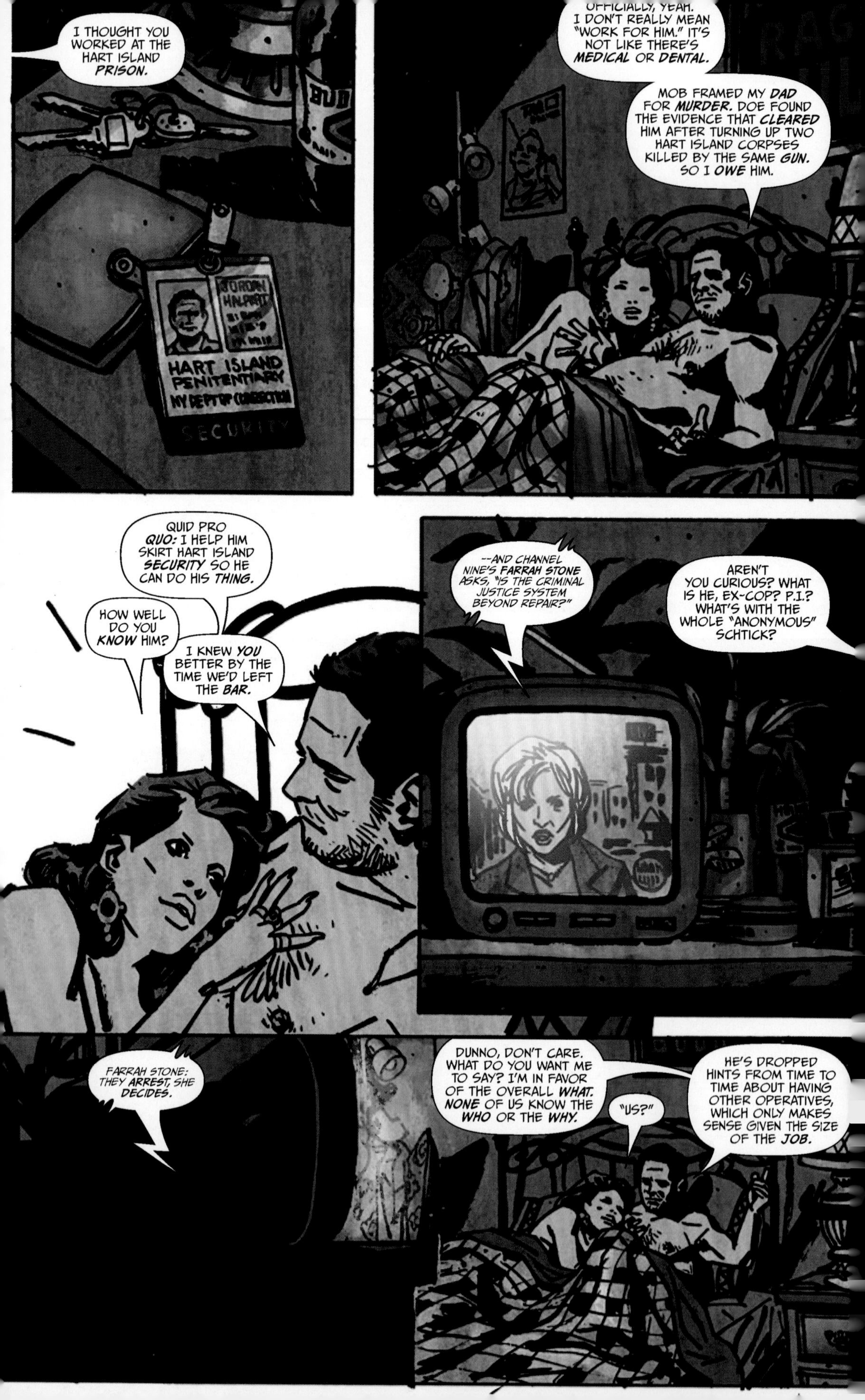
I THOUGHT YOU WORKED AT THE HART ISLAND PRISON.
JORDAN HALPART
HART ISLAND PENITENTIARY
NY DEPT OF CORRECTION
SECURITY
OFFICIALLY, YEAH. I DON'T REALLY MEAN "WORK FOR HIM." IT'S NOT LIKE THERE'S MEDICAL OR DENTAL.
MOB FRAMED MY DAD FOR MURDER. DOE FOUND THE EVIDENCE THAT CLEARED HIM AFTER TURNING UP TWO HART ISLAND CORPSES KILLED BY THE SAME GUN. SO I OWE HIM.
HOW WELL DO YOU KNOW HIM?
QUID PRO QUO: I HELP HIM SKIRT HART ISLAND SECURITY SO HE CAN DO HIS THING.
I KNEW YOU BETTER BY THE TIME WE'D LEFT THE BAR.
--AND CHANNEL NINE'S FARRAH STONE ASKS, "IS THE CRIMINAL JUSTICE SYSTEM BEYOND REPAIR?"
AREN'T YOU CURIOUS? WHAT IS HE, EX-COP? P.I.? WHAT'S WITH THE WHOLE "ANONYMOUS" SCHTICK?
FARRAH STONE: THEY ARREST, SHE DECIDES.
DUNNO, DON'T CARE. WHAT DO YOU WANT ME TO SAY? I'M IN FAVOR OF THE OVERALL WHAT. NONE OF US KNOW THE WHO OR THE WHY.
"US?"
HE'S DROPPED HINTS FROM TIME TO TIME ABOUT HAVING OTHER OPERATIVES, WHICH ONLY MAKES SENSE GIVEN THE SIZE OF THE JOB.

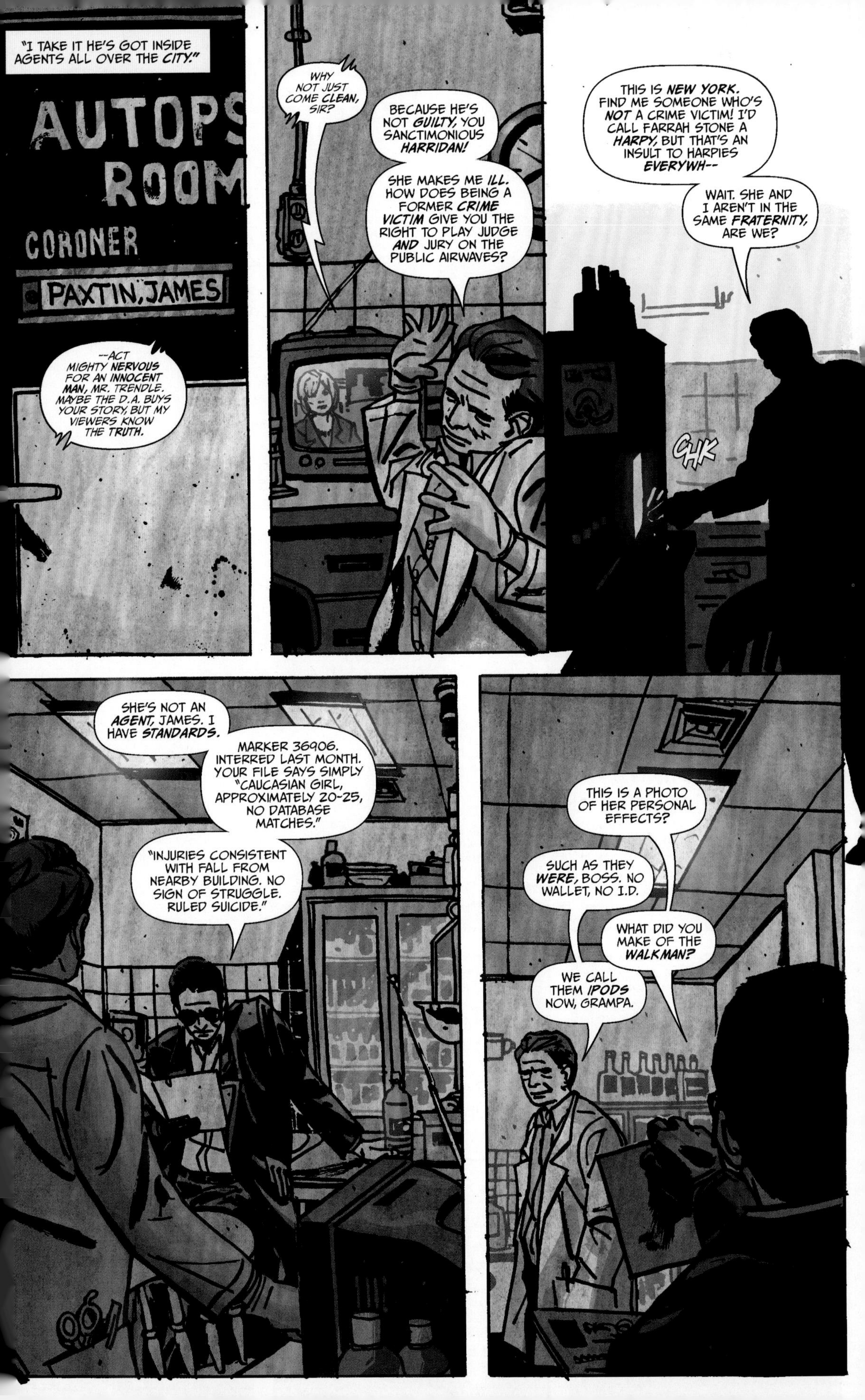
"I TAKE IT HE'S GOT INSIDE AGENTS ALL OVER THE CITY."
AUTOPS ROOM
CORONER
PAXTIN, JAMES
--ACT MIGHTY NERVOUS FOR AN INNOCENT MAN, MR. TRENDLE. MAYBE THE D.A. BUYS YOUR STORY, BUT MY VIEWERS KNOW THE TRUTH.
WHY NOT JUST COME CLEAN, SIR?
BECAUSE HE'S NOT GUILTY, YOU SANCTIMONIOUS HARRIDAN!
SHE MAKES ME ILL. HOW DOES BEING A FORMER CRIME VICTIM GIVE YOU THE RIGHT TO PLAY JUDGE AND JURY ON THE PUBLIC AIRWAVES?
THIS IS NEW YORK. FIND ME SOMEONE WHO'S NOT A CRIME VICTIM! I'D CALL FARRAH STONE A HARPY, BUT THAT'S AN INSULT TO HARPIES EVERYWH--
WAIT. SHE AND I AREN'T IN THE SAME FRATERNITY, ARE WE?
CHK
SHE'S NOT AN AGENT, JAMES. I HAVE STANDARDS.
MARKER 36906. INTERRED LAST MONTH. YOUR FILE SAYS SIMPLY "CAUCASIAN GIRL, APPROXIMATELY 20-25, NO DATABASE MATCHES."
"INJURIES CONSISTENT WITH FALL FROM NEARBY BUILDING. NO SIGN OF STRUGGLE. RULED SUICIDE."
THIS IS A PHOTO OF HER PERSONAL EFFECTS?
SUCH AS THEY WERE, BOSS. NO WALLET, NO I.D.
WHAT DID YOU MAKE OF THE WALKMAN?
WE CALL THEM IPODS NOW, GRAMPA.

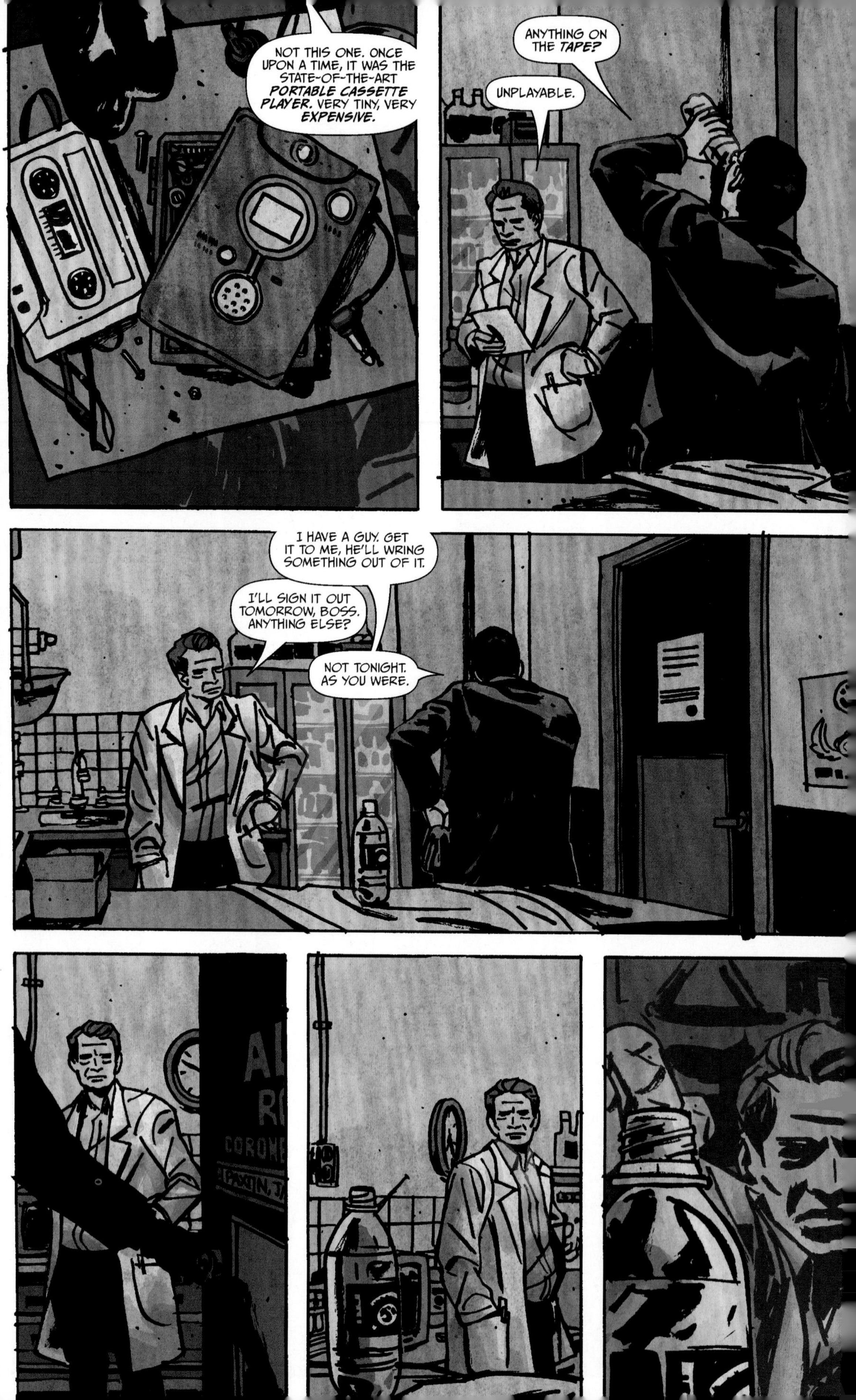
NOT THIS ONE. ONCE UPON A TIME, IT WAS THE STATE-OF-THE-ART *PORTABLE CASSETTE PLAYER.* VERY TINY, VERY *EXPENSIVE.*
ANYTHING ON THE *TAPE?*
UNPLAYABLE.
I HAVE A GUY. GET IT TO ME, HE'LL WRING SOMETHING OUT OF IT.
I'LL SIGN IT OUT TOMORROW, BOSS. ANYTHING ELSE?
NOT TONIGHT. AS YOU WERE.

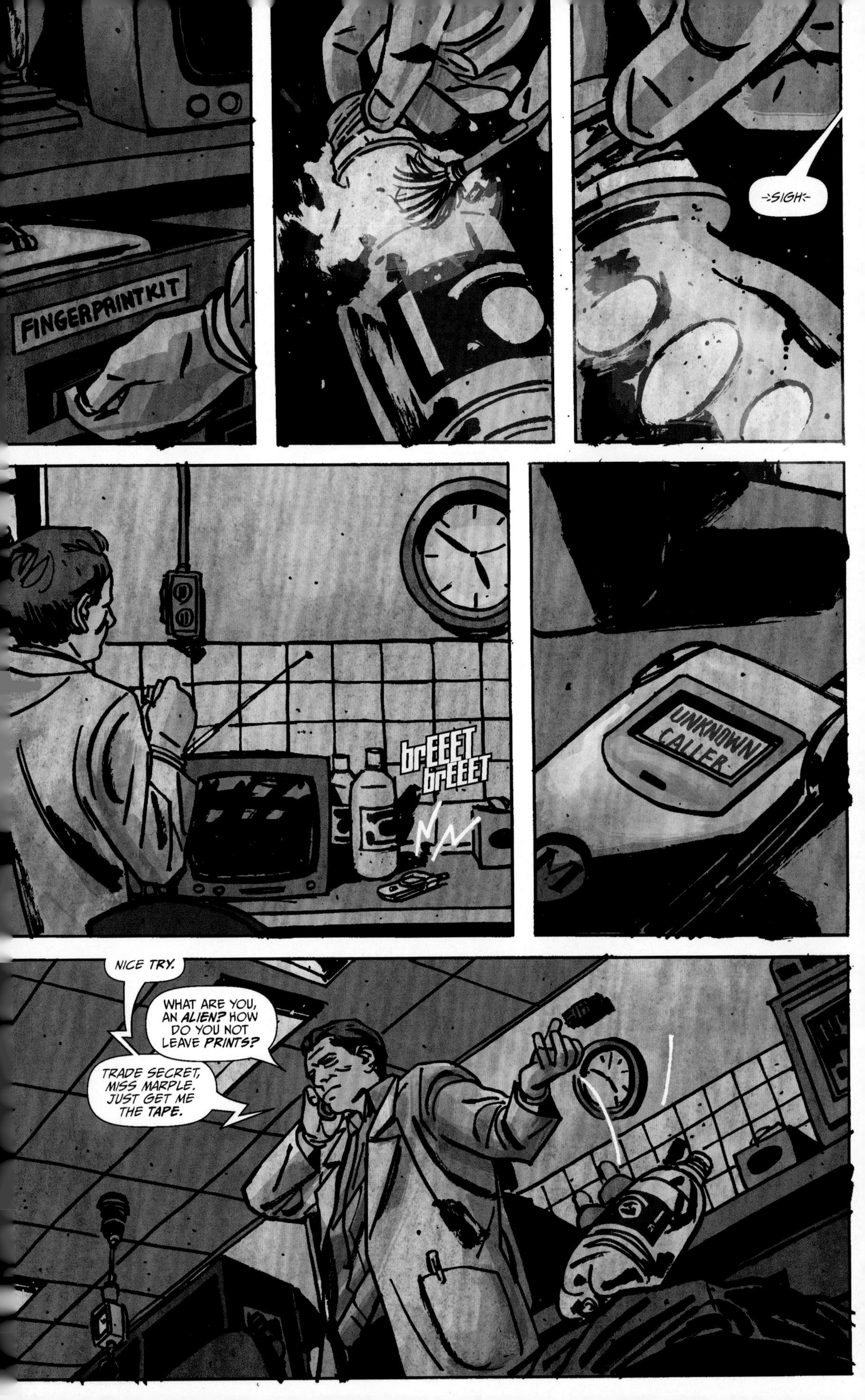
FINGERPRINT KIT
-SIGH-
brEEET brEEET
UNKNOWN CALLER
NICE TRY.
WHAT ARE YOU, AN ALIEN? HOW DO YOU NOT LEAVE PRINTS?
TRADE SECRET, MISS MARPLE. JUST GET ME THE TAPE.

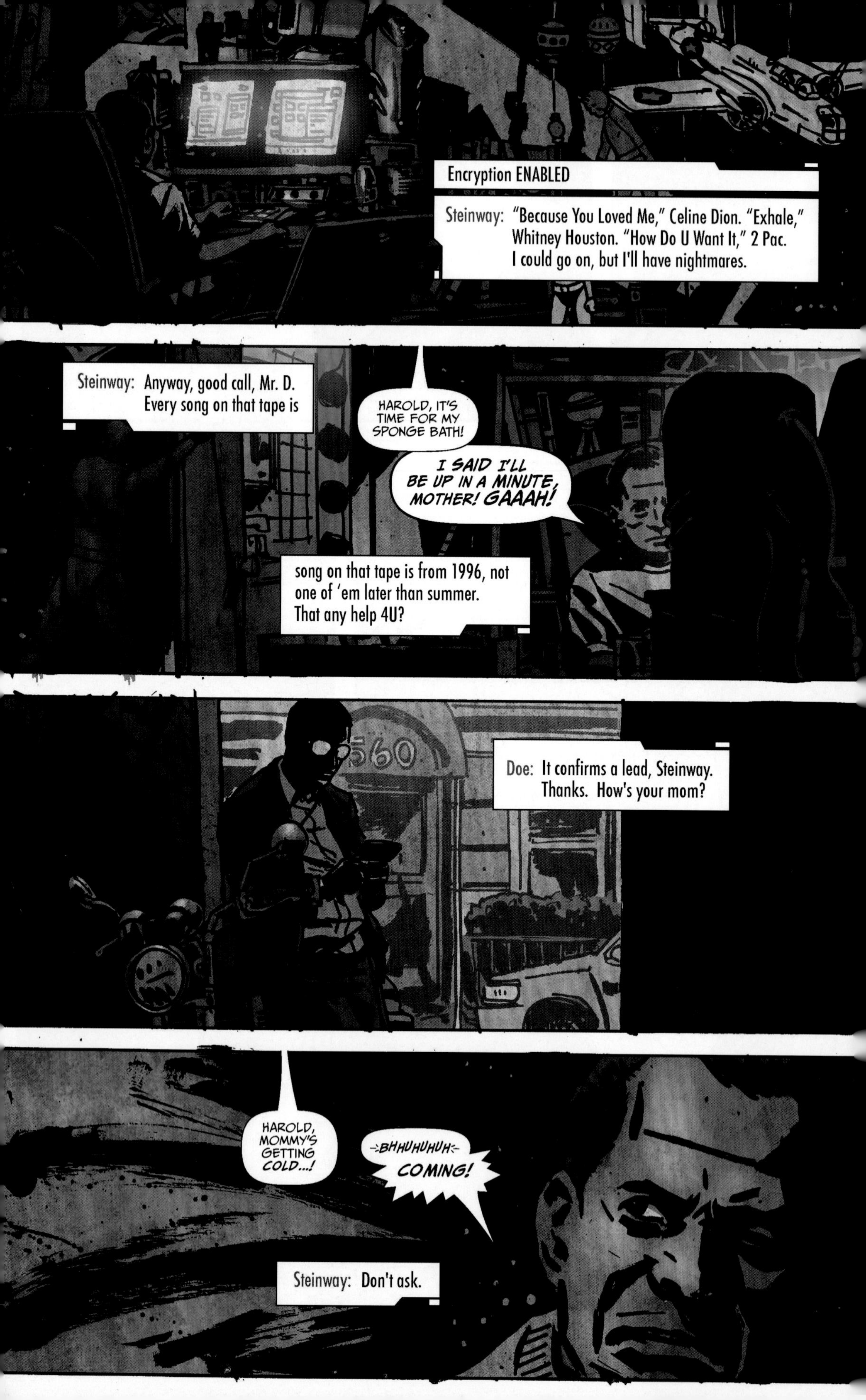
Encryption ENABLED
Steinway: "Because You Loved Me," Celine Dion. "Exhale," Whitney Houston. "How Do U Want It," 2 Pac. I could go on, but I'll have nightmares.
Steinway: Anyway, good call, Mr. D. Every song on that tape is
HAROLD, IT'S TIME FOR MY SPONGE BATH!
I SAID I'LL BE UP IN A MINUTE, MOTHER! GAAAH!
song on that tape is from 1996, not one of 'em later than summer. That any help 4U?
560
Doe: It confirms a lead, Steinway. Thanks. How's your mom?
HAROLD, MOMMY'S GETTING COLD...!
-BHHUHUHUH-
COMING!
Steinway: Don't ask.

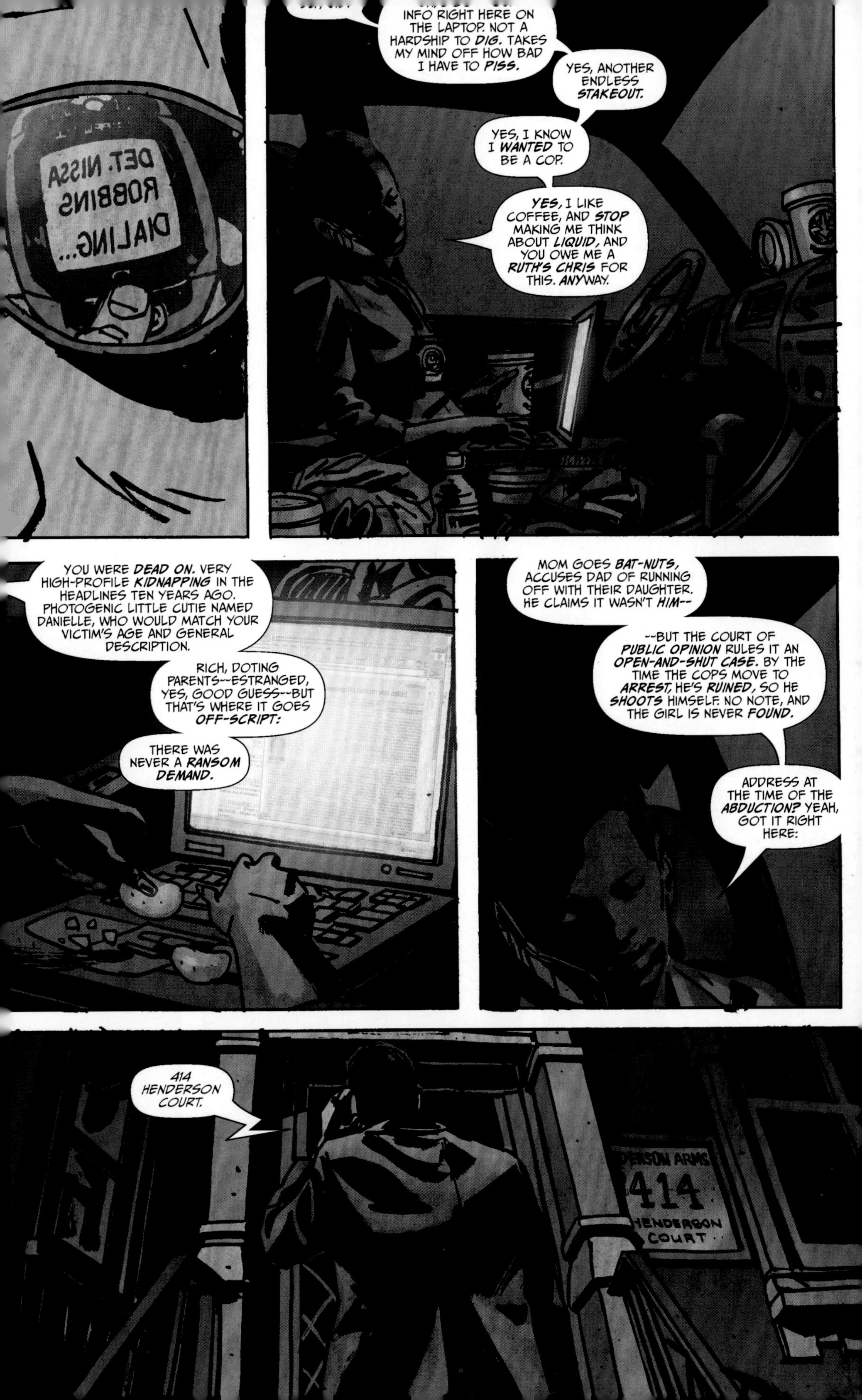
DET. NISSA ROBBINS DIALING...
INFO RIGHT HERE ON THE LAPTOP. NOT A HARDSHIP TO DIG. TAKES MY MIND OFF HOW BAD I HAVE TO PISS.
YES, ANOTHER ENDLESS STAKEOUT.
YES, I KNOW I WANTED TO BE A COP.
YES, I LIKE COFFEE, AND STOP MAKING ME THINK ABOUT LIQUID, AND YOU OWE ME A RUTH'S CHRIS FOR THIS. ANYWAY.
YOU WERE DEAD ON. VERY HIGH-PROFILE KIDNAPPING IN THE HEADLINES TEN YEARS AGO. PHOTOGENIC LITTLE CUTIE NAMED DANIELLE, WHO WOULD MATCH YOUR VICTIM'S AGE AND GENERAL DESCRIPTION.
RICH, DOTING PARENTS--ESTRANGED, YES, GOOD GUESS--BUT THAT'S WHERE IT GOES OFF-SCRIPT:
THERE WAS NEVER A RANSOM DEMAND.
MOM GOES BAT-NUTS, ACCUSES DAD OF RUNNING OFF WITH THEIR DAUGHTER. HE CLAIMS IT WASN'T HIM--
--BUT THE COURT OF PUBLIC OPINION RULES IT AN OPEN-AND-SHUT CASE. BY THE TIME THE COPS MOVE TO ARREST, HE'S RUINED, SO HE SHOOTS HIMSELF. NO NOTE, AND THE GIRL IS NEVER FOUND.
ADDRESS AT THE TIME OF THE ABDUCTION? YEAH, GOT IT RIGHT HERE:
414 HENDERSON COURT.
DERSON ARMS
414
HENDERSON COURT

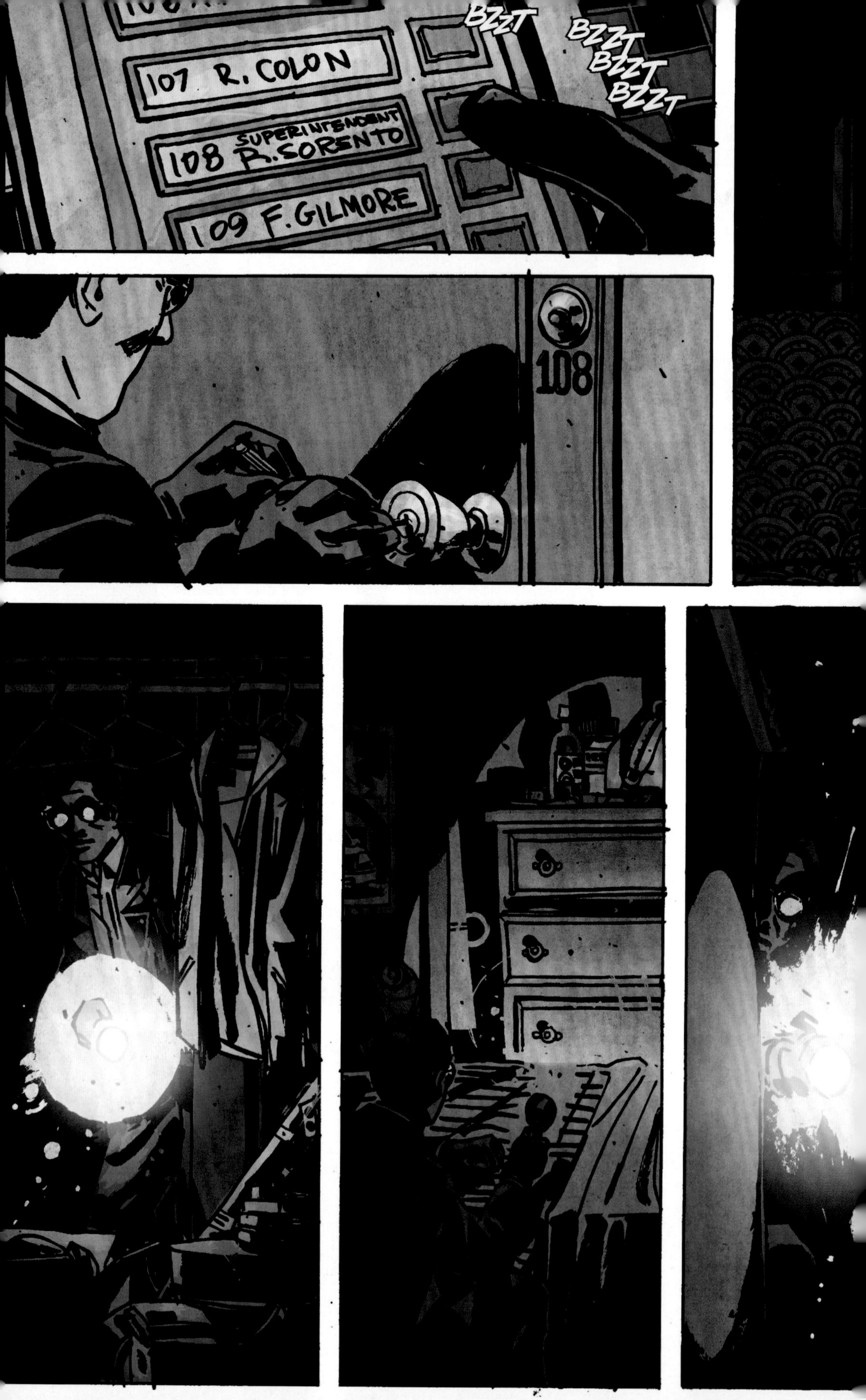
107 R. COLON
108 SUPERINTENDENT R. SORENTO
109 F. GILMORE
BZZT
BZZT
BZZT
BZZT
108

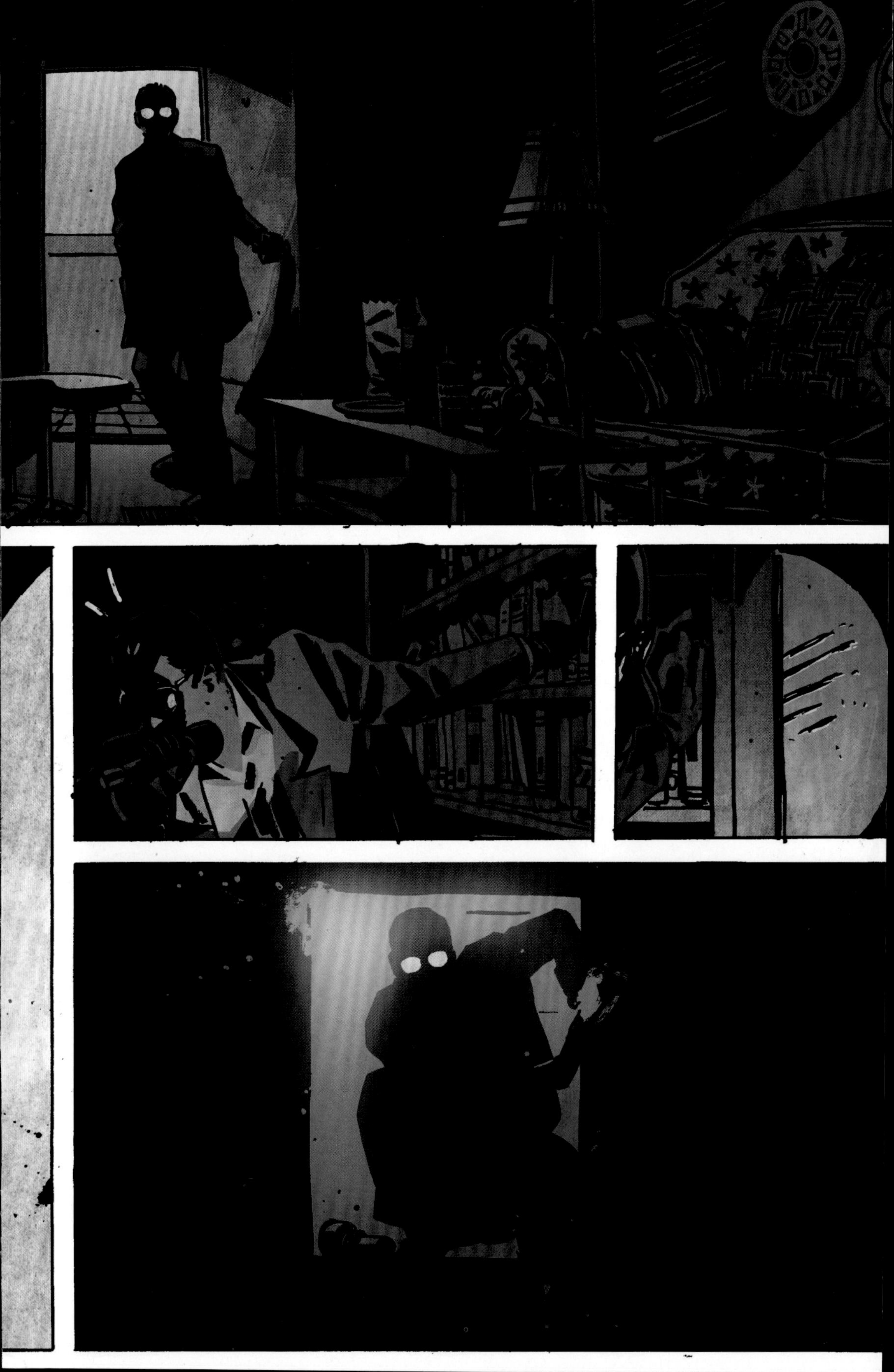

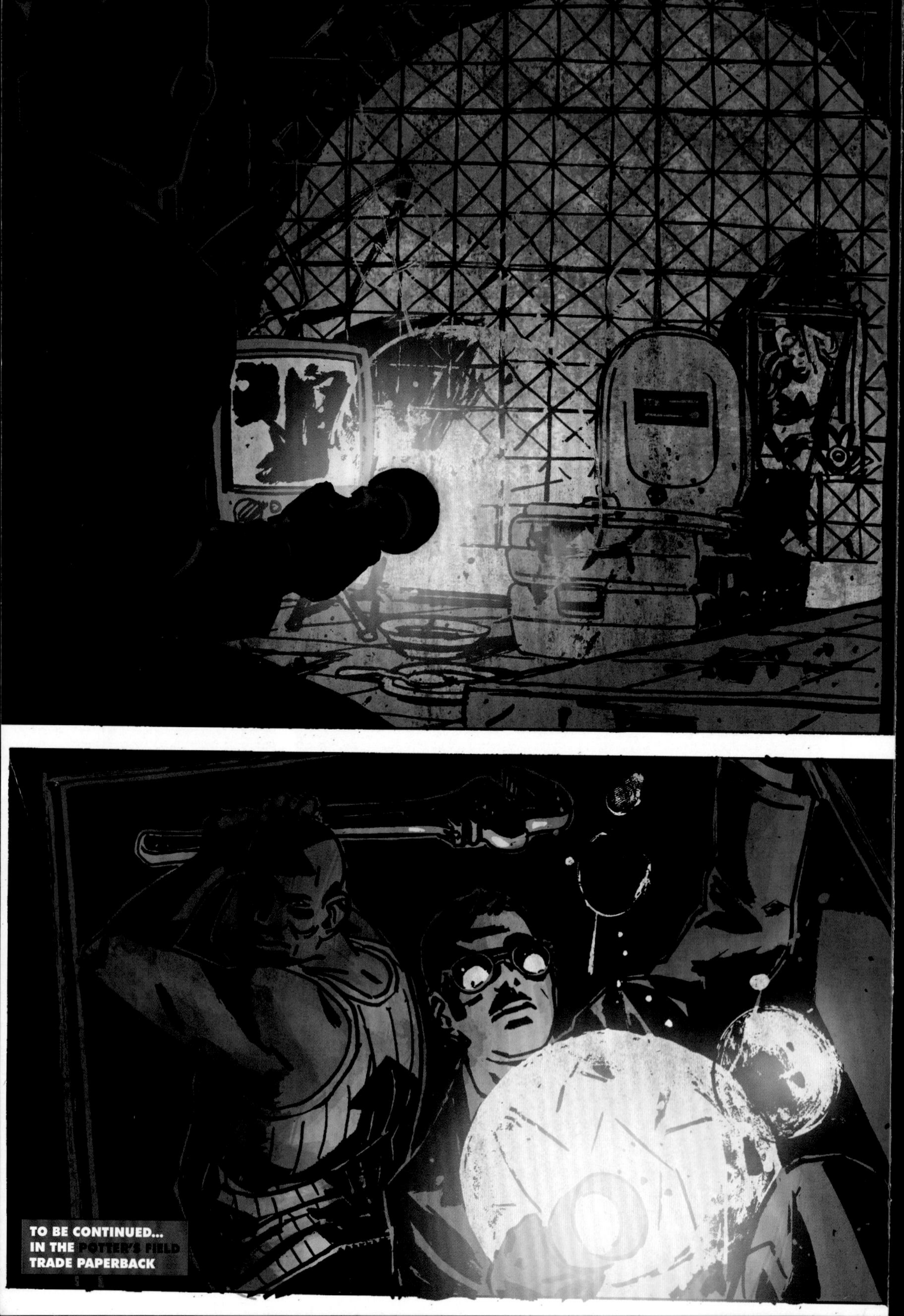
TO BE CONTINUED...
IN THE POTTER'S FIELD
TRADE PAPERBACK

MD

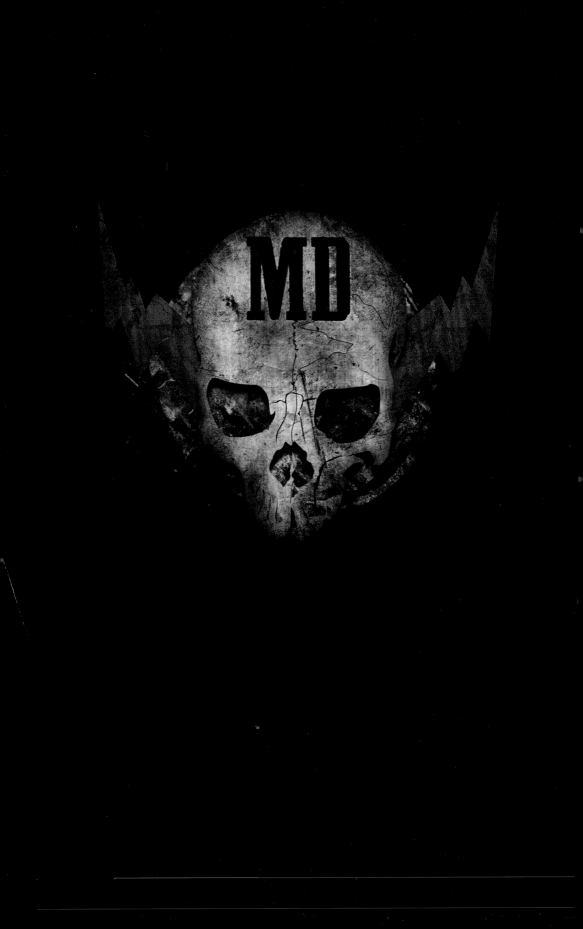